The Business Case for Corporate Governance

This book goes beyond the 'what and how' of corporate governance to explore the impact and benefits of good governance for companies and their investors. The contributors are leading market practitioners, investors, academics and consultants who offer their own views based on a wealth of experience. Topics covered include what makes for an effective board and is the unitary board sustainable? The contribution of governance to financial performance – is the research conclusive? Managing risk and reputation – how do boards ensure they are trusted by their shareholders? The benefits of market-led standard setting – do US and EU regulatory initiatives threaten the traditional UK approach? The book looks to dispel the belief that governance is a burden on companies that adds little value by demonstrating the contribution it makes to board effectiveness and corporate performance.

KEN RUSHTON is a former Director of Listing, Financial Services Authority and Company Secretary ICI.

The Business Case for Corporate Governance

Edited by

KEN RUSHTON

CAMBRIDGE
UNIVERSITY PRESS

CAMBRIDGE UNIVERSITY PRESS
Cambridge, New York, Melbourne, Madrid, Cape Town, Singapore, São Paulo, Delhi

Cambridge University Press
The Edinburgh Building, Cambridge CB2 8RU, UK

Published in the United States of America by Cambridge University Press, New York

www.cambridge.org
Information on this title: www.cambridge.org/9780521871068

© Cambridge University Press 2008

First published 2008

Printed in the United Kingdom at the University Press, Cambridge

A catalogue record for this publication is available from the British Library

Library of Congress Cataloguing in Publication data

The business case for corporate governance / Edited by Ken Rushton.
    p.   cm.
Includes index.
ISBN 978-0-521-87106-8 (hardback)
1. Corporate governance – Law and legislation – Great Britain.   2. Corporate
governance – Great Britain.   I. Rushton, Ken.   II. Title.
KD2088.B87   2008
346.41′0664 – dc22   2008013705

ISBN 978-0-521-87106-8 hardback

Contents

Contributors

Will Chalk
Addleshaw Goddard

Hans-Christoph Hirt
Hermes Investment Management

David Jackson
BP plc

Keith Johnstone
Addleshaw Goddard

Simon Lowe
Grant Thornton

Charles Mayo
Simmons & Simmons

Colin Melvin
Hermes Investment Management

Peter Montagnon
Association of British Insurers

Stilpon Nestor
Nestor Advisors

Sir Bryan Nicholson
Formerly Financial Reporting Council

Sir Geoffrey Owen
London School of Economics

Ken Rushton
Formerly Imperial Chemical Industries PLC

Murray Steele
Cranfield School of Management

Acknowledgements

I would like to thank a number of people who have helped me to produce this book. First, my commissioning editor, Kim Hughes, who has been patiently supportive and with good humour. Julia Casson, a former Company Secretary colleague, who helped with some of the editing and Gill Franklin who helped to type some of my own contributions. Above all, I want to thank my authors for their contributions and for accepting my changes, where needed, with good grace. I am particularly indebted to those Company Chairmen, past and present, who gladly gave their time to talk to me about their jobs. These included: Martin Broughton, Sir Christopher Gent, Sir Ronald Hampel, Peter Hickson, Sir Christopher Hogg, Sir David John, Richard Lapthorne, Sir Robert Margetts, Lord Oxburgh and Sir Peter Walters. Finally, I want to thank Sir Robert Worcester and the Institute of Business Ethics for hosting a discussion with some of these Chairmen.

Introduction

KEN RUSHTON

This book is not intended to be another handbook or primer on corporate governance. Although readers will find chapters, such as those by Charles Mayo and Stilpon Nestor, that describe recent developments in laws and regulations, the main purpose of the book is to describe corporate governance in practice from the viewpoints of the principal players, including the board of directors, the regulator and the investor. Contributors have focused on the benefits of good governance and a number have written about events and their own experiences that demonstrate governance in action: both positive and negative examples.

I hope that the book will appeal not only to lawyers but also to those working in listed companies. Those who are directors may identify with the views of Sir Geoffrey Owen and many of the Chairmen I interviewed who believe that boards are becoming more professional. The role of director, whether executive or non-executive, can no longer be considered simply as a promotion for a successful senior manager or a reward for doing a good job running another business. Being a director is a job in its own right that demands specific skills and individual qualities. Aspiring directors will gain an appreciation of the value of good governance for their business and should understand the importance of high-performance effective boards for corporate success. Colin Melvin and Hans-Christoph Hirt from Hermes Investment Management have written about the academic and professional studies that show that good governance leads to improved corporate performance.

Similarly, I hope institutional investors who read this book will understand the benefits of responsible activism. Peter Montagnon writes that the relationship between companies and their investors on governance should not be confrontational, but that the quality of the dialogue must be improved. As Melvin and Hirt contend, positive engagement with investors results in more value-creation for companies.

UK regulators, supported by Government, take the view that the public interest is best served by market-based solutions to governance issues rather than by regulation. Sir Bryan Nicholson points out that voluntary codes, reinforced by the Listing Rules, are more flexible and more aspirational than laws and regulation. Laws require compliance with minimum standards while codes focus on raising standards. Sir Bryan, and other contributors, compare the UK principles-based approach favourably with the US rules-based approach and

1

criticise the knee-jerk reaction of US legislators following Enron, World Com *et al.* Although it is easy to criticise the Sarbanes-Oxley Act, it has helped to restore investor confidence in the US. Furthermore, it is arguable, as the chapter by Keith Johnstone and Will Chalk suggests, that corporate scandals on the scale of Enron in the UK would place enormous pressure on government to pursue a legislative response rather than continuing to rely on a voluntary code enforced by the market. The Government was sensible, following Enron, to call in regulators and market professionals to review what steps should be taken to reduce the risks of a similar scandal occurring in the UK. This review resulted in worthwhile measures for improving the effectiveness of oversight of audit and accounting.

What is corporate governance?

The classic definition was provided by Sir Adrian Cadbury in 1992: 'Corporate governance is the system by which companies are directed and controlled.' Although this definition focuses usefully on the board of directors, it is a somewhat narrow and mechanistic view of governance. Ira Millstein, the US lawyer whose views on corporate governance command international respect, defined corporate governance in 2003 as:

> that blend of law, regulation and . . . voluntary private sector practices which enables the corporation to attract financial and human capital, perform efficiently . . . generating long-term economic value for its shareholders while respecting the interests of stakeholders and society as a whole.

Millstein recognises that good governance requires both regulation and voluntary measures, and he draws attention to the benefits for companies of good governance practices. This was also reflected in the 1998 Hampel Review in the UK which emphasised the importance of corporate governance for its contribution to business prosperity as well as to accountability. Millstein's work has influenced the OECD and when they published their revised Principles of Corporate Governance in 2004 they defined corporate governance as follows:

> Corporate governance involves a set of relationships between a company's management, its board, its shareholders and other stakeholders. Corporate governance also provides the structure through which the objectives of the company are set and the means of attaining those objectives and monitoring performance are determined.

In this last sentence, we find the link between governance and performance clearly expressed. It is this positive aspirational definition that is more likely to capture the enthusiasm of directors and managers as opposed to a definition calling for structures and processes that appear to be designed solely to police bad behaviour by boards of directors.

Sir Adrian Cadbury himself moved somewhat in this direction when he redefined corporate governance in 2003:

> In its broadest sense, corporate governance is concerned with holding the balance between economic and social goals and between individual and communal goals. The governance framework is there to encourage the efficient use of resources and equally to require accountability for the stewardship of those resources.

Corporate responsibility and ethics

Sir Adrian Cadbury refers to 'holding the balance between economic and social goals' while Millstein mentions 'respecting the interest of stakeholders and society as a whole'. Although the Company Law Review rejected the stakeholder model for a company when considering directors' duties in favour of the 'enlightened shareholder value' model, as discussed by Charles Mayo, it is notable that the formulation of the legal duty to promote the success of the organisation in effect requires directors to 'hold the balance between economic and social goals'. The enhanced Business Review, also discussed by Mayo and others, then requires directors to report annually on how they have fulfilled their responsibilities towards stakeholders.

When the OECD Principles referred to corporate governance involving a set of relationships between management, the directors, shareholders and other stakeholders, they articulated four basic principles to govern those relationships:

- accountability – to shareholders
- responsibility – to stakeholders
- transparency – in all actions
- fairness – in treatment of shareholders.

Follow these principles, the argument goes, and companies will be rewarded by a lower cost of capital as they will be seen to be less risky. Their performance will benefit from better information flows and more rigorous decision-making. Investors will have more confidence in companies that respect their rights and produce fewer bad surprises. In essence, the proposition is that well-governed companies offer investors better returns on their investments. In addition, good governance produces superior operational performance through more considered allocation of resources creating more wealth.

I am delighted that a number of contributors (including Owen, Montagnon, Johnstone and Chalk, and Melvin and Hirt) have chosen to emphasise how corporate (social) responsibility is now a key component of corporate governance and reputation management. In conversations with business leaders about good governance, the word 'integrity' is often mentioned. I agree with Murray Steele when he picks out good judgement and integrity as essential qualities for directors. I have always thought of corporate governance and corporate

3

responsibility as sub-sets of business ethics. My interest in all these areas stems from my passion for business. From my days at university, I bought into the argument that business creates much of the wealth the country needs to provide public services and high living standards. I continue to be dismayed that business generally has a poor image and I have always felt that the media give business a raw deal.

Looking back, it seems that companies were slow to appreciate that competitive advantage could be gained by articulating strong values and insisting these values are lived up to and that high ethical standards are maintained by those working in the organisation, especially by those at the top of the organisation. Words like 'values' and 'ethics' were not often heard in boardrooms and might have been regarded as 'soft' issues only fit for Personnel or Communications departments to worry about.

Readers may not like the idea of linking values and ethical standards with competitive advantage. While I have never doubted that most business leaders have high integrity, I found in my short time at the Institute of Business Ethics that it was easier to command their attention if I used the language of business rather than the language of academic ethics which is rooted in philosophy.

Increasingly, talented people who can choose for whom they want to work, and thoughtful consumers who elect to choose from whom they will purchase goods and services, are adopting ethical criteria to inform their decisions. We are also seeing some institutional investors taking ethical considerations into their investment decisions. So companies should seek to gain a reputation for ethical and responsible behaviour because they appreciate it makes good business sense. Companies need to appreciate, however, that this is a high-risk area, as fine words and glossy communications, though helpful, are not sufficient if the leadership ignores reputation risks when making business decisions, or if those at the top of the organisation put self-interest ahead of the interests of shareholders and other stakeholders. The old adage 'actions speak louder than words' is never more true than when it comes to defending corporate reputation. To my mind, the disciplines of corporate governance, as captured in this book, should help a business leadership that is committed to ethical behaviour and reputation risk management.

Role of the board

Although corporate governance is sometimes criticised for being obsessed with structures and processes while it is understood that people and their behaviour are usually the cause of scandals, if those structures and processes are effective they can go a long way to ensuring that employees do act in the best interests of the company and comply with corporate policies.

I appreciate this is making corporate governance appear to be no more than a monitoring tool, and those responsible for the stewardship of corporate governance are often referred to as watchdogs or corporate policemen. A number of the contributors to this book discuss whether the role of the board is to monitor compliance with the law and recognised standards, such as the Combined Code, or whether it is rather to raise the performance of the business while supervising management. The answer, surely, must be that the board is responsible for both. I agree, however, that boards who perceive corporate governance merely as another compliance obligation are missing the point that good governance is good business. David Jackson, as a Company Secretary, sees his role as assisting his Chairman and the non-executive directors to use the corporate governance framework as a means of getting more effective performance and more value from the board. Jackson points out with delight that the focus on corporate governance has promoted the Company Secretary from being a mere servant of the board to being chief of the Chairman's staff.

As the authors have shown, board evaluation has become commonplace since Sir Derek Higgs reported. It would be valuable, as Sir Geoffrey Owen suggests, if there was a better way of measuring the performance and contribution of the board. The German Society of Investment Analysis and Asset Management in 2000 developed a corporate governance scorecard based mainly on the German corporate governance code. Although the scorecard was intended to be used mainly by investors, it can also be used by boards to evaluate the quality of their own governance frameworks. It would be interesting to see if such scorecards could be developed for UK companies to use as part of their board evaluation process.

Is corporate governance working?

The evidence from the reviews of the Combined Code carried out in recent years by the Financial Reporting Council is encouraging. Many countries use the UK as their model for developing corporate governance regimes, as the US is no longer seen as the gold standard. The absence of a developed institutional shareholder base may mean that other countries look for tougher enforcement mechanisms. Simon Lowe points out in chapter 11 that only 10 per cent of the FTSE 350 companies comply in full with the Combined Code. However, the Code is promoted on the basis of comply-or-explain and is not intended to be applied as a one size fits all set of rules.

A greater concern has been that companies could be defaulting to compliance with the provisions of the Code rather than risk having to justify deviations to their investors or other critics. Companies criticise box-ticking by proxy voting agencies and others whom they accuse of having little interest in finding out the reasons why boards might choose not to implement certain Code provisions. However, some companies regrettably choose to adopt a box-ticking approach themselves when implementing the Code and when describing their corporate governance arrangements in their annual reports. Those that do choose to explain why they are not complying with a provision often use boilerplate, me-too language rather than providing a customised explanation appropriate to the circumstances of the company.

I would like to see more companies use the corporate governance statement to investors to describe how they have applied the principles of the Combined Code. This is currently a Listing Rule requirement, and I suggest that if investors had a better understanding of a board's strategy for implementing corporate governance requirements, this would improve the quality of the dialogue between companies and their investors around departures from Code provisions. Peter Montagnon accepts that the quality of this dialogue is sometimes deficient and he lays the blame on the way both companies and investors tend to compartmentalise their communications. I agree there are situations which can be defused by earlier contacts between Chairmen or senior independent directors and Chief Investment Officers rather than leaving the corporate governance specialists to conduct the engagement for too long. As Montagnon recognises, there is still a weakness in that the governance and investment processes in institutions are insufficiently joined up. This results in board members often seeking to bypass the governance specialists. Also, in smaller companies it is often the case that governance is regarded mainly as a compliance activity to be managed by a senior official such as the Company Secretary rather than a board responsibility.

Contribution of non-executive directors

Another hallmark for governance is to assess the effectiveness of non-executive directors. This is not easy as one has to rely on anecdotal evidence. It is certainly true that boards are taking more trouble to appoint suitable non-executive directors. The nomination committee has assumed far more importance and the process for recruitment and appointment has become more sophisticated. It is remarkable that the pool of talented candidates for non-executive director appointments remains so deep given the risk–reward ratio and the time commitment to do the job properly. Murray Steele considers that many investors are slow to challenge companies with weak performance and rely instead on non-executive directors to provide challenge to the 'acceptable under-performance' mindsets of their executive colleagues. I recall one highly regarded US activist investor saying at a conference that there were certain eminent non-executive directors in the UK whom he felt confident would do a good job in looking after shareholder interests, and if he saw their names on a board he was more relaxed.

My own experience confirms that a conscientious non-executive director can really make a valuable contribution both to fulfilling the board's monitoring responsibilities and to the quality of its decision-making. Much will depend on his level of commitment to understanding the business and his willingness to ask the awkward questions, as well as on his individual skills and experience. It worries me, however, that commentators and some investors have unrealistic expectations of what non-executive directors can achieve, following the Higgs review. Their limitations were dramatically exposed in the Equitable Life and Northern Rock collapses, which demonstrated that it remains true that it is the Chief Executive and his management who run the business.

I am also concerned that a number of UK boards are moving towards the US model of having a minority of executive directors and appointing more non-executive directors. Although I welcome the trend for smaller boards, I have always believed that a balanced board comprising roughly equal numbers of executive and non-executive directors is desirable. The Chief Executive should be supported by a few executives who share responsibility for board decisions. This serves as a useful check on the powers of the Chief Executive who might otherwise be tempted to be selective in the information he shares with the board, and also gives the board a close-up view of potential successors to the Chief Executive. Choosing the Chief Executive is, arguably, the most important decision a board will make; firing a failed Chief Executive runs it a close second.

Sanctions

The topic of sanctions is well covered by Keith Johnstone and Will Chalk who have introduced the interesting concept of the Virtuous Circle. It will be fascinating to see how the population in the Circle might change over time. One sanction which I consider to have been underdeveloped is the power to disqualify errant directors for serious breaches. I am pleased that Johnstone and Chalk appear to support my view. When I was Head of the UK Listing Authority, I failed to persuade the then DTI that such a power would be a helpful addition to our armoury. I am not convinced that the sanction of a fine, even though unlimited, is a sufficient deterrent for Chief Executives or Chief Financial Officers who are determined to mislead investors, possibly for their own personal gain. Such serious breaches of the Listing Rules demonstrate that the individual directors concerned lack integrity and are not fit for office. An alternative is to introduce a licensing system for directors of listed companies on the lines of the 'approved persons' regime for financial services organisations. I believe that the disqualification power is a preferable option. It is not easy to convince enforcement authorities that are not courts or tribunals to bring actions against individuals in breaches of Listing Rules cases. The hurdles are set high and I believe the alternative of seeking a disqualification order from the Companies Court should be explored again. Given the choice, I believe the market would prefer to see proceedings brought against a reckless director rather than punishing the shareholders (possibly for a second time) by pursuing the company for a fine in respect of the behaviour of one or more of its directors.

The future of corporate governance

Stilpon Nestor describes regulatory trends in the US and the EU in his chapter. A number of influential commentators in the US are calling for principles-based regulation and comparing the approach of US regulators, such as the SEC and the New York Stock Exchange, unfavourably with our own. UK companies that remain listed in New York (and a number have delisted in recent years) face the costs and complexities of compliance with the Sarbanes-Oxley Act, though some of the burdens have been lifted for foreign registrants.

In the EU, the Company Law Action Plan at one time appeared to threaten our market-based approach to corporate governance. Our Government have so far done well in Brussels in influencing the implementation of the Action Plan so that, by and large, the UK approach to corporate governance has not been impaired. We have been helped by the philosophy of Commissioner McCreevy, a strong believer in better regulation, which means the need to demonstrate market failure that can only be remedied by regulation before going down the road of legislation. While his approach should be applauded, it remains to be seen whether it will be maintained when there is a change of Commissioner.

The EU Commission would like to see greater convergence of national corporate governance codes, though it no longer talks of an EU-wide code. Although convergence would be consistent with a single market, the differences in national laws and structures of companies and their ownership make such an outcome unlikely.

In the UK, it is generally agreed that we have a code that is fit for purpose. It is regularly reviewed and minor changes are made, often to suit the needs of smaller companies. The Financial Reporting Council is rightly focused on how well the Code is being implemented by companies and shareholders alike. There are concerns that the effectiveness of comply-or-explain would be damaged if both companies and shareholders lapsed into a box-ticking approach to compliance. Contributors to this book urge companies to provide more thoughtful corporate governance statements in their annual reports, particularly when they are explaining why they have departed from the Code's provisions. Similarly, investors need to be more active in their engagement activities with companies if the comply-or-explain approach is to be sustained. The benefits of responsible constructive activism are demonstrated by the success of focus funds, as described by Melvin and Hirt. As Montagnon relates, the UK Government supported the market-based approach rather than regulation of corporate governance because it saw shareholder power being more business friendly, but it still requires shareholders to use their powers sensibly. Melvin and Hirt provide an interesting case study in Premier Oil which shows how a thoughtful, long-term engagement between investors and the most senior board members helped to turn a company round. It is also a good example of how a company Chairman can influence his board by listening to his investors.

One direction which corporate governance could take is to lay down more rules regarding the responsibilities of institutional shareholders. I think it is unlikely that the Financial Reporting Council will wish to pursue this line. There is already some criticism that Section 2 of the Combined Code, which deals with institutional investors in terms of their voting responsibilities, the role of activism and the need for careful evaluation of company disclosures, sits uneasily in a Code that is aimed at the behaviour of companies. As implementation of the Code relies on policing by shareholders, when it comes to the responsibilities of shareholders themselves one has to ask 'quis ipsos custodiet?' (who guards the guards?). It is commendable that shareholder bodies such as the Institutional Shareholders Committee and the International Corporate Governance Network have published statements of shareholder responsibilities. It is perhaps now time for these bodies to consider how compliance with these policies should be monitored and whether sanctions are necessary for non-compliance.

Challenges

Sir Bryan Nicholson and Peter Montagnon highlight further challenges to corporate governance, including:

- The growing influence of hedge funds, many with short-term interests in ownership compared with institutional investors and therefore less interest in governance.
- The increase in ownership of UK companies by foreign investors who have different experiences and expectations of good governance.
- The possibility that institutional investors, when they see that their influence over boards is diminishing, will become apathetic about engagement, which might also result in companies taking even less care with their governance disclosures.
- Boards of directors may become confused about their role and the unitary board itself could be threatened. It may become more difficult to find strong Chairmen and effective non-executive directors who are willing to give the time to challenge underperformance and weak internal controls.
- Small companies may find the burden of corporate governance so great that they desert the main market and find refuge on AIM or other markets. But that begs the question of how long those markets can continue without raising their standards of corporate governance.

1

The role of the board

SIR GEOFFREY OWEN

Introduction

Since the early 1990s we have seen three important changes in the composition
and behaviour of boards of directors in UK public companies: first, the decision
by most though not all large firms to separate the posts of Chairman and Chief
Executive and to appoint to the chairmanship an outsider, that is, someone who
is not, and has not previously been, an employee of the company; second, the
increase in the number and influence of independent or non-executive directors,
who now occupy at least half and usually a majority of board seats, and dominate
board committees; and, third, the greater emphasis on the monitoring function
of the board, both in evaluating the performance of the executive team and
in ensuring that the company complies with what has become an increasingly
onerous set of corporate governance guidelines or rules.

These three changes, taken together, represent a distinctively British
approach to corporate governance. In the US, most companies combine the roles
of Chairman and Chief Executive Officer in a single person, although there is
some pressure from corporate governance reformers for separating them.[1] US
public company boards usually contain no more than one or at most two executive members (the Chief Executive and the Chief Financial Officer), whereas the
executive component of the typical British board is larger, often including heads
of major divisions and/or managers with functional responsibilities. In France,
power in most large companies continues to be concentrated in the hands of the
Président-Directeur Général, although the status and influence of non-executive
directors appear to be increasing. Germany remains committed to its two-tier
board structure, whereby the tasks of the supervisory board are separated from
those of the managing board. While there is dissatisfaction within the German
business community over some aspects of this system (for example, the fact that
the co-determination arrangements exclude non-German employees from seats
on the supervisory board), the prospects for radical reform to bring German
corporate governance into line with Anglo-American practice are remote.

---

[1] See, for example, Paul W. McAvoy and Ira M. Millstein, *The Recurrent Crisis in Corporate
Governance*, New York: Palgrave, 2003. For a defence of the combined Chairman/CEO role
see James A. Brickley, Jeffrey L. Coles and Gregg Jarrell, 'Leadership Structure: Separating the
CEO and Chairman of the Board', *Journal of Corporate Finance* 3 (1997), 189–220.

How well is the British system working? Part of the rationale behind the proposals contained in the Cadbury Report, published in 1992, was the perceived
need to restrain overpowerful Chief Executives. Several corporate scandals
at the end of the preceding decade had highlighted the apparent inability or
unwillingness of some boards of directors to prevent dominant leaders from
riding roughshod over the interests of shareholders in pursuit of their private
ambitions. This restraining role has been an important strand in the subsequent evolution of corporate governance in the UK, but it has been subsumed
within the broader objective of making the board an effective instrument for
improving the quality of decision-making and bringing about better financial
performance.

How well boards achieve these goals is hard to measure, since board composition is only one of a large number of factors which affect how a company
performs. Some companies have done outstandingly well over a long period,
despite having board structures which are not in accord with approved corporate governance principles. Critics of recent corporate governance reforms use
such cases to question the value of what they see as unnecessary constraints on
enterprise, driven largely by political correctness.[2] Nevertheless, most Chairmen, most directors and probably most investors believe that a well-organised
board, with an appropriate mix of skill and experience, can make a positive
contribution to the success of the business.

It is certainly true that a vast improvement has taken place in the professionalism of British boards since Cadbury reported. This applies most obviously to
the non-executive directors, who take the job more seriously than in the past
and devote more time and effort to it. The days when a director might be seen
opening his board papers as he walks into the board meeting, remarking to the
Chairman 'I have to be away by 12', are long since over, as is the tendency
for companies to fill their boards with 'the great and the good' – people who
might add lustre to the company by virtue of their distinction in other fields, but
have little to contribute to the business. The process by which potential non-
executive directors are identified and selected is more rigorous than it used to
be. Companies are looking for people whose skills are relevant to the business,
and who have demonstrated the strength of character and independence of mind
that are necessary to do the job well.

Yet these changes do not in themselves ensure that boards perform better
than they did before the changes were introduced. Building an effective, British-
style unitary board that genuinely adds value to the business calls for much
more than simply adhering to the new corporate governance requirements. Nor
should one ignore the persistent lack of clarity, both among directors and in the
outside world, about what boards are for. There are ambiguities in the role of

---

[2] An early critic of the Cadbury approach was Sir Owen Green, former chairman of BTR. See
his Pall Mall Lecture to the Institute of Directors, 'Corporate Governance, Great Expectations',
24 February 1994.

non-executive directors which, even if they cannot be removed, should at least be openly recognised. Moreover, while most boards now submit themselves to some form of annual self-examination, the improvements that result from these exercises generally relate to style rather than substance. A better approach needs to be developed whereby boards can set realistic goals for themselves and measure how well they have been achieved.

The Chairman's role

The practical problems start with the Chairman. It is his job to manage the board and, assuming that the post is not combined with that of Chief Executive, a great deal depends on how he handles two potentially awkward relationships: with the Chief Executive and with the other non-executive directors.

On the first, a clear division of responsibilities is essential, written down, agreed by the two individuals and approved by the board as a whole. But an agreed document is only the beginning. What matters even more is that the Chairman and Chief Executive should complement each other – in skills, knowledge and experience, and preferably also in personality and style. There has to be mutual respect between the two individuals, and a recognition by the Chief Executive that his hold on the job depends in the last resort on how well the Chairman, advised by the other directors, thinks he is doing it. There is plenty of anecdotal evidence to suggest that the relationship between these two people can easily become dysfunctional, either because the Chairman stands back too far or because he interferes too much, or simply because the two individuals have been unable to develop a constructive working relationship. There is a further discussion on this relationship in the chapter on the role of the Chairman (chapter 2).

Given that the Chairman is normally inevitably closer to the Chief Executive, and spends more time with him, than he is to the non-executive directors, there is a danger that proposals will come to the board 'pre-cooked', agreed in advance between the Chairman and the Chief Executive. In these circumstances, the other directors may be reluctant to express a contrary view, and the board serves merely to rubber stamp what has already been decided. The most effective Chairmen are those who involve the non-executive directors in major decisions at the earliest possible stage, so that they have the opportunity to debate them from every angle and to ensure that any reservations are fully aired. Involvement can be increased by developing a secure website for use by board members, so that non-executive directors can be kept fully abreast of developments between formal board meetings.

The executive/non-executive relationship

A second set of relationships which can be problematic is that between the executive and non-executive members. Many companies encourage non-executive directors to supplement their attendance at board meetings with visits to the businesses and discussions with functional heads and line managers. In one large retailing group, for example, directors are assigned to particular stores, which they are encouraged to visit on a regular basis. In some cases directors may be selected for their specific skills – in brand management, for example, or in the human resources field – which are put to use in mentoring the relevant executives within the company. The danger here is that such close relationships may blur the distinction between executive and non-executive roles; the outside director may lose his objectivity and become a spokesman for the part of the company with which he is most closely linked.

Outside directors, most Chairmen agree, should be regarded not as consultants, but rather as broadly based individuals who can take an intelligent and objective view of the company as a whole; there are other ways for the company to access specialist expertise than by appointing specialists to the board. If the specific skills of directors are to be used, it is better to use them on issues that cut across divisional or functional responsibilities, rather than attaching them to a particular department.

The ideal is for the board to act as a cohesive group of well-informed and active participants who know enough about the business to make a full contribution to the discussion. That knowledge cannot be obtained purely by attending monthly board meetings. But how much knowledge is needed? This question highlights one of the ambiguities in the role of non-executive directors on a unitary board. How can they be both independent of the business and sufficiently well informed about it to contribute intelligently to decision-making?

As two American commentators have pointed out, most part-time independent directors are busy with other activities, and they find it hard to acquire more than a rudimentary knowledge of their companies' affairs; it may take several years before they begin to understand the business, and in the meantime they are almost entirely dependent for information on the Chief Executive and his senior colleagues.[3] They may supplement this source by talking to industry experts and analysts, but a little knowledge is a dangerous thing, and directors have to resist the temptation to second-guess the executives in areas where their expertise is superficial at best.

It is true that, if they want to be more than remote monitors, directors do need to get to know the company, and that involves more interaction with management than is possible at formal board meetings. But their value depends not so much on how much they know about the company and its industry, as on their ability to identify and focus on the small number of key issues on which the success of the business depends. How well they do so depends to a considerable extent on the direction they get from the Chairman. For more discussion on the role of the non-executive director, read Murray Steele in chapter 3.

---

[3] Colin B. Carter and Jay W. Lorsch, *Back to the Drawing Board*, Cambridge, MA: Harvard Business School Press, 2004, p. 45.

The board agenda and the number of meetings

Since the outside director has only a limited amount of time to devote to the company, that time must be used constructively. A crucial task for the Chairman is to structure the agendas of board meetings in a way which ensures that the board focuses on important issues and has the opportunity to engage with the executives on policy.

In one large company, the Chairman has ruled that each board meeting should allocate an appropriate amount of time to the following topics:

- a report on operational and financial performance against plan
- an update on markets, competitors, customers and investors
- progress on strategic issues
- developments on important people issues
- a review in depth of one key strategic issue
- a short presentation from one senior or high-potential leader.

Other topics, for example the strength of the brand, succession plans and longer-term scenario development, are dealt with on a periodic basis. In this company, the Chairman also ensures that at the end of the meeting at least five minutes are set aside for an assessment of how well the board has handled the agenda and how useful the discussion has been. This is a good discipline since many board meetings tend to overrun their allotted time span, leading to hurried treatment of the last few items on the agenda. The Chairman has to steer a path between sticking rigidly to a specific time slot for each item and allowing a free-flowing discussion. As the size of the agenda tends to expand, partly because of the growing importance of corporate governance issues, many companies are finding that a morning meeting followed by lunch is no longer enough; an all-day meeting is becoming common practice, often followed or preceded by an informal dinner.

The Chairman's ability to manage board meetings efficiently depends to a considerable extent on the support he receives from the Company Secretary. This is a role which has become more central to good corporate governance. Apart from the responsibility for organising and distributing the board papers (preferably at least a week before the meeting), for taking the minutes and for providing a full record of the discussions, the Company Secretary has to keep the Chairman and the board abreast of new developments in corporate governance, and to ensure that all statutory requirements are fulfilled.

What can sometimes seem to be pedantic interventions on the Company Secretary's part can irritate directors who want to get on to what they regard as more interesting topics, but scrupulous attention to detail is an essential ingredient in the board's deliberations. The importance of the Company Secretary's role is reflected in the decision by British Petroleum to detach the post from the

Chief Executive and make it part of the Chairman's office. Under this arrangement, the Company Secretary is not part of the executive management. He reports to the Chairman and 'provides support to all the non-executive directors, ensuring that board and board committee processes are demonstrably independent of the executive management of the group'.[4] More on this can be found in David Jackson's chapter on the role of the Company Secretary (chapter 4). While this system may not be appropriate for smaller firms, it underlines the need to provide the Chairman and the outside directors with adequate administrative support.

As for the number of board meetings, most companies have eight or nine regular meetings per year, usually supplemented by a two-day strategy discussion away from the head office. Such a schedule can cause problems for companies with extensive international operations and with several directors based outside the UK; having fewer meetings with 100 per cent attendance is clearly preferable to having more meetings with irregular attendance. Moreover, there is a danger with too many meetings that the discussion takes on a routine character, with the directors spending most of their time in passive mode, listening to reviews of the previous month's results.

Board committees

The time commitment of non-executive directors has been increased by the additional duties that have been given to board committees, principally the audit committee, the remuneration committee and the nomination committee.

The audit committee is responsible for ensuring the adequacy of the company's financial controls and the robustness of its external and internal audit arrangements. At least one member of the audit committee is required by the Combined Code to have recent and relevant financial experience. The other members need to be knowledgeable enough to understand the accounts and the financial reporting rules that have to be followed. Following the Enron affair and the passing of the Sarbanes-Oxley Act, British boards, whether or not their company's shares are listed in the US, have become much more aware of their responsibilities in the area of financial control. This has meant, among other things, a closer relationship between the audit committee and the external auditors. The auditors increasingly regard the chairman of the audit committee as their boss (and paymaster), rather than the company's Chief Financial Officer. Audit committees are also looking more closely at the balance between the auditing firm's audit and non-audit fees, and seeking to ensure that the latter are not so large as to jeopardise the auditor's independence.

---

[4] *BP Annual Review 2003*, p. 39.

Membership of the remuneration committee has also become more demanding. Members have to wrestle with the increasing complexity of executive remuneration packages and with the knowledge that their decisions will be scrutinised critically by institutional investors and the press. Most companies now offer their senior executives a range of incentive schemes tied to the achievement of specific performance targets. Remuneration committee members rely on consultants to advise on the incentive effects of these schemes and on how they compare with those offered by other companies. Whether the complexity of these schemes is justified by their impact on executive performance is open to question, but the fact remains that setting remuneration packages has become a difficult and time-consuming process, calling for sensitivity on the part of committee members, both to the wishes of investors and to the effect of their decisions on morale within the company.

Inevitably the largest burden falls on the chairmen of these two committees, and this is reflected in the size of their fees, but it is important to ensure that other members play more than a minor role. They need to be fully engaged in the reviewing and decision-making process and, again, this means devoting more time to the meetings of the committee and to preparations for them.

The nomination committee, concerned with identifying and selecting new non-executive directors, meets less frequently than the audit and remuneration committees. Its task is to ensure that the board has an appropriate mix of skills and experience and that succession plans for retiring directors are organised well in advance. A tricky issue is the degree of influence that should be wielded by the Chief Executive in the appointment of new directors. The Combined Code states that new directors should be independent, having no previous business connection with other members of the board, and most companies go to great lengths to avoid any hint of cronyism in their appointments. Yet there is still a tendency to go for candidates who will fit in with the established culture of the board, and to steer clear of people who may be thought to be too aggressive or in some sense too awkward in their approach.

The Chief Executive has every right to object to nominees who, in his view, are unlikely to work constructively as part of a team, but this should not preclude the appointment of strong-minded individuals who are capable of challenging the Chief Executive's proposals. Hence it is important that the nomination process is not dominated by the Chairman and the Chief Executive; other board members must be fully involved. That a new Chairman should be compatible with the current Chief Executive goes without saying; whether the Chief Executive should have the right of veto, as is the case in some companies, is another matter.

The nomination committee is sometimes also given responsibility for corporate governance, in the sense of monitoring on the board's behalf any new corporate governance rules or guidelines, keeping abreast of the corporate governance debate and ensuring that the board is alerted to significant developments.

Size and composition of the board

Taking into account the responsibilities which now fall on non-executive directors, how many of them should there be? What is the optimum size of the board, and what is the appropriate mix of executive and non-executive members?

Most Chairmen agree that, as a minimum, the Chief Executive and the Chief Financial Officer should be on the board. Whereas in the US that is generally regarded as a maximum, many British companies take the view that other senior managers such as the Chief Operating Officer, if there is such a post, or functional directors like the heads of R & D or human resources, or the heads of major divisions should also be considered for board membership.

Some Chairmen believe that managers who are answerable to the Chief Executive should be not be members of the board since they are placed in an impossible position. As managers, they cannot express views which might imply lack of confidence in the Chief Executive; yet as directors they are required to take an objective view of what is in the best interests of shareholders. Others believe that the presence on the board of two or three executives in addition to the Chief Executive and the Chief Financial Officer strengthens the sense of a balanced team at the top of the company, working together to drive the business forward. Such an arrangement, according to this view, gives the non-executive directors greater exposure to potential successors to the current Chief Executive, and the executive directors are obliged to think more broadly about the company as a whole. This is particularly relevant in international companies where several divisions are based outside the UK; the divisional heads may be central to the success of the business, but if they are not on the board they may have little contact with the head office and little understanding of the pressures to which the directors are exposed.

As one Chairman has put it:

> to have a meaningful executive representation you have to have the heads of the key divisions there, not to talk narrowly about their own operations, but to be involved in broader issues of strategy, and in such matters as dividends, share buy-backs, feedback from shareholders. Divisional executives learn a great deal about governance, which is a good preparation for becoming Chief Executive, and their contribution goes way beyond their divisional responsibilities.[5]

The balance between executive and non-executive director membership has implications for the size of the board. The tendency over the past fifteen years has been for boards to get smaller, and for the executive component to go down. According to a study by Deloitte, the average FTSE 350 board had ten members in 2005/6, comprising six non-executive directors (including the

---

[5] Quoted in Geoffrey Owen and Tom Kirchmaier, *The Changing Role of the Chairman*, London: Chairmen's Forum, 2006, p. 25.

Chairman) and four executives. In FTSE 100 companies, the size range went from seven directors to eighteen in 2005/6, compared with a range of six to twenty-two in the previous year.[6] The number of very large boards, in excess of twenty, appears to be declining, although there is still a wide divergence in board size.

How big can a board become before it becomes dysfunctional? In a recent survey of company Chairmen, we found a majority, though by no means unanimous, view that anything beyond twelve members would pose problems. It is hard to see how a board of, say, fifteen or more members can engage in the kind of free-flowing discussion, with all directors taking part, which a unitary board on the British model requires. There is some evidence from the US that the turnover of Chief Executives is higher with smaller boards, as long as those boards have a clear majority of outside directors.[7] Smaller boards are likely to be more collegiate than large ones, and better able both to evaluate performance and to contribute to the strategy-setting process.

The board and the shareholders

It has been said that the balance of power in a publicly quoted company rests on three critical anchors: shareholders, management and the board of directors. 'Each of these has important responsibilities of its own, but their interactions are the key to effective governance. When they work together as a system they provide a powerful set of checks and balances. But when pieces of the system are missing, or not functioning well, the system as a whole can become dangerously unbalanced.'[8]

This comment comes from an article written by two American observers who noted that a great deal of attention had been paid to two of the relationships: between management and shareholders and between management and the board. They noted that substantial improvements had been made in the flow of information between them and in mutual understanding. The third relationship, between the board and its shareholders, was more problematic.

> Transparency and accountability, which rest at the heart of good governance, are essentially missing in this relationship. The exchange of information between these two players is poor, and shareholders, for various reasons, have failed to exert much influence over boards. In short, directors don't know what shareholders want, and shareholders don't know what directors are doing.

[6] Deloitte and Touche, *Board Structure and Non-executive Directors' Fees*, September 2006.

[7] Benjamin E. Hermalin and Michael S. Weisbach, *Boards of Directors as an Endogenously Determined Institution: A Survey of the Economic Literature*, Economic Policy Review, Federal Reserve Bank of New York, April 2003.

[8] Cynthia A. Montgomery and Rhonda Kaufman, 'The Board's Missing Link', *Harvard Business Review*, March 2003, p. 88.

Although the concern of these writers was with corporate governance in the US, the point they make is relevant to the UK. In principle, all members of the board of a British company, whether executive or non-executive directors, are answerable to shareholders, but the dominant owners, the institutional investors, are not directly represented on the board. They rarely play a direct role in the appointment of directors (although they may object to nominees whom they regard as unsuitable), and they almost never have face-to-face meetings with the non-executive directors; the annual general meeting, which could provide a forum for such meetings, is not usually attended by the big investors. The dialogue with institutions, fund managers and analysts is generally conducted by the Chief Executive and the Chief Financial Officer. This is justified on one side by the need for the company to present a consistent message to the outside world and, on the other, by the desire of investors to speak with the people who are most fully informed about the business.

There have been proposals, in the UK as well as the US, that the institutions, individually or as a group, should engineer the appointment of professional outside directors who would have specific responsibility for monitoring the company's performance on their behalf and would report back to them.[9] However, as Paul Davies of the London School of Economics has pointed out, there are powerful legal and political obstacles to closer involvement along these lines. The legal risks relate mainly to the insider trading rules, both statutory and in the listing obligations, which reduce the institutions' freedom to buy and sell shares in the market. On the political side, the more the institutions are connected with the choice of directors, the more likely they are to be held accountable if the company fails.[10]

Institutions do become directly involved in the event of a financial crisis, or if they are seriously dissatisfied with the way the company is being managed. In these circumstances, the large investors will wish to express their views directly to the Chairman, to the senior independent director or perhaps to other non-executive directors who have contacts with particular institutions. In the absence of such a crisis, is the gap between board and shareholders too wide? The gap is partially filled by the regular flow of information from the Chief Executive and the Chief Financial Officer in the meetings they hold with investors and analysts; their reaction to road shows, the publication of interim and final results, visits by analysts to company facilities, and so on. In this way, the board builds up an understanding of how the company is regarded in the financial community and of what are shareholders' expectations. But is this enough?

Part of the problem is that shareholders' expectations differ. While it is generally accepted that the primary focus of the board should be on maximising

---

[9] See, for example, Allen Sykes, *Capitalism for Tomorrow: Reuniting Ownership and Control*, Oxford: Capstone, 2000.

[10] Paul Davies, 'Board Structure in the UK and Germany: Convergence or Continuing Divergence?', *International and Comparative Law Journal* 2 (2001), 435–56.

shareholder value, there are differing views about how that objective should be pursued. Large companies may have on their shareholder register investors with widely different aims: from hedge funds mainly interested in short-term gains to pension funds which have a longer-term orientation. Companies may also find themselves the target of attention from activist shareholders who have a different view from the board about the direction and management of the business.

What matters is that the board should have a clear view, communicable to the outside world, of how its strategy will generate long-term shareholder value. The directors should have sufficient confidence in the strategy, not to ignore what investors are saying, but to resist calls for action that might push the share price up in the short term but will ultimately damage the business. They also need to keep their feet on the ground when, as can happen during bull markets, their shares are temporarily overpriced. In the euphoria of the late 1990s, some companies, in the UK as well as in the US, used their high-priced shares to make acquisitions that they later came to regret.[11]

A focus on the underlying value of the business is particularly important in hostile takeovers where boards can be faced with a choice between accepting an offer from the bidder, usually at a substantial premium to the pre-bid price, and siding with the Chief Executive and his team who may wish to maintain the company's independence. In recent years there have been a large number of bids for British firms from foreign acquirers, and some critics suggest that boards may have surrendered too readily. Paul Myners, a leading authority on institutional investment and corporate governance, has pointed out that it is easier for directors to accept a bid that offers a premium of, say, 20 per cent to the pre-bid price than to reject it on the grounds that shareholders will do better in the long term if the company remains independent.[12] Outside directors, Myners wrote, need to show more courage. 'Those who want an easy life or are fearful of upsetting big names in the City can be seduced into recommending a marginal offer. This can lead to tensions around the boardroom table if other directors are more resolute. Financial advisers also have a strong vested interest in managing the merry-go-round of corporate acquisitions.'

How best to ensure the right degree of accountability from the board to the shareholders, while allowing directors the necessary freedom to run the business, has been the subject of an acrimonious debate in the US. Some shareholder groups, backed by influential academics, believe that the board is too insulated from investor pressure; they are arguing for changes which would make it easier for shareholders to elect new board members in place of the incumbents, and allow more decisions to be subject to shareholder vote.[13]

---

[11] Michael C. Jensen, 'Agency Costs of Overvalued Equity', European Corporate Governance Institute, Finance Working Paper No. 39/2004, April 2004.

[12] Paul Myners, 'We're Selling Britain Too Cheaply', *Sunday Telegraph*, 19 February 2006.

[13] See Lucien A. Bebchuk, 'Letting Shareholders Set the Rules', Harvard Law School, Discussion Paper No. 548, March 2006.

These initiatives have been described by Martin Lipton, a leading New York lawyer who has been a redoubtable defender of board autonomy, as an attack on the fundamental building blocks of the American corporation. Corporations, he wrote, are not intended to be run by town meetings. 'Instead, corporations are designed to be risk-taking collections of capital in which those putting in the capital – the shareholders – surrender day-to-day control of the corporation but are granted immunity from liability as a way of encouraging risk.'[14]

This is an argument which has not so far spread to the UK, perhaps because the power relationship between boards and shareholders is more balanced than in the US. Investing institutions in the UK are not directly involved in selecting directors, but they do have the power to intervene in a company which they think is poorly managed, not least by calling an extraordinary general meeting. Partly for that reason, boards of directors are more responsive to what the institutions are saying. Nevertheless, it is still open to question whether the incentives for non-executive directors to put the interests of shareholders first are strong enough.

Most boards operate by consensus, and it is hardly surprising if directors pay more attention to what is being said by their colleagues around the board table than to the views of distant and unknown shareholders. 'The determined pursuit of an issue on behalf of shareholders requires the expenditure of political capital and emotional energy – potentially big costs to a director with few compensating benefits. When time pressures and lack of adequate information are added into the mix, the path of least resistance can become very tempting.'[15]

The dual role of British boards

The issue of accountability to shareholders is linked to the central paradox in the British approach to corporate governance. Can the British-style unitary board combine the monitoring function, geared to the interests of shareholders, with the strategy-setting, business-developing, advisory role? Should one accept that, thanks to the development of corporate governance since the Cadbury Committee reported in 1992, the typical British board has acquired, de facto, the character of a German-type supervisory board, monitoring the decisions of the executive committee – effectively a German-type managing board – below it?

There was a period, in the 1960s and 1970s, when many people in the UK believed that the German two-tier board had substantial advantages over what appeared to be the poorly functioning British-style unitary board. For the Left, the main attraction of the German system was the presence on the

---

[14] Martin Lipton, 'Twenty-Five Years after *Takeover Bids in the Target's Bedroom*; Old Battles, New Attacks and the Continuing War, *The Business Lawyer* 60, 4 (August 2005), 1369–82, at p. 1378 .

[15] Montgomery and Kaufman, 'The Board's Missing Link'.

supervisory board of trade union and worker representatives, which ensured that the interests of employees were taken into account in the company's decisions. There was also a view within parts of the business community that the separation of supervision and management was logical and even desirable, since it avoided the ambiguity inherent in the British system.

Admiration for the German system waned during the 1980s and 1990s, partly because of the poor performance of the German economy, but also because a series of corporate scandals highlighted the weaknesses in German corporate governance. Because of the excessive size of the supervisory board, its infrequent meetings, and the limited flow of information to it from the managing board, empire-building Chief Executives were able to destroy shareholder value without any serious interference from their nominal supervisors. It was also recognised that the German two-tier structure had evolved over a long period in response to particular economic circumstances; it formed part of a financial system, and a political and legal environment, which was very different from the British situation, and could not be replicated in the UK.

Nevertheless, even if the German system has lost much of its appeal, the question remains: can monitoring be combined with collegiality? Most British directors and Chairmen answer this question strongly in the affirmative. They accept that their primary task is to ensure that the company is well led, but that does not have to be an exclusive preoccupation. As one experienced director has put it, 'if the Chairman picks the right non-executives and really wants to use them, they can bring an extra dimension to decision-making. They exert an invisible disciplinary pressure because the executives know that if a weak proposal is put to the board it will be torn apart.' According to this view, a good mix of involved non-executive directors goes well beyond the monitoring and controlling function. 'Often the Chief Executive may not have 100 per cent of the answers when he brings a proposal forward – though he may have 100 per cent of the questions. Good non-executives help to provide what is missing.'[16]

The chief complaint among some British directors is that the pendulum has swung too far in the direction of monitoring. The corporate governance agenda, they say, has become so time-consuming as to crowd out what they see as their most important contribution: working with the executives to drive the business forward. The situation may not have gone as far as in the US, where, to quote Martin Lipton, 'directors are under pressure from a multitude of directions, with federal securities laws, federal sentencing guidelines, stock exchange governance requirements, state attorneys general and shareholder activism acting to mandate or suggest new director responsibilities'. The demand for improved compliance, governance and transparency, Lipton warns, 'unless judiciously applied, is more likely to make boards less rather than more effective, and in

---

[16] Owen and Kirchmaier, *The Changing Role of the Chairman.*

extreme cases will so overburden boards with process that they become dys-functional'.[17] It is not hard to find echoes of these sentiments in the UK.

Is there a danger that, as the number of rules and regulations increases, boards will spend their time monitoring compliance rather than performance? There is no disputing the fact that in the UK, as in the US, the monitoring role of boards has now acquired greater importance, and to that extent the colle-giate, advisory role has been downgraded. But one does not have to exclude the other. The challenge for boards, and most importantly for the Chairman, is to find the right balance: encouraging the executive and non-executive directors to work together as a team, and not allowing the corporate governance agenda to crowd out other issues. Yet neither the Chairman nor the outside directors should forget that in the last resort their single most important task is to hire and fire the Chief Executive. They must always be alert to signs that the Chairman and Chief Executive may be going off the rails and be ready to take appropri-ate action. In that sense monitoring must always take precedence over other functions.

Yet the ambiguities remain. As several commentators have pointed out, outside directors are not just involved in monitoring and advising. They have a third role: decision-making. They are in the curious position of participating in major decisions and sitting in judgement on the managers who are carrying them out. When things go wrong, it is usually managers who get the blame, not the outside directors.

The board and the company's stakeholders

The balancing act which boards and directors have to perform is further com-plicated by the pressure on companies to demonstrate their commitment to cor-porate social responsibility (CSR). This term can be defined in several different ways, but the thrust of today's CSR movement is that companies should not concern themselves exclusively with maximising shareholder value but should pay regard to the interests of their employees, local communities and society at large. The CSR agenda has been pushed by a range of non-governmental organ-isations, many of which are concerned with issues such as poverty alleviation, human rights and environmental protection.

Some companies have responded by adopting what has been called triple bottom line reporting, covering the economic, social and environmental aspects of their activities. Others – especially those operating in the natural resource sectors which have been a particular target for CSR campaigners – have gone to considerable lengths to demonstrate their concern for the countries and regions where they operate, and their commitment to the highest standards of ethical behaviour.

[17] Martin Lipton, 'Some Thoughts for Boards of Directors in 2006', Wachtell, Lipton, Rosen and Katz, 1 December 2005.

While these policies have been adopted voluntarily in response to pressures from unofficial bodies, there are signs that the company's obligations to non-shareholder constituencies could become part of the statutory framework. During the Parliamentary debates which took place in 2006 over the new Company Law, there was considerable controversy over provisions in the bill that would require directors to 'promote the success of the company' and to have regard for the interests of customers, suppliers, the community and the environment. Business organisations feared that directors could be pursued in the courts for their alleged failure to discharge their expanded duties to non-shareholder groups. At the same time non-governmental organisations criticised the bill for being too soft, and urged that the responsibilities of directors should be spelt out more explicitly.

Although the bill in its final form did not depart from the principle that the interests of shareholders must come first, the argument highlighted an issue that is likely to be of growing concern to boards of directors. How much of a conflict is there between shareholder and stakeholder interests, and how should boards resolve them? Sir Andrew Likierman, a professor at the London Business School, has urged companies to recognise that the pressures from stakeholder groups are constraints to pursue shareholder value, not alternatives to it. 'The fact that these pressures are now stronger than before does not alter the requirements for a company to pursue shareholder value.' This does not mean, he writes, that companies should ignore the claims of other stakeholders. 'On the contrary, for many organisations listening to, acknowledging and, if required, meeting these claims is essential for them to carry on their business successfully.'

As Likierman points out, a company that is seen to act irresponsibly is increasingly likely to run into reputational risk problems. 'It will find it difficult to attract the best recruits. It could be subject to consumer boycotts. It might just be the subject of unwelcome scrutiny by government. It is very much in the company's self interest to act responsibly – more so now than ever before.'[18]

The board has to take a balanced view of the demands that are coming at the company from the CSR activists. It should report accurately and fully on those CSR issues that are relevant to its business – for example, its record on environmental damage in the case of companies which have potentially polluting production facilities – but it should be prepared to ignore or rebut complaints that have no basis in fact.

A commitment to shareholder value is not incompatible with a concern for the interests of stakeholders. That does not imply that stakeholder demands should be given the same weight as those of shareholders. Boards of directors have a difficult enough job as it is; to give them the additional task of balancing

[18] Sir Andrew Likierman, 'Stakeholder Dreams and Shareholder Realities', *Financial Times*, 16 June 2006.

the needs of several different constituencies is a recipe for blurred accountability and poor performance.

What value does the board add?

When publicly quoted companies are taken private by private equity firms, most or all of the outside directors are normally replaced with people directly linked to the new owners. According to a recent US study, the boards of private equity-owned companies are fundamentally different from the public boards that are the focus of governance activists. 'They are typically smaller and consist only of representatives of private equity owners whose explicit job is to help managers create and execute strategy; many directors fulfil both roles.' As a result, according to this view, the board is far more involved in assisting the company.[19]

Does this imply that the conventional public company board in the UK, with its mix of inside and outside directors, adds little value? Do boards exist mainly to satisfy corporate governance codes and listing requirements?

A cynical view might be that the board is marginal to the real business of the company, that it is largely reactive rather than active, and that the executive team derives little that is useful from its deliberations. A more positive view is that a good board adds value in three main ways: it acts as a check on the executive team; it provides advice; and it improves the overall quality of the company's decision-making. On the first, boards do this part of the job more effectively than they did fifteen years ago. Whether their influence is more positive than negative – it is easier to say no to a risky proposal than to understand it fully and support it – is open to question. On the second, there is not much doubt that an improvement has taken place. Because of the stringent criteria that are now applied to the appointment of outside directors, the skills and experience around the board table are more relevant and potentially more useful than used to be the case. The biggest uncertainty is over the third function: does the board improve the quality of decision-making?

The prevailing view among current Chairmen is that a well-managed board, made up of independent-minded people who work as a team, are committed to the success of the business and are knowledgeable about it, can make a valuable contribution.

Yet before accepting this favourable verdict, two reservations need to be stated. First, it is a mistake to exaggerate what boards can do. The composition and behaviour of boards are not the principal determinants of a company's performance, and it is wrong to look to improved corporate governance as the key to raising the level of British industrial performance. In this context, one might question the assertion in the introduction to the Higgs Report that

---

[19] Geoffrey Colvin and Ram Charan, 'Lessons of Private Equity', *Fortune*, 27 November 2006.

effective boards will help in closing the productivity gap between the UK and its major competitors.[20]

Second, any assessment of the value of the British-style board has to take into account the difficulty of its task. Companies cannot be run by committee. Leadership has to be vested in the Chief Executive, and that person has to be given the authority and freedom to lead. Second-guessing on the part of the board is a recipe for confusion or inertia.

Companies can get into trouble for two main reasons: a single bad decision that throws the business seriously off course, and a slow decline that stems from deteriorating performance on the part of the Chief Executive and his team. In theory, the board should be able to prevent both eventualities, but there are many reasons why they do not do so. On the first, it is not easy for outside directors to reject proposals that are strongly supported by the Chief Executive and, probably, also the Chairman, as well as by external advisers.

Take, for example, a major acquisition designed to transform the fortunes of the company and take it into a new, high-growth market – perhaps a 'bet-the-company' decision. Boards can examine the costs, risks and potential benefits of such a deal in detail, but when the arguments are finely balanced, should the board overrule the Chief Executive or give him his head? Again, the board may be faced with a proposal to commit large funds to a new product at a time when neither the future market nor the manufacturing costs can be precisely assessed. The easy response might be to delay the decision until there is less uncertainty, but would the company then forgo its first-mover advantage?

Since the outside directors are less well informed about the details of these projects than the management team, they will need to be very certain of their ground if they are to turn them down. They also have to recognise that a risk-averse board which consistently restrains an ambitious Chief Executive is unlikely to add value.

A situation of slow decline presents problems that are hardly less difficult. To remove a Chief Executive when his performance is falling short of expectations requires the board to be convinced that the problems are the fault of that individual, and not due to circumstances outside his control. The factors causing the company to perform poorly may be complicated and hard to assess, particularly if they involve unexpected changes in technologies or markets. Moreover, dismissal will be a disruptive event, damaging morale within the company and causing uncertainty among investors, customers and suppliers.

Underlying these problems are the ambiguities which have been touched on earlier in this chapter. To whom are the non-executive directors responsible and, to the extent that they have multiple responsibilities, how should they be balanced? As several commentators have pointed out, a great deal of attention has been paid in recent years to making directors independent of management.

---

[20] DTI, *Review of the Role and Effectiveness of Non-executive Directors*, The Higgs Report, January 2003, p. 11.

Much less attention has been paid to making them accountable to shareholders. While directors recognise that they are ultimately responsible to shareholders, in their relationship to the company their main loyalty is to the Chairman and the Chief Executive, and their instinct is to support them, not to stand in their way.

How do boards know whether or not they are doing a good job? Most companies now go through an annual self-evaluation process and this exercise has helped to identify where board processes could be improved, how meetings can be made more productive, and so on. The improvements that result from these exercises tend to be useful rather than fundamental, and this reflects uncertainty about the criteria that should be used to assess board effectiveness.

It is not difficult to draw up a list of board responsibilities which would be acceptable to most directors. How exactly are these responsibilities to be fulfilled, and which ones are the more important? Boards vary in the way they approach their task; the differences may be due to the personalities of the Chairman and Chief Executive, to the particular stage which the company has reached or to the external market situation which it faces at the time.

A useful distinction has been made between the board as watchdog and the board as pilot. The former implies a strong focus on monitoring and oversight while the latter is much more active, gathering a great deal of information and involving itself directly in decisions.[21] One can envisage a spectrum of board styles ranging from watchdog at one end to pilot at the other, and there is a strong case for boards thinking hard about where along that spectrum they want to be. The two American commentators quoted earlier, Colin Carter and Jay Lorsch, argue that each board must define the value it intends to provide. 'It must explicitly choose the role it will play, and its choice must be informed by a good understanding of its company's specific situation and its own capabilities and talents.'[22]

An appraisal of board performance should start with the recognition that all boards are not alike and that directors should decide for themselves what sort of board the company needs. The choice will be influenced by several factors, both internal and external: whether, for example, the Chief Executive is recently appointed or nearing retirement, or whether the external environment is turbulent or stable. Whatever the choice, it should be discussed and agreed by the directors, and their performance should be judged against the criteria which have been worked out.

Such an exercise, probing more deeply than the typical annual self-appraisal, does not necessarily make the task of the board easier. The fundamental appraisal which is suggested here would have the value of exposing these ambiguities to the scrutiny of the board as a whole. Moreover, individual directors,

[21] Ada Demb and F.-Friedrich Neubauer, *The Corporate Board: Confronting the Paradoxes*, Oxford: Oxford University Press, 1992, p. 55. These issues are also discussed in Carter and Lorsch, *Back to the Drawing Board*.

[22] Carter and Lorsch, *Back to the Drawing Board*, p. 61.

many of whom often feel uneasy about whether they are making a significant contribution to the board, would find it easier to assess their own performance if it could be related to a set of agreed goals for the board as a whole.

Some unresolved questions

An effective board of directors is the central element in any properly functioning corporate governance system. Most of the corporate governance reforms that have taken place in the UK since Cadbury have been concerned with the role of the board, its composition and its mode of operation. That improvements have been made is not in doubt, but there is a danger of complacency about what has been achieved. It is true that the UK has not had its Enron or its Parmalat. Relations between boards of directors and investors are more balanced than, for example, in the US. But it does not follow that the UK has got everything right. There are legitimate questions to be asked about the British system. How should the responsibilities of the non-executive Chairman be defined, and what sort of person is best qualified to carry them out? Do non-executive directors have a sufficiently strong incentive to act on behalf of shareholders? What is the appropriate balance between independence and knowledge of the business?

The fact that these questions still need to be asked does not imply that the British system is seriously flawed. The point rather is that the issue of how to make boards work better needs continuous attention from practitioners, regulators and academics. The biggest challenge for researchers is to find a better way of measuring the performance of boards and the contribution they make, or fail to make, to the performance of the company. Even if definitive answers cannot be reached, the attempt must be made, if only to establish a more robust foundation for corporate governance reform.

2

The role of the Chairman

KEN RUSHTON

Introduction

In the UK over 90 per cent of listed companies split the roles of Chairman and Chief Executive, whereas in the US the reverse is true. It is said that in the US a Chief Executive's vanity is hurt if he or she is not also the Chairman. A number of Chief Executives in the UK might feel this way, and arguably, for successful companies that can avoid rough water, it might be feasible for a gifted person to combine the two roles effectively. More than one Chairman told me that if the company's strategy and management are good, the job is easy. However, I firmly believe that the conventional wisdom that there are two distinct roles – running the board and managing the business – is sound.

The Chairman is properly seen as one of the checks and balances on the authority of the Chief Executive. This does not always work in practice. For example, Enron (although a US company) had separate Chairman and Chief Executive. Astonishingly, Hewlett Packard reacted to its boardroom debacle by appointing its Chief Executive to be Chairman.

Another argument for separating the roles is the additional responsibilities created by all the corporate governance requirements that have been imposed. Better to let the Chairman, assisted by his Company Secretary, deal with 'all the compliance stuff' than distract the Chief Executive from his operational duties.

Sir Derek Higgs suggested the Chairman is responsible for:

- leadership of the board, ensuring its effectiveness on all aspects of its role and setting its agenda
- ensuring the provision of accurate, timely and clear information to directors
- ensuring effective communication with shareholders
- arranging the regular evaluation of the performance of the board, its committees and individual directors
- facilitating the effective contribution of non-executive directors and ensuring constructive relations between executive and non-executive directors.

After talking to a number of present and recently retired FTSE 100 Chairmen, I believe Sir Derek's list is a good one. What has struck me is how much the role

29

of Chairman has changed during my time in industry. One Chairman summed it up like this:

> If you look back to the 1960's and 1970's and you think how boards were run then, we are in a different world. The Chairman's position has been professionalised and it has become not just possible, but in many cases obligatory, to talk about things that boards never talked about before. The interaction of directors, the judgement of boards collectively and individually, conflicts of interest . . . all these things make it necessary to redesign the board . . . the next decade should be the decade of the Chairman when they actually assert themselves and show how boards can be run well.

These remarks highlight two points made by most of the Chairmen with whom I spoke: the role has become more professional; and the principal task is to build an effective board.

Due diligence

Before considering these points in more detail, I suggest that 'professionalism' starts with the due diligence process when a Chairman is first approached to see if he is interested in the job. As one Chairman remarked, 'If you are not comfortable with the Company, don't take the job.' Putative Chairmen will enquire about the company's values and ethics. After all, one of their concerns, if they become Chairman, will be to protect the company's reputation and preserve its integrity. The putative Chairman will also seek to discover how much trust there is between the directors and how effective are the relationships between executive and non-executive directors. He will want to talk to every director and to the company's professional advisers including the auditor. He is likely to spend most of his due diligence time with the Chief Executive for, as we shall see, that relationship between Chairman and Chief Executive is critical for an effective board and, arguably, for a successful company.

It is common for a Chairman to be appointed from among the board's non-executive directors, in which case due diligence becomes more straightforward. A number of those I spoke to thought their previous experience as a Chief Executive (though in a company in another sector) had helped them to run the board and to manage their relationships with their own Chief Executive.

Professionalism

The responsibilities of Chairman most frequently mentioned to me, apart from building an effective board, were:

- setting the agenda and running the board meeting
- promoting good governance in the company
- creating an effective relationship with the Chief Executive
- sustaining the company's reputation
- succession planning.

Setting the agenda and running the board meeting

Chairmen rightly consider that it is their job to ensure the board spends its time considering issues that really matter. It is too easy to overload the agenda with routine, administrative matters and regular reports from committees. It is particularly important that sufficient board time is given to developing and reviewing the business strategy. Although the Chief Executive and his executive team are primarily responsible for preparing the strategy, the Chairman must see to it that contributions and challenges are sought from the non-executive directors. These more independently minded board members are more likely to test the assumptions, coherence and affordability of the proposed strategy.

One Chairman told me he had to bring in a new Chief Executive to convince the management that a comprehensive business strategy was needed. That company had previously been used to fighting for survival and coping with short-term problems. In that case, despite the Chairman's dislike of committees, the board created one comprising the Chairman and two non-executive directors in order to support the executive team develop a strategy over a period of one year. The strategy was finally presented to the board over dinner the evening before a board meeting. Interestingly, in this case, the strategy identified that among the key weaknesses in the company were the absence of any succession planning and skill gaps in management as well as on the board itself.

Another Chairman told me that his board spent two days considering strategy at the beginning of each planning cycle so, later in the cycle, they were able to take a more informed view on the individual business strategies. The board was better able to determine how the company, as 'owner', would add value to each of its constituent businesses.

Chairmen of highly regulated and high-technology companies are especially sensitive to the need to allow sufficient board time for non-executive directors to understand the complex environment in which the company operates. Some of this education should be done outside board meetings, but Chairmen are aware of the lack of knowledge and involvement that most of their non-executive directors will have.

Getting the agenda to be relevant and appropriate, and ensuring the board minutes are reliable, are essential to create a climate of transparency in the board and also for laying effective audit trails should something go wrong and the question is asked 'what was the board doing at the time?' This has become even more important with the broader definition of directors' duties contained in the Companies Act 2006 discussed by Charles Mayo in chapter 7. Every director needs to take care that his Chairman is using the board's time in a way that is consistent with his duty 'to promote the success of the company'. All directors, not just the Chairman, could be exposed if agendas and board papers fail to include those matters that are material to the company's success.

In setting the agenda, the Chairman will also take care to see that board time is not wasted considering proposals or other items that can properly be decided by management. The Company Secretary should be able to advise the Chairman by referring to the company's schedule of reserved powers that lays down those matters that only the board can decide.

So far as running the meeting is concerned, the effective Chairman will allow the Chief Executive and his executive colleagues to present proposals or reports that will usually have been pre-agreed by management. The Chairman will see to it that presentations are not so long as to leave inadequate time for discussion. It is up to the Chairman to set a tone at the board meeting that encourages non-executive directors to contribute. The quality of debate is often dependent on the quality of the board papers and the presentations. A number of companies have introduced rules or guidelines for papers and visual aids. One Chairman limits presentations to a maximum of four slides (I recall when he was an executive director, his presentations were notorious for the excessive number of slides). A number of Chairmen consider it is helpful to invite professional advisers to attend board meetings when complex proposals are being decided or when there are serious legal or financial issues to be considered. This is viewed not as undermining management but as a necessary safeguard for the board and helpful in reaching the right conclusions. As one Chairman put it, 'external advisers provide a reality check to make sure we are not kidding ourselves'. On the other hand, a Chairman with direct experience of crisis management told me he was grateful not to have been surrounded by an army of advisers. In that case he was happy with the internal support made available to him and for the space he was given to work through the crisis.

Another Chairman said he is never rigid about sticking to agendas so long as the weighty issues such as strategy and budget are taken first. He is content if information items or even governance matters are squeezed out. He argues that the Chairman's priority is to ensure that all views from around the board table are heard without the agenda or the timetable limiting free discussion.

Promoting good governance

I am encouraged by the number of Chairmen who confirmed it is their job to ensure high standards of corporate governance are followed by the company, the board and its committees. They take this responsibility on their shoulders rather than burdening the Chief Executive. Some may see it as a compliance task but most appear to accept that governance is a feature of good management and will both help performance and enhance the company's reputation with investors and the media. Of course, some complain about various provisions in the Combined Code, particularly the limit on the number of FTSE 100 chairs (which is now likely to be changed), but I found most of those I talked to believe the Code is operating 'surprisingly well'.

A common complaint from Chairmen used to be that compliance issues, including corporate governance matters, took up too much board time. I would make no apology for boards of regulated firms being required to spend a fair amount of board time on internal control and risk management issues. However, it seems to me that the case against governance dominating board agendas was always overstated. I recall Sir Digby Jones (as he then was), when Director General of the CBI, suggesting such matters typically took up 60 per cent of board time.

One Chairman, whose company is also listed in New York, told me that the first item on his board agenda is a report from the Company Secretary that includes recent developments in corporate governance and company law in the UK and the US. He considers it essential to keep his directors up to date and he does not see corporate governance as a necessary evil. He fully supports the need for clear accountabilities and greater transparency. He is convinced that his own accountability for promoting governance is not just about compliance, but also requires him to ensure the board is functioning effectively in support of the management and that the relationships between executive and non-executive directors is constructively tensioned.

Another Chairman sees his priorities for promoting governance as including the need to 'systematise' board processes such as agendas, papers and minutes so that directors are fully aware of all relevant issues. His concern for transparency is evidenced by the four questions he asks each year of his senior independent director:

- How do you regard the quality of the relationship between the Chairman and the Chief Executive?
- How open has the Chief Executive been with the board?
- How visible are the checks and balances on the executive directors?
- Have all the questions asked by the non-executive directors been appropriately addressed?

Chairmen usually look to their Company Secretaries for support in fulfilling their responsibility for promoting governance. This has increased the visibility of the Company Secretary dramatically, as David Jackson describes in chapter 4. One Chairman said he regards his relationship with his Company Secretary as extremely important and that he allows the Company Secretary to challenge him on governance issues. Sir Geoffrey Owen, in his research for the Chairmen's Forum, suggested that Company Secretaries might be attacked by directors for being too pedantic. One Chairman told Sir Geoffrey, 'It is always good to have one pedant around the board table.'

Creating an effective relationship with the Chief Executive

When the Chairman was also the Chief Executive there was no issue about relationships, but now management of their relationship is a top priority for both. None of the Chairmen I spoke to would admit to having any difficulty in this regard, but a number had witnessed the catastrophic results when such a relationship breaks down. As one Chairman said, where communications or trust breaks down, one of them has to leave and sometimes the solution is for both to leave. Another Chairman I spoke to is a 'part-time executive Chairman' but he still has to manage his relationships with three managing directors.

Since few Chairmen seem to have job descriptions (why is that?), Chief Executives may have their hands full should their Chairmen try to be too interventionist. This seems to be more of a risk in smaller companies or where the Chairman was formerly the Chief Executive. Most Chairmen do work at good communications with their Chief Executives and avoid excessive interference. Many have weekly private meetings which may last two hours or more and are designed to build trust between the two colleagues. Sometimes the senior independent director may attend these meetings keeping a watchful eye on the relationship. Where there is a risk of a breakdown, the senior independent director may intervene. In other cases, he may have to be the bearer of the message from the board that either the Chairman or the Chief Executive has to leave.

Although the Chairman may see himself as the mentor or coach to the Chief Executive, one told me that when he was first appointed he looked to his experienced Chief Executive for guidance. After a while he asked the Chief Executive for feedback as to how he was doing and was surprised to hear 'I wish you were a little more paternal and a lot less fraternal.' There are times when a Chairman needs to direct his Chief Executive, but normally the Chief Executive will decide when he needs his Chairman's advice and whether to take that advice. The Chief Executive is responsible for running the business and cannot abdicate that responsibility by saying 'I followed my Chairman's direction.' He must not be made to feel he is obliged to act on the Chairman's advice or he will quickly stop raising issues with the Chairman. When there is a significant policy disagreement between them, that issue needs to be raised with the board. One Chairman told me that if he did not support his Chief Executive's proposal, he would not allow it to be considered by the board. If he was merely doubtful, he would always let it go to the board.

All Chairmen stress the need for their relationships with Chief Executives to be totally open. A number had had difficulties over the issue of remuneration and these had been best handled when the Chairman had been frank and direct.

Although 'non-executive' or part-time Chairmen are not expected to attend executive team meetings, many cannot resist the occasional visit. This is often justified as helping with succession planning. While the Chairman might hope he is a fly on the wall at such meetings, he is more likely to be seen as a piranha in the pond unless he clarifies why he is there.

As Sir Geoffrey Owen's research concludes, 'the goal is a partnership in which the Chairman and Chief Executive have complementary, clearly defined roles, as well as complementary skills, qualities and experience'. The Chairman and the senior independent director need to be aware of the risk of that partnership breaking down and act accordingly.

Sustaining the company's reputation

A Chairman, when asked by his wife to describe his job, replied 'to stand above the parapet and take the flak when everybody else is down in the trench'. Chairmen accept that they are accountable for upholding the company's reputation. This gives them a dilemma and they need to find answers to questions such as:

- What issues might affect the company's reputation?
- How and when does he get involved in these issues without undermining the Chief Executive's authority to run the business?
- Are there circumstances in which the company's reputation is so much at stake that the Chairman must effectively 'take over the reins'?

Chairmen usually prefer to keep a low public profile and leave their Chief Executive in the spotlight. When things go wrong, or are at risk of going wrong, then the Chairman has to intervene. At all times he needs to be aware as to how the company is perceived by its stakeholders and he should keep in touch with the mood of investors and the press. He will also sense the mood of the employees since a loss of confidence inside the company can be as damaging as a weakening of external reputation. One Chairman put it to me that 'Chairmen tell employees what they can't do while Chief Executives tell them what they must do.'

In times of crisis the Chairman is likely to be a key player and his effective management of the board at this time is essential if the company is to handle the crisis successfully. At such times, when the eyes of the world are watching the company, attention is focused on the board and its responses (remember Marconi?). Increasingly, investors and the media are asking 'Where is the Chairman?' During the crisis at Northern Rock, this question was being asked by the press, taking advantage of the fact that its Chairman, Dr Ridley, was not well known in the City. The difficulty for the Chairman is to decide whether to focus on ensuring the board is supervising (in some cases controlling) crisis management while supporting the Chief Executive, or whether he himself needs to be the main company spokesperson. Where the crisis is on the board, the Chairman needs to lead the investigation and get to the truth quickly and resist any temptation to bury bad news. A confident, respected and well-briefed Chairman can calm the nerves of anxious stakeholders at times of crisis.

Similarly, there are times when a Chairman needs to be restrained from exercising his natural inclination to be seen publicly to be doing something. Think of the Chairman of Union Carbide's ill-timed visit to India after Bhopal which led to his arrest. It was understandable that he should feel the need to go there but he should have been better advised.

On a smaller scale, I recall advising my own Chairman at ICI to delay making a visit to the scene of an explosion in Peterborough when one of the company's vans carrying commercial detonators caught fire. Sadly, a fireman had died and there was much damage to property. Media attention was intense for a brief period and a visit by the Chairman at that time was more likely to result in angry scenes and unsympathetic publicity as emotions were running high. When the Chairman visited a few days later, it received little publicity but was locally seen as being considerate and well timed.

In large international companies it is unrealistic to expect the board to be so close to all facets of the business that it should be held accountable for every incident or accident. It is fair to look to the board to supervise management's handling of such an event, if its scale is so great that it puts corporate reputation at risk. Beyond this, it is also vital, as well as a requirement of corporate governance, that the effectiveness of internal controls are kept under review. In the UK, these requirements do not relate only to financial controls. Although the board usually delegates this review to its audit committee, I believe that the Chairman should take a particular interest. I would encourage him to attend the meeting of the audit committee when the internal control review is discussed each year. I also believe the review should embrace issues like crisis management; the defence plan in the event of a takeover threat; and external communications, particularly with financial markets. These reviews are an essential part of reputation risk management and the Chairman should participate as necessary to discharge his responsibility for sustaining the company's reputation.

It is interesting that BP, after its run of bad news such as Texas City and Lord Browne's resignation, decided that the board itself, rather than a board committee, should assume responsibility for keeping the company's reputation under review. Similarly, in Shell, after the damage caused by the overstatement of oil reserves and the dismissal of the Chairman, the incoming Chairman saw his main task in restoring the company's reputation as being to rebuild trust with employees, investors and the media. As Lord Oxburgh told me, his main concern was to get the day-to-day business back on track as quickly as possible. I give him the last words on this topic: 'the Chairman's personality and interaction with the outside world are immensely important for the value of the company . . . the Chairman must be approachable and trusted'.

Succession planning

The Higgs review emphasised the need 'to ensure that the board as a whole has an appropriate mix of skills and experience . . . to be an effective decision-making body'. Although the Combined Code requires that a nomination committee of the board should lead the process for board appointments, and that this committee should be chaired by an independent non-executive director, I believe that in practice the Chairman will be very influential in its decisions. This is hardly surprising given his responsibility for running the board.

Chairmen agree that succession planning for board appointments is one of their main concerns. In particular, they think about succession to the Chief Executive and future non-executive directors. The Chairman will also consider potential executive directors with the Chief Executive and, privately, with the non-executive directors.

Chairmen go to some trouble to ensure that managers who are included in succession lists for board appointments are given opportunities to interact with the board, both at business meetings and in a more social environment. Many Chairmen take the opportunity to drop in at executive meetings to see how brightly the future stars are shining.

The nomination committee, which Sir Derek Higgs suggested was the least developed of the board's committees, has now become more generally recognised as having an important role. Boards understand more clearly the contribution non-executive directors can make and how difficult it is to find good ones. The time it takes to obtain the right person is often long, so the committee needs effective procedures. In large companies, the days are over when the Chairman could appoint someone informally from his 'old boys network'. Nevertheless, an effective nomination committee is an important safeguard to avoid a Chairman picking non-executive directors in his own mould. It is reasonable for the Chairman to want to find directors who will blend with the rest of the board: chemistry and collegiality are acceptable qualities to look for while cronyism is not. It is good practice for the Chairman, perhaps in consultation with the Chief Executive, to prepare a succession plan for board appointments for discussion with the nomination committee.

An effective succession plan requires the board and the nomination committee to be clear on the skills needed and the skills gaps among the board and senior management. Chairmen find that they can assess skills needs from their insights into corporate strategy which should identify the challenges and opportunities facing the company. This not only holds true for board appointments but applies equally to senior management. Skills gaps at board level are also identified in the board evaluation process. This is one reason why board evaluation is now proving popular with Chairmen.

Exposing well-regarded senior managers to the board is not risk-free. One Chairman told me that when he and some of the non-executive directors decided that two of the senior managers did not cut the mustard, he had to tell a surprised Chief Executive to remove them.

Another Chairman told me he did not believe in formal succession planning for the board. Indeed, he doubted that it really existed in practice. He certainly did not advocate a transparent process since his experience had been that the more visibility given to potential candidates, the more likely it was they would be poached by his competitors.

Building an effective board

Chairmen identified the following factors necessary for creating an effective board:

- finding the right people
- getting the communications right

- making good use of non-executive directors
- using board committees effectively
- protecting the unitary board
- creating a climate of trust
- making good use of external advisers
- promoting the use of board evaluation and director appraisal.

They accept it is their job to ensure these building blocks are in place. Most use their previous experience as board members, often as Chief Executives, to understand what can make boards work better and what inhibits effective working.

Finding the right people

Getting the right balance of skills and experience on the board is critical, as is the need to refresh the board from time to time by introducing new blood.

I found Chairmen to be divided about the wisdom of the nine-year limit for the tenure of non-executive directors. In practice, companies wishing to retain effective non-executive directors beyond nine years usually succeed in convincing their shareholders to re-elect them at the annual general meeting. One Chairman said he considered that after nine years it was time to introduce fresh thinking, with the exception of a good chairman of the audit committee. Such skills are hard to find so he was reluctant to let a good one go. The starting point for determining the skills needed on the board is the strategy. If the company intends to enter new markets or business sectors, it may need to bring onto the board directors with experience in these markets and sectors. When I was in ICI, during a period when the company was becoming more international, the board included an American, a German and a Hong Kong Chinese businessman. Earlier there had also been a Japanese non-executive director. Although managing a board which includes directors from all round the world in different time zones is more difficult, given modern communications these difficulties are certainly outweighed by the benefits their wider experience brings to the board.

At one time, Chairmen would use their contacts, or those of other members of the board, to find suitable non-executive directors. Quite often the company's advisers were used as sources for introductions. Now, the more formal procedures adopted by nomination committees involve role profiles being prepared and specialist search firms being engaged. In many cases, candidates will be totally unknown to the Chairman. Given the risks involved in being a non-executive director (largely to reputation) and the relatively low rewards, it is surprising that so many talented people are prepared to serve. The expectations of what non-executive directors can do are becoming increasingly unrealistic and their exposure ever greater. Although lip service is paid to the need for more diversity on boards, the evidence does not show that changes are happening quickly. There are more overseas directors but Chairmen prefer to have people who have run business on their boards. The spider's web of cross-directorships remains a tangled one. Nevertheless, companies in consumer goods recognise that many of their customers are women, so women are now better represented on boards of companies in this sector. However, as one Chairman said, 'diversity is great in theory but impractical given the skills required to be a non-executive director. They need to understand the business and be able to read a balance sheet.' He obviously thought that these skills are unlikely to be found in a woman. It is unsurprising but sad that less than 10 per cent of non-executive directors of FTSE 350 companies are women.

One Chairman told me he did not want 'virgin non-executive directors' on his team. He preferred to find non-executive directors who understood what was expected of them and could make an immediate value-adding contribution to the business. Although he considered the gene pool is still deep (though not all his colleagues agree), he was unhappy about the quality and experience of many he had seen. While he needed experience on his board, he rejected arrogant or outspoken candidates. In common with most Chairmen, he looked for team players with the time to be effective as well as the required skills and experience. As another Chairman put it, 'getting the right culture and social interaction is important for an effective board'. Most Chairmen emphasise personality and behaviour of a director as more important than structure or process on a board. A threat to the availability of good non-executive directors (as well as effective Chairmen) is coming from the growth in private equity. The rewards and lack of transparency (though this looks like changing) in private equity is attractive to many. One FTSE 100 Chairman has noticed the impact of private equity on the talent pool. He says that colleagues are being lured into private equity to make money, get out of the glare of the spotlight and escape the short-term focus of fund managers.

All the Chairmen I spoke to had found that the board evaluation process (discussed later) had been valuable not only in checking if the board was operating effectively but also in determining what skills were missing and whether directors needed to be replaced.

Getting the communications right

This ingredient has a number of facets. First, if the Chairman chooses to be a spokesperson for the company he needs to be good at it. A wise Chairman will normally expect his Chief Executive to handle the media and be the principal channel to the investors. Where a Chairman handles communications badly or ignores the media and investors in good times, they will find ways of getting back at him should he run into trouble later. A spectacular example of this was Philip Watts at Shell. Much criticised for his offhand treatment of the press and investors, he was vilified in the press during the reserves scandal which led to his downfall after the board and investors lost confidence in him.

A Chairman also needs to keep in regular contact with his board colleagues between board meetings and make himself available to his Company Secretary. A Chairman might give access for colleagues to his electronic diary so he can be contacted, either directly or through the Company Secretary, in an emergency. The need for good communications with the Chief Executive has been discussed earlier in this chapter, and David Jackson refers to the relationship between Chairman and Company Secretary in chapter 4. The Chairman also needs to keep in touch with the non-executive directors to make them aware of any important business developments or to alert them to any stories about the company that might appear in the media. The 'no surprises' rule is one that a Chairman needs to keep in mind. One Chairman I spoke to believed he was not sufficiently conscientious about keeping his non-executive directors up to date, and his company is one that is seldom out of the media spotlight. Another makes a point of not reading the business press himself (his wife makes sure he knows what the press are writing about him or his company), but he also makes sure his media team alert him when he needs to inform his non-executive directors about any particular news item. A number of Chairmen put in place ground rules for communications with colleagues so all are clear as to when they can expect to be informed or consulted.

A further facet of good communications is the need to ensure the board is receiving the right information at the right time. This is something the Chairman needs to work at with his Company Secretary and is an issue that can be checked out in a board evaluation. Chairmen are increasingly taking more interest in the flow of information between management and the board, and from the company to the financial markets. This should be welcomed and is consistent with the Chairman's responsibility for sustaining the company's reputation.

Making good use of non-executive directors

Having recruited non-executive directors, it is the Chairman's responsibility to make sure they are used effectively. It is sensible to try to set out the board's expectations of the non-executive director in his letter of appointment. This will be particularly useful for performance appraisal, which is now more common for non-executive directors. It is only fair that they should be told how well or badly they have performed and how the Chairman believes they can improve their contribution. Similarly, the non-executive directors will be monitoring the Chairman's performance and should be prepared to advise him of any shortcomings and, *in extremis*, if he should make way. The bringer of such bad news is usually the senior independent director, acting as *primus inter pares* (and now so recognised in his remuneration) for the non-executive directors.

Chairmen plan a series of private meetings with their non-executive directors during the year. Typically, these will be dinners the evening before a board meeting. One may be chaired by the senior independent director and will be used to appraise the Chairman's performance in his absence. Another dinner will be used to review the performance of executive directors and consider board succession plans. Chairmen encourage non-executive directors to open up on these occasions and express views about the company or the board that they might be reluctant to share 'on the record'. They are clearly considered to be important occasions and can provide early warning signals to the Chairman if there is any unease or discontent.

Chairmen should want their non-executive directors to gain as full an understanding of the business as is reasonably possible. Induction programmes for newly appointed directors have become the norm and are supervised by Chairmen. These usually include meetings with senior management and site visits. I think it is important that non-executive directors keep up to date by paying site visits and these can often be programmed into their business trips rather than made into special journeys. A curious non-executive director can get under the skin of a company by visiting the factory, the store or the sales office and asking intelligent questions. However, he should always ask the Chairman's permission before making such a visit.

Where a non-executive director has been appointed for his specialist skills, there may be a temptation for the Chairman to align him more closely to a particular business or function in the company that will benefit from his knowledge. This needs careful handling as it risks the director being seen as an advocate for that part of the organisation. In any case it is preferable in such cases to be open about the arrangement and recognise the additional contribution expected from the director by having a formal consultancy agreement which is transparent both inside the company and to investors.

The Chairman will also give a lot of thought as to how he will deploy his non-executive directors on board committees. There will be at least three committees: nomination, remuneration and audit. Some boards create additional committees such as risk, ethics and corporate social responsibility, safety, health and environment and so on. These additional committees may include both executive and non-executive directors together with senior management.

When I was a Company Secretary and there were fewer non-executive directors, it was quite common for all the non-executive directors to be on all the committees. Now the increased workload and the time required are simply too much and it is unusual for a non-executive director to be on more than two board committees. However, the former practice did have the benefit of preserving greater board unity.

Appointing the appropriate people to chair the audit and remuneration committees is critical. The audit committee is expected to be chaired by someone with financial experience who might be a retired senior partner from one of the major audit firms or a Chief Financial Officer from another company. This position can become very exposed should there be a serious fraud, failure of internal control or misstatement in the company's accounts. Committee chairmen need to be reminded, or reassured, that their committees are committees of the board which has the ultimate accountability and where all directors share responsibility for decisions. Although that might be the legal position, investors and the media will point the finger at the audit committee when there is any whiff of a financial scandal. So the committee chairman needs to be resilient and unlikely to buckle in the face of criticism. It is surprising that it is not more difficult to find non-executive directors who are willing to take up the position. When the day comes when a chairman of an audit committee is sued by investors we may find this position changes.

Similarly, the chairman of the remuneration committee must be able to manage investor reaction when it is necessary to gain acceptance for a controversial incentive scheme. The committee chairman also needs to be able to defend the pay packages of his executive colleagues. Sometimes, he will be required to support the Chairman in facing down the excessive pay demands of a greedy Chief Executive. It is not surprising that the senior independent director often chairs the remuneration committee. The decision of the Financial Reporting Council to amend the Combined Code and allow the Chairman to be a member of the remuneration committee was welcomed by Chairmen. It recognises the reality that Chairmen are highly influential in determining the pay and conditions of board members, and particularly those of the Chief Executive. The Chairman is also a key player in appraising the performance of his board colleagues.

Using board committees effectively

Chairmen seem generally content with the existing structures of board committees and believe that the appropriate issues are being considered. They appreciate that service on these committees requires a greater commitment on the part of the non-executive directors. However, such committee work is seen as a positive way in which non-executive directors can add value.

A number of Chairmen seem to attend meetings of the audit committee, which have become an increasingly important part of the board's programme. If the company is in an industry which is highly regulated, the audit committee meeting may be nearly as important as the board meeting and can last even longer. It is unrealistic to expect the audit committee to be a guarantee against fraud or other financial irregularity, although this appears to be the expectation of some investors. Where there is a fraud or financial scandal, it is often the audit committee that is called upon to supervise an investigation. This places a heavy burden on part-time non-executive directors, and Chairmen I spoke to who had experienced such investigations were not always complimentary about the contribution of their audit committees. Also such responsibilities confirm to management that non-executive directors are expected to behave more like policemen.

One Chairman told me how he was able to energise his benign audit committee by bringing in a new committee chairman who was an experienced Chief Financial Officer. The committee chairman set about rebuilding the internal audit team, visiting sites and talking to management. He upset a number of managers by the many procedural changes that quickly resulted from his appointment. The Chairman considered it was his job to encourage his audit committee chairman while reassuring the management that the changes made were in the best interests of the company.

Another Chairman, who was concerned about the unrealistic expectations investors had of his audit committee, said the blame for failure should lie with management unless the audit committee had failed to ask for proper information or had not asked the right questions.

Although a good deal of attention has focused on audit committees, some Chairmen consider it is the remuneration committee where the non-executive director can make the most valuable contribution. There have been too many examples of Chief Executives being able to negotiate excessive pay and incentives. Sometimes the excesses are tucked away in pension benefits but investors are getting wise to this tactic. A Chairman should look to the remuneration committee for support in striking a fair bargain with the Chief Executive. Should the Chief Executive fail and be asked to leave, the world will be looking to see what severance terms are agreed and whether the Chief Executive is required to mitigate any compensation for loss of office. Payment for failure will always be a hot topic but the board's main concern will be to remove a failed Chief Executive as quickly as possible even if to do so means reaching agreement on departure terms that appear to be generous. There is a tension between treating a failed Chief Executive decently while making sure he is replaced speedily. The handling of such a situation requires effective teamwork on the part of the Chairman, the chairman of the remuneration committee and the senior independent director, where he is not also the chairman of the remuneration committee.

Most remuneration committees take advice from specialist consultants whose contribution is particularly valuable for the design of complex incentive schemes. The Chairman, however, will want to be sure that the committee's recommendations for board and top management remuneration are consistent with the needs of the business and not just competitive with the company's peer group. This is an area where experience matters and I expect that service on a remuneration committee will become an increasingly attractive selling point for non-executive directors.

Protecting the unitary board

When the Cadbury Committee reported, it stressed that the unitary board was a strength of the UK corporate governance system. The Committee did not wish to see its proposals for creating board committees and additional responsibilities for non-executive directors as undermining the unitary board. Successive revisions to the Code have reinforced the monitoring role of board committees and non-executive directors adding to the threats to the coherence of the unitary board.

Most Chairmen see it as part of their responsibility for managing an effective board to protect the integrity of the unitary board. Some feel this fight is being lost. One said:

> I think we are almost creating a two-tier complex within our unitary board for which we used to pride ourselves, but now we have snoopers, patrollers and policemen, with the non-executive directors spending far too much time being policemen, and insufficient time being concerned with the strategic direction of the company. We also now have a fragmentation of the non-executive directors with the senior independent director spying on the non-executive Chairman and being entrusted to deal with the shareholder.

In the same discussion, another Chairman expressed what I believe is the more popular view:

> it seems to me that the main job of the Chairman is to get the board working as a team . . . I have seen situations where board committees have really gone off on their own, doing something that the rest of the board doesn't approve of because of slavish adherence to the rules rather than using their common sense. I think it's the Chairman's job to get everyone to understand that, while the Code has to be followed, at the same time we have to run the company. That is what we are accountable for and a lot depends on using our common sense.

If anything similar to Sarbanes-Oxley legislation were to be enacted in the UK, I believe the unitary board could be seriously threatened. One Chairman, who is also a director of a US company, told me that, following Sarbanes-Oxley, US board meetings had doubled in length and most of the meeting was attended by the company's legal advisers. That part of the meeting he regarded as being more of a box-ticking exercise. In a UK context, we would expect most of this compliance-driven business to be delegated to board committees but we could reach a point where the business of the committees became more onerous and more time consuming than that of the board.

Another Chairman, while confirming that it is his responsibility to protect the unitary board, did not feel that board committees threatened its coherence. He regarded the committees as looking after governance and, in any case, they report to the board. In practice, he said, the board did not generally have to review what was being done in the committees, and executive directors were encouraged to attend the audit committee when the quarterly results were being considered.

A further threat to the unitary board could come from shareholders seeking to exercise their rights to nominate their own directors. Chairmen run their boards as collegiate teams and this would become more difficult if the board itself had not chosen the team. UK Chairmen will be monitoring developments in the US in this area.

Creating a climate of trust

I found it reassuring in my conversations with Chairmen that they put great emphasis on their responsibility for ensuring that board relationships are built on trust. For them, personally, a trusting relationship with their Chief Executives is essential. Equally important is the need for the non-executive directors, collectively, to trust the executive directors and the management. Unfortunately, there are examples where trust breaks down when matters go badly wrong in a company. The Chairman needs to pick up the early warning signals by using his antennae and then nip the problem in the bud. To my mind, breakdowns in trust in companies are not usually the result of any betrayal but are more often caused by poor communications. One Chairman who had experience of such a breakdown on his board gave me a copy of a speech he read to his executive and non-executive directors in two groups. He was not sure that it had been effective but I believe it is worth quoting from extensively: 'An exemplary board', he wrote, 'is one which is a robust, social grouping of individuals which is capable of challenging one another's conclusions through open communications in an atmosphere of respect, trust and candour.'

This captures the spirit of the board as a collegiate team.

He goes on: 'You have to guard against your executive directors interpreting the governance guidance as "management is not to be trusted" or "the board's responsibility is to police management on behalf of the shareholders". If this is communicated to a management team from the behaviour of the Chairman . . . then you destroy all hope of a unitary board.'

Although Chairmen feel they need to be aware of any sign of a lack of integrity amongst management, there are more subtle ways of picking up such signs than behaving like policemen. The encouragement of whistle-blowing procedures is a positive feature now introduced into most large organisations.

The Chairman, in his speech, then identified problems that can arise for a Chairman. For example:

- where his predecessor dominated the board and there was an unwillingness to dissent from his view
- where the Chief Executive does not trust the board enough to share information
- where a whistle-blowing report is suppressed
- where management is nervous about communicating 'near misses' in safety reports
- where non-executive directors develop individual lines of communication to management because they receive insufficient or unreliable information or have their own agendas
- where 'political' factions develop on the board.

This is a good list of signals of a breakdown in trust, many of which have poor or ineffective communications as their source. Many can be resolved by open dialogue among board colleagues, perhaps in those meetings between the Chairman and Chief Executive or between the Chairman and the non-executive directors. Where they cannot be resolved, they must not be allowed to fester and the Chairman needs to recognise that board changes must be made.

Finally, my Chairman in his speech proposes measures for creating a climate of trust on the board:

- neutralise political cliques
- insist on proper, timely reports to the board
- ensure bad news travels quickly up to the board
- fully brief new non-executive directors – 'warts and all'
- encourage non-executive directors to listen more
- ensure board members understand the difference between dissent and disloyalty – beware 'group-think'.

He could have added measures such as articulating the values of the company and living up to those values by your behaviour and your actions; having a code of ethics and embedding it in the culture of the company; treating employees with respect and dealing with them fairly. However, his focus on maintaining trusting relationships at board level is entirely appropriate as that is where the Chairman can have the most influence. Furthermore the integrity of the company starts with the board, which needs to set the correct tone from the top.

Making good use of external advisers

The Combined Code provides that board committees should be able to call in advisers at the company's expense. Remuneration consultants have made a good living advising remuneration committees and, some would argue, helping Chief Executives and their executive colleagues grow rich by getting them paid 'above median' salaries plus generous incentives for average performance.

Nomination committees call in search firms to find candidates for board vacancies, while audit committees increasingly find themselves looking to lawyers and accountancy firms to help carry out investigations. One recalls Davis Polk and Wardwell, US attorneys, assisting the Shell audit committee with its reserves scandal or Lord Woolf investigating British Aerospace's business practices in the light of the alleged bribes for contracts in Saudi Arabia.

One Chairman I spoke to believes boards and their committees should make greater use of advisers. His company is highly regulated, with substantial interests in the US market. As previously mentioned, another Chairman was grateful that his company did not surround him with advisers when his board was in the midst of an enormous crisis.

One risk of engaging advisers is that it increases the chances of a leak to the press. This is particularly true in the case of corporate actions such as takeover bids, where a company cannot help using advisers though the number can be controlled. Leaks of commercially sensitive information that can create a disorderly market in the company's share price are far too common in these situations. The finger is often pointed at the advisers though far from easy to prove. It is up to the Chairman to make it clear to advisers that the chances of getting future business from the company are nil if such a leak can be shown to come from them. Also, if there should be a leak, the Chairman must make sure it is thoroughly investigated. While I was Company Secretary at ICI during a period of hyperactivity on the mergers and acquisitions front, I can only recall one possible leak. I am sure it helped that our advisers knew precisely what would happen in the event of a leak being traced to their firm.

In my final years at ICI it sometimes felt that the company had been overrun by advisers. Management consultants and investment banks would be invited to many of the board meetings. This did not go unnoticed by management, who asked the question 'Who is running the company?'

As a former regulator (after leaving ICI), I am pleased, of course, that boards do take professional advice on issues relating to their listing obligations or other technical issues where the consequences of wrong decisions could seriously damage the interests of shareholders or other stakeholders. There are many other board decisions where directors are being rewarded for using their judgement and experience. Chairmen should not easily concede the collective wisdom around the board table to the advice of a consultant, who has little to lose, unless the issue is beyond the competence of the board.

Promoting the use of board evaluation and director appraisal

The Higgs review of the Combined Code advocated more rigorous board evaluation procedures and offered guidance as to how this might be done. At the time, many Chairmen considered that such a requirement was, at best, a waste of time and, in any event, demeaning to the intelligence and experience of those who serve on boards of quoted companies. Where Chairmen supported the proposal, they were frequently met with resistance from their board colleagues.

Now, board evaluation is seen as one of the best things to come out of the Higgs review. There are many ways of carrying out an evaluation, but what is more important is that the process will not be effective unless it is fully supported by the Chairman. Indeed, in many companies, it is the Chairman who leads the process supported either by an external facilitator or by the Company Secretary. Evaluation not only is designed to review board effectiveness but also may look at the performance of individual directors, including the Chairman. One Chairman considers the idea of a peer review of individual directors' performance as 'cobblers'. Companies differ as to how they appraise their directors, but the Chairman's performance will usually be reviewed by the non-executive directors led by the senior independent director.

In some board evaluations, when the performance of individual directors is being scored by their peers, these scores will be disclosed to the Chairman and may also be shared with the whole board. One Chairman was quite explicit in saying he used the process to get rid of weak non-executive directors.

Investors also confirm that they regard board evaluation as useful and prefer to see it being facilitated by external consultants as a check on the Chairman's influence. Investors make the point that evaluations are only as useful as the actions that result. It is essential that the board, under the Chairman's leadership, develops an action plan following the evaluation and that the action plan is regularly reviewed by the board so that improvements in board performance are monitored.

Qualities of an effective chairman

I asked most of the Chairmen I spoke to what they regard as the qualities of an effective Chairman. I was struck by the variety of characteristics suggested. The most common one quoted was leadership but that begs the question of what qualities make up good leadership. The list below shows all the characteristics that were mentioned:

leadership	transparent
coach	objective
visionary	ethical
strategic thinker	confident
approachable	trustworthy
integrity	consistent
assiduous	decisive
knowledgeable	adaptable
accountable	courageous

Small wonder that effective Chairmen are not easy to find. Also, it is supposed to be the Chairman's job to make his Chief Executive look a hero but, surely, a person with all the above qualities would be a god. One attribute I might have added is a sense of humour. In my opinion, courage ranks high on the list of desirable qualities and the list excludes the quality which I would suggest is the most important for a Chairman and for any director: good judgement. For a Chairman it is often his ability to judge people that will make him more successful, rather than his business judgement. As one Chairman said to me, 'It's managing the people that matters, the issues are usually relatively straight-forward.' Another said:

> Ultimately the good boards have good judgement and good companies are those where the boards have made the right judgements in terms of strategy, management, and execution. We must not forget we are all individuals, we all have our faults. We must not let the requirements of corporate governance let us forget about our thoughts or forget about our judgement.

If judgement is so important, this suggests that Chairmen cannot be made more effective by special training. This is certainly the view of most Chairmen I met. Although they accept that induction is useful when they first join the board and they appreciate being updated on legal or other technical developments, they consider their previous experience on boards of companies has sufficiently equipped them for the job. One Chairman said he would regard a training programme as insulting and would be 'teaching grandmother to suck eggs'. Another said you are not asked to be a Chairman unless you have demonstrated you have the necessary skills. Chairmen have created their own more informal support groups of fellow Chairmen meeting once or twice a year, which they find useful.

In conclusion, in arguing that the role of the Chairman is vital for effective governance, I would quote another of the Chairmen I have interviewed for this chapter: 'The Combined Code can only supply a structure; it can't supply the soul of the board. Governance depends on how well the board works, and that depends first and foremost on the Chairman.'

3

The role of the non-executive director

MURRAY STEELE

Introduction

I am frequently asked: 'What is the role of a non-executive director (NED)?' In 1996, when we were undertaking research prior to launching the Cranfield NED Seminar, the answer was far from clear. We were told jokes such as: 'What's the difference between an NED and a supermarket shopping trolley?' Answer: 'One can hold large amounts of food and drink while the other is useful for taking the shopping home and occasionally has a mind of its own.'

This lack of awareness, in conjunction with recent corporate scandals and growing shareholder activism, has put a greater focus on the role of the NED. The role was significantly clarified by the Higgs Report in 2003. Today I believe the answer to the question is much clearer and can be best summed up by the following quotation: 'The fundamental job of NEDs is to see that the company is properly run, but not to run the company.' I am unaware of the source of the quotation, but I believe it describes accurately and appropriately what is a complex and demanding role.

The importance of the NED has changed significantly over time. This quotation sums up how the role used to be viewed:

> Coote got me in as a director of something or other. Very good business for me – nothing to do except go down to the City once or twice a year to one of those hotel places and sit around a table where they have some very nice new blotting paper. Then Coote or some clever Johnny makes a speech simply bristling with figures, but fortunately you needn't listen to it – and I can tell you, you often get a jolly good lunch out of it.

How complex and demanding the role is today is aptly portrayed by this job advertisement:

> Experienced professional required for demanding role in small but influential team. Although the role is part time (up to 18 days a year) there is scope to make a significant contribution to a multi-million pound operation. Commensurate with this, the successful candidate will need to be fully versed in stakeholder issues and may be required to fall on his or her sword as appropriate.
>
> To be successful, the candidate must have an extensive working knowledge of corporate finance, business planning, financial analysis, auditing,

regulation and compliance, human resources, remuneration policy, organisational theory and change management.

On a personal level, he or she will be an experienced diplomat, negotiator, lateral thinker, communicator, trouble shooter, and will have the drive and energy to ensure successful outcomes.

Pay and benefits negligible. Risks potentially enormous.

Role of a non-executive director

This chapter is intended to bring alive both what is the role of an effective NED and the personal qualities required to be successful in the role. The Higgs Report provided a clear summary of the role of an NED:

> *Strategy*: NEDs should constructively challenge and contribute to the development of strategy.
>
> *Performance*: NEDs should scrutinise the performance of management in meeting agreed goals and objectives and monitor the reporting of performance.
>
> *Risk*: NEDs should satisfy themselves that financial information is accurate and that financial controls and systems of risk management are robust and defensible.
>
> *People*: NEDs are responsible for determining appropriate levels of remuneration of executive directors and have a prime role in appointing and, where necessary, removing senior management, and in succession planning.

This summary caused some consternation among company executives, particularly the item on strategy. This is best described by a personal experience. Since the 1980s, I have facilitated numerous board strategy awaydays. During the planning I would always inquire who would be attending. Invariably the conversation went something like this:

> MS: So who'll be attending the strategy awayday?
>
> CEO: Myself, the Finance Director, the HR director, the marketing director and the two divisional directors.
>
> MS: So only executive directors. What about inviting the NEDs to attend?
>
> CEO: Why would we want to invite them? We've always found that they don't make much contribution to the strategy debate when there is the opportunity to do so.
>
> MS: So the executives will go on the strategy awayday, develop the bones of a strategy, come back and the FD will flesh it out. At the next board meeting you'll present it to the NEDs, almost as a fait accompli.
>
> CEO: That's a good way of describing it

Higgs concluded that NEDs can bring valuable insights to the strategy development process, but only if they are involved from the beginning. They can make significant contributions through effective challenging of executives as a result of their relative distance from day-to-day operations combined with their

51

external experience. However, to do this effectively they have to be engaged with the business, which means they should have an understanding of:

• the company's operating environment, particularly the major forces which could impact the company's prospects such as technological change; legal and regulatory developments
• the essential dynamics of the industry in which the company operates
• competitors – who are the key ones; what is the basis of their competitive position?
• customers – which are the key customer segments, how are they changing, what are the forces that shape changing demand?

Without this knowledge and understanding it will be difficult for NEDs to establish their credibility with the executive directors. In addition to developing their own understanding, effective NEDs should be satisfying themselves that the executive directors are keeping their own knowledge up to date.

In many instances, challenging the executives means getting them to distinguish between their prejudices and the facts. There is a temptation, especially where executives have worked together over an extended time, for management to lapse into Acceptable Underperformance. This occurs when members of a management team have roughly the same mindset which manifests itself in the belief that the effort required to improve performance cannot be justified: 'Where we are is good enough and cannot be improved upon.' A typical Acceptable Underperformance conversation between an NED and a marketing director might be as follows:

NED: What's our current customer service rating?
Mkt. Dir.: The last survey we did showed that we had a 90% level of satisfaction.
NED: Are you happy with that? Where does it place us relative to our customers?
Mkt. Dir.: It's OK. We're in the second tier, probably second percentile.
NED: What would it cost to improve our satisfaction level to say 95% and what would the return be?
Mkt. Dir.: It wouldn't be worth the effort. Everybody knows that.
NED: Have you got any empirical analysis to support your views?
Mkt. Dir.: Well no, but the board are all agreed . . .

This situation could be acceptable if the executive directors had hard evidence to support their views, but, as so often happens, all they have is the strength of their convictions based on their experience. The basis of effective challenging is therefore to ask good questions.

Importance of the role of non-executive director

Figure 3.1 explains the importance of the role of NED. Corporate boards are responsible for the governance of their companies, and executive boards (or

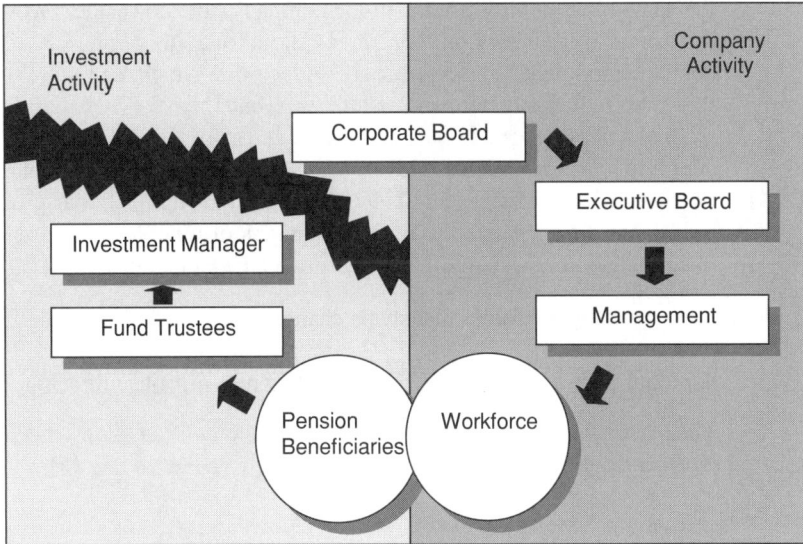

Source: Hermes

Figure 3.1 The importance of the role of non-executive director

committees) are responsible for the management and performance of the company. Both have a significant responsibility for generating shareholder value. Why is shareholder value so important in today's economic climate? Companies have workforces who will ultimately be pension beneficiaries. The pension fund trustees invariably delegate the management of the fund to professional investment managers, and what do they invest in? Companies, either listed on stock markets or privately held through private equity or venture capital funds/companies. Unfortunately this is where the cycle breaks down, as few investment managers are interested in engaging effectively with the companies in which they have invested to improve their performance, thus driving up shareholder value for the benefit of all of us as current and future pensioners. Sadly, they are mere 'renters' of shares, selling them at the slightest hint of trouble and thus passing the problem on to another investment manager. This approach was summed up nicely by a senior investment manager who said: 'No one ever washes a rental car.'

Consequently the role of the NED is both vital and complex. Institutional investors expect NEDs to bridge the gap between themselves and the companies in which they invest. They expect them to be both the promoters and the custodians of shareholder value through the application of effective corporate governance, whilst at the same time fulfilling their duties as directors of the company. The law does not recognise any distinction between executive and non-executive directors. NEDs can suffer from schizophrenia in that they should be encouraging the development of the company, 'the upside', while at the same time monitoring risk to the company, 'the downside'. Working with the executive directors on these areas should lead to greater success for the company and hence enhanced shareholder value which, as Figure 3.1 shows, flows through into better pensions for everyone.

In the non-corporate sector there has been a growth in demand for independent NEDs in areas such as Government departments, the NHS, education and charities. Since its election in 1997, the Labour Government has promoted the usefulness of independent NEDs as members of top management teams both to strengthen their capabilities and to undertake a monitoring role on behalf of stakeholders.

Personal skills and attributes of an effective non-executive director

The personal skills of an effective NED fall into two categories – technical and interpersonal.

Technical

Effective NEDs should have a sound understanding of:

1. *Strategy and development*, including an understanding of:
   * the company's external environment
   * the dynamics of the industry in which the company operates
   * the markets in which the company operates
   * the requirements of its customers
   * the nature of its competitors and their strategies
   * risk management
2. *Legal, regulatory and corporate governance*, including an understanding of:
   * the principles of strategic change
   * relevant developments in the Companies Act and securities laws
   * developments in regulation, such as health and safety; competition and employment
   * the trends in corporate governance
3. *Finance*, including an understanding of:
   * the principal components of the Annual Report and Accounts – profit and loss account, balance sheet and cash flow statements
   * operating financial reports, the financial information discussed at board meetings
   * the economic model of the company
   * raising capital, appropriate capital structures and cost of capital
   * evaluating investment decisions
   * the drivers of shareholder value
   * shareholder relationships.

That a lack of understanding in these areas can be dangerous was brought home to me in a seminar I organised for members of audit committees of listed companies. During a discussion, I commented that all directors, regardless of whether they were executives or non-executives, shared the same responsibilities and liabilities in the eyes of the law. To my astonishment, a director of a large company, supported by four of his colleagues, told me in no uncertain terms that I was talking utter rubbish. This small example highlights a level of ignorance which could damage the individual director's credibility.

Interpersonal

The technical skills outlined above will only be of value to a board if the individual NED also has the interpersonal skills to utilise them appropriately. This is summed up perfectly in the Higgs Report: 'The key to NED effectiveness lies as much in behaviours and relationships as in structure and processes.'

It is important to establish a spirit of partnership and mutual respect on the board. This can only be done if NEDs make effective contributions which enable them to gain the trust of the executives. This can be difficult given the fundamental tension that exists in the split role of an NED: both to support executives in their leadership of the business and to monitor and supervise their conduct.

Essential personal attributes for effective NEDs are integrity and high ethical standards, which are a prerequisite for all directors. Sound judgement and an inquiring mind are also essential. So situations in which NEDs can find themselves rarely conform to any predictable pattern. Relying on judgement, developed from experience, is often the only route available to NEDs, who should have the ability and willingness to challenge and probe the executive directors. This requires them to have sufficient strength of character to seek full and satisfactory answers. A critical area of judgement for an NED is how far to push questioning if they are not receiving acceptable answers. Not pushing far enough may mean they are not fulfilling their obligations as a director; pushing too far could mean destabilising relationships and upsetting the collegiality of the board. The basis for NEDs challenging the executives should be their relative distance from day-to-day matters combined with their external experience.

Summarising the personal skills and attributes of effective NEDs, they should:

- question intelligently
- debate constructively
- challenge rigorously
- decide dispassionately.

All are equally important.

Importance of independence

A non-executive director, according to the Higgs Report, is considered independent when the board determines that the director is independent in character and judgement and there are no relationships or circumstances which could affect, or appear to affect, the director's judgement.

Such adverse relationships or circumstances would include where the director:

- is a former employee of the company or group unless employment (or any other material connection) has ended five years earlier
- has, or has had within the last three years, a material business relationship with the company either directly, or as a partner, shareholder, director or senior employee of a body that has such a relationship with the company
- has received or receives additional remuneration from the company apart from a director's fee, participates in the company's share option or a performance-related pay scheme, or is a member of the company's pension scheme
- has close family ties with any of the company's advisers, directors or senior employees
- holds cross-directorships or has significant links with other directors through involvement in other companies or bodies
- represents a significant shareholder
- has served on the board for more than nine years.

Investors view independence as a safeguard against conflicts of interest that might allow executives to 'capture' NEDs and restrain them from challenging executives because they share their mindsets.

Non-executive director dilemmas

There are three fundamental dilemmas which NEDs face:

Engaged and non-executive

NEDs' effectiveness stems from their degree of engagement with the company. Today it is no longer sufficient just to turn up at board meetings. Research has shown that executives on boards attach great weight to NEDs having previous executive experience but this can lead to problems.

An example was a FTSE 350 company with a young Chief Executive of whom the board had high hopes that he would lead the company into the FTSE 100. The Chairman, through search consultants, managed to persuade a Chief Executive of a FTSE 100, upon his retirement, to become an NED of the company. This would be his first NED position and the Chairman and the rest of the board hoped that he would mentor their young Chief Executive. At his first board meeting, the first item on the agenda was a decision that the board needed to make about an investment. The discussion had gone on for two hours when the former Chief Executive made his first contribution to the meeting by shouting loudly across the boardroom table at the young Chief Executive: 'Good God, sonny, it's ∗∗∗∗ing obvious, just do it.' After the meeting the Chairman had a quiet word with the new NED and this turned out to be his first and last board meeting, as he had clearly crossed the line between being an executive and a non-executive director.

Challenge and support

The essence of effectiveness of an NED comes from skilful challenge which stimulates action by executives and forces them to reflect on their future actions. Such challenge should set standards for executive performance and conduct. For example, when executive directors are preparing investment proposals to the board, they are more likely to be of a higher quality if they know they are going to be skilfully challenged by the NEDs. Effective challenge by NEDs has to be seen by the executive directors to be well informed, and needs to be motivated by a concern to enhance executive performance and not to promote the NEDs' egos.

Independence and involvement

NEDs' independence is viewed by executives as their having the ability, as outsiders, to see things differently: an independence of mind that allows NEDs to challenge executive thinking on the basis of their external experience. This independence offsets the potential capture of NEDs' thinking by executives. Boards never function optimally when everyone thinks along similar lines. Independence should encourage greater openness which should lead to the full use of NED experience and judgement.

Barriers to NED effectiveness

Research undertaken for the Higgs Report identified two major barriers to NED effectiveness. These were that 25 per cent of NEDs believed the main barrier to their effectiveness was their own lack of time or commitment to the company; and that a lack of knowledge or understanding of the company was cited by 10 per cent of NEDs and 19 per cent of executive directors as a barrier to effectiveness.

This first point leads to two very important questions for NEDs and companies. *How much time does it take to be an effective NED? Is it worth it?*

The 2006 Independent Chairman and Non-Executive Director Survey from Independent Remuneration Solutions (IRS) sheds some interesting light on these questions as shown in Table 3.1. IRS estimates that the amount of time NEDs are spending on their duties has increased by approximately 20 per cent since the publication of the Higgs Report in 2003. Typically for an NED, the

Table 3.1 The number of days spent by non-executive directors at company meetings						
	Company sales £M					
	<10	*11–30*	*31–100*	*101–500*	*501–1000*	*1000+*
Formal meetings:						
Board	9	8	9	9	9	8
Strategy	1	2	2	2	3	3
Audit committees	1	2	2	2	3	4
Remuneration committees	1	2	2	2	3	3
Nomination committees	0	1	1	1	2	3
Other	1	1	1	2	2	2
Preparation committees	3	4	4	4	4	5
Visits and research	1	1	2	2	4	4
Total	**17**	**21**	**23**	**24**	**30**	**32**

Source: IRS, 'Independent Chairman and Non-executive Director Survey', 2006.

time commitment can be estimated as two days per month, broken down into one meeting per month plus one day's preparation. Chairmanship or membership of board committees or attending strategy development sessions would be additional.

The amount of time depends on a number of circumstances. Cranfield research has shown that an executive director becomes ineffective as an NED if, in addition to executive duties, he also has more than two NED appointments. The general rule of thumb is that if you are a full-time NED then five, possibly six, appointments are doable. However, this is based on the assumption that the companies are all performing satisfactorily. If one or more of the companies gets into difficulty, then management of the NED's personal diary becomes an issue. Numerous directors in this situation suddenly find the need to cancel holidays. There are significant pitfalls if you do not devote sufficient time to the role of an NED as the following example shows.

One NED, who had many such appointments, frequently read the board papers during the journey to the meeting. On one particular day he caught an early train for a board meeting and during the journey felt he had familiarised himself with the papers. The first item on the agenda was a review of the previous month's performance. The NED challenged the Finance Director about an aspect of the company's performance. The FD appeared to have difficulty answering the NED's questions. The more the FD was unable to respond the more intense became the questioning from the NED. The atmosphere was becoming distinctly uncomfortable until another NED, who was sitting next to the assertive questioner, leaned across him, looked at his board papers and said: 'It would appear that you have the board papers for another company.' In his haste to catch his train, the NED had picked up the papers for his next board meeting, two days hence. Needless to say, he contributed

Table 3.2 The remuneration of NEDs in relation to size of company

	Company sales £M									
	<10		11–30		31–100		101–500		501–1000	1001+
	Q	P	Q	P	Q	P	Q	P	Q	Q
Lowest, £000s	5	3	8	8	15	12	20	18	30	32
Highest, £000s	30	15	35	22	35	27	42	40	50	85
Daily rate, £	950	500	1040	540	1080	670	1190	1080	1250	1410

P= Private company, Q = Quoted company.
Source: IRS, 'Independent Chairman and Non-executive Director Survey', 2006.

little to the remainder of the meeting and had to work very hard to regain his credibility.

Is it worth being an NED? The simple answer is that in purely financial terms it almost certainly is not worth it. Table 3.2, again taken from the IRS 2006 Survey, shows the remuneration of NEDs in relation to size of company sales. In the quoted company sector, NED fees have increased significantly in recent years to attract the increased number of independent NEDs required by the Higgs Report recommendations, and to compensate for the greater risks associated with the position. In the unlisted sector, remuneration is lower, with the equivalent of £1000 per day being a good rate for the job. However, IRS believes that the rate of increase in NED fees in private companies has been catching up with that of quoted companies, reflecting the growing awareness of the importance and responsibilities of the role.

It is still a reasonable conclusion that the financial rewards for NEDs do not match the risks and liabilities associated with the position.

The second barrier to effectiveness, concerning an NED's lack of knowledge or understanding of the company, highlights one of the problems of being an NED: the potential for a difficult relationship with the executive directors. Cranfield research has shown that executive directors dislike professional NEDs.

A significant, and probably most important, part of the Chairman's role is to ensure effective functioning of the whole board. In many cases the linkage between the executive and non-executive directors is at best weak or even non-existent. Executives feel that NEDs do not have the same commitment to the company as they do and consequently that they are not objective. In many cases, executives believe that they run the business while NEDs are responsible for all the corporate governance 'stuff' which the executives perceive as a hindrance to effective management.

The senior independent director (SID)

The role of the senior independent director was first proposed in the Hampel Report in 1998 and its value was reiterated in the Higgs Report to the extent that it is now enshrined in the Combined Code. Prior to the Hampel Report, there had been a number of situations where boards had been in dispute and one of the NEDs had taken the initiative to work with the members of the board to resolve the conflict.

A good example of this was Sir Peter Middleton at United Utilities during 1997 when a serious dispute over executive remuneration arose, not only in the board but also between the board and the institutional investors. Sir Peter worked diligently, mainly behind the scenes, to resolve the dispute. This prompted a number of institutional investors to lobby the Hampel committee to propose the role of the SID. Previously the duties of the SID may have been carried out by the Deputy Chairman but the institutional investors wished to have a role which carried greater independence. So what is the role?

In simple terms, it is an alternative to the Chairman, particularly where there is a possibility of the Chairman's thinking being captured by the executive directors, thus potentially compromising the effective working of the board. The SID should be available to shareholders, if they are concerned that they cannot resolve issues through the normal channels of contact with the Chairman or Chief Executive. Additionally, the SID should chair meetings of non-executive directors when the Chairman does not attend.

NEDs and board committees

A significant time commitment for NEDs is membership of the principal board committees – nomination, remuneration and audit. Nearly all companies in the FTSE 350 have these committees and they are growing in number outside that sector. Similarly, private companies, especially those which are private equity or venture capital backed, are introducing audit and remuneration committees.

Both remuneration and audit committees have had increased scrutiny in recent years: remuneration committees because of the media's fixation with the 'fat cat' syndrome and audit committees because of their responsibility for the accuracy of the company's annual report and accounts. Greater scrutiny of audit committees has been created by the Sarbanes-Oxley Act, which led to much greater oversight of published accounts.

The Smith Report into audit committees, which was released at the same time as the Higgs Report, states that the audit committee should consist of at least three independent NEDs, one of whom should have significant, recent and relevant financial experience. These requirements, together with the greater scrutiny caused by Sarbanes-Oxley, have affected the willingness of NEDs to serve on audit committees. In the Ernst & Young Corporate Governance Survey published in January 2005, two-thirds of NEDs stated that they were less likely to accept the position of chairman of the audit committee than twelve months previously.

Board evaluation

Another relatively recent issue facing NEDs is that of board evaluation. The Higgs Report recommended that board evaluation should be introduced and it was included in the Combined Code. The principles are listed below:

- The board should undertake a formal and rigorous annual evaluation of its own performance and that of its committees and individual directors.
- Individual evaluation should aim to show whether each director continues to contribute effectively and to demonstrate commitment to the role (including commitment of time for board and committee meetings and any other duties). The Chairman should act on the results of the performance evaluation by recognising the strengths and addressing the weaknesses of the board and, where appropriate, proposing new members be appointed to the board or seeking the resignation of directors.
- The board should state in the annual report how performance evaluation of the board, its committees and its individual directors has been conducted. The NEDs, led by the senior independent director, should be responsible for performance evaluation of the Chairman, taking into account the views of executive directors.

Prior to the introduction of these principles only a handful of the UK's largest companies conducted any form of board evaluation. Whilst regular appraisal and evaluation of executives and managers was an accepted practice throughout the vast majority of companies, it was not in the boardroom.

There appear to be two approaches to board evaluation in the UK: one welcomes the use of outside expertise; the other does not. A typical performance evaluation statement is shown below.

> With the full support of the Board, the Chairman led a formal evaluation of the performance of the Board and its key committees. The process, which included interviews with each Director and the Company Secretary, was conducted by an external independent consultant. The review concluded that the Tesco Board is highly effective and that there have been significant improvements in the Board's culture, dynamics and administrative processes during the year. *Tesco Annual Report*

Other companies make similar statements but do not necessarily state explicitly that outside consultants have been used. Clearly, for many boards the thought of opening themselves up to outside scrutiny is just too difficult to contemplate. This is another issue that is not going to go away. The CEO of a major institutional investor remarked, at the time of the launch of the revised Combined Code, that board evaluation would be a big issue for them in the coming years.

Board evaluation is starting to make an impact. In a recent conversation with an experienced Chairman who sits on the boards of a number of FTSE 350 companies, he commented that he was now seeing very few 'duds' in boardrooms, and he considered that NEDs were much more professional than they were five years previously.

Training for NEDs

NED training is an interesting but sensitive issue. The Higgs Report made two statements on NED training. First, 'There should be a step change in training and development provision for board members.' As a result of this observation, there was an initial rush of training providers into the market. In 2006 very few remained. Despite the encouragement of Higgs, there has not been a step change in demand by NEDs for training. Second, '62 per cent of NEDs in listed companies have never received any training for their role.' Given the research that Cranfield conducted prior to launching its NED Seminar in 1997, it is likely that this percentage should be closer to 92 than 62.

Why is there such antipathy and even hostility among directors to NED training? The situation was summed up in an interview with an NED as part of the research to establish the appropriate content of the Cranfield NED Seminar. He said that if we called the event a course or programme no self-respecting NED would attend, but a seminar was acceptable. Hence the Cranfield NED Seminar is called just that and its creation has been supported by Hermes. To launch the Seminar, the Chairman of Hermes wrote to the Chairman of every company in the FTSE All Share Index. A number of Chairmen responded by complaining that the calibre and integrity of their NEDs had been impugned by the receipt of an invitation to attend a seminar which they obviously did not need. There seems to be a belief among directors that if you join a board as an NED you are displaying weakness by suggesting that you require training for the role. Most companies would develop their executive directors for senior positions but this logic does not seem to apply to NEDs.

Diversity

Over the last few years the issue of diversity on boards has been debated extensively. The Higgs Report highlighted the lack of diversity and his research concluded that previous board experience is often seen to be the main, and sometimes only, competence demanded of potential NED candidates. In 2003, NEDs were typically white males nearing retirement age, with previous board experience. Other statistics for the FTSE 100, were:

- Fewer than twenty NEDs (in total) were under 45.
- 7 per cent of NEDs were non-British.

- 1 per cent were from black and ethnic minority groups.
- Women constituted 30 per cent of the managerial population but only 6 per cent of NEDs.
- There were two female FTSE 350 chairmen.

Higgs concluded that the qualities required to make an effective contribution to the board can be acquired from a variety of backgrounds and a further investigation into the pool of potential NEDs was undertaken by Laura Tyson, Dean of the London Business School. The Tyson Report supported Higgs and argued the case for diversity:

> The best boards are composed of individuals with different skills, knowledge, information, power and time to contribute. Given the diversity of expertise, information, and availability that is needed to understand and govern today's complex businesses, it is unrealistic to expect an individual director to be knowledgeable and informed about all phases of business. It is also unrealistic to expect individual directors to be available at all times and to influence all decisions. Thus, in staffing most boards, it is best to think of individuals contributing different pieces to the total picture that it takes to create an effective board.

Higgs had recommended that a list should be developed of 100 individuals from the non-commercial sector with the relevant experience and skills that contribute to being an effective NED. Tyson declined to create such a list, citing the need to consider every NED appointment on its individual merits.

The case for greater diversity in board composition was further strengthened in December 2004 when the DTI published *Building better boards*. This argued strongly, supported by a number of case studies, that more diverse boards performed more effectively than less diverse boards.

So, with all this debate, have UK boards become more diverse?

Since 2000, Cranfield School of Management's Centre for Developing Women Business Leaders has been producing its Female FTSE Report. Whilst gender is only one dimension of diversity, it is the one that has been subject to the most in-depth research.

In the 2005 Female FTSE Report, seventy-eight FTSE 100 companies, a new record number, had women directors, up 13 per cent on the previous year. The new female directors are more likely to be international, have board experience and have much richer, more varied work backgrounds than the men. Six FTSE 100 companies had appointed their first ever woman director. However, only eleven FTSE 100 companies now had female executive directors, down from thirteen in 2004. Twenty-two of the FTSE 100 boards were still all-male. Table 3.3 shows the development of women directors in the FTSE 100 companies from 2000 to 2005. Diversity on boards in the UK is an issue that is not going to go away for NEDs.

Table 3.3 Women directors in the FTSE 100 companies, 2000–2005						
	2005	2004	2003	2002	2001	2000
Female-held directorships	121	110	101	84	75	69
	(10.5%)	(9.7%)	(8.6%)	(7.2%)	(6.4%)	(5.8%)
Female executive directorships	14	17	17	15	10	11
	(3.4%)	(4.1%)	(3.7%)	(3.0%)	(2.0%)	(2.0%)
Female NEDs	107	93	84	69	65	60
	(14.5%)	(13.06%)	(11.8%)	(10.0%)	(9.6%)	(9.1%)
Women holding FTSE directorships	99	96	88	75	68	60
Companies with women executive directors	11	13	13	12	8	10
Companies with at least one woman director	78	69	68	61	57	58
Companies with no women directors	22	31	32	39	43	42

Source: Cranfield School of Management, 'The Female FTSE', November 2005.

Conclusion

The role of NEDs today is vital for all of us. Their performance on company boards has a direct bearing on the shareholder value of the company and ultimately the security of our pensions. In the public sector, effective NEDs also have a direct influence on both our welfare and our wealth. As directors of public sector organisations they can exert significant influence on the expenditure of taxpayers' money.

Consequently, as a result both of their responsibilities and of the rapidly changing environment in which companies operate, the NED role today is complex and demanding. It requires skills, experience, integrity, and particular behaviours and personal attributes. NEDs have to deal with interesting dilemmas: they need both to challenge and to support the executive directors; be both engaged and non-executive; and be both independent and involved. Independence, in particular, has become an increasingly important attribute for NEDs. The exercise of independent thought and judgement is generally regarded as likely to lead to more effective boards.

The operating climate for companies and their directors shows no sign of a reduction in the rate of change. An example of this is the new Companies Act. These changes, and the significantly increased responsibilities of directors in general, mean that being an effective NED is no longer a job for the lucky amateur. NEDs, to remain effective, will have to be prepared to acquire and develop the relevant technical and interpersonal skills. This takes time. It is no longer acceptable just to turn up for board meetings having read the board papers the day before.

Previously NEDs performed their functions without any evaluation of their performance; indeed they frequently saw their role as being the evaluators of performance of others. Today, like any other director, NEDs must expect their performance to be subject to, at least, annual review.

A positive trend around the role of NEDs is that there is now much greater clarity than there was in 1996. Similarly, there is more training and general assistance available to NEDs. Key to this was the Higgs Report published in 2003.

It is worth repeating that 'the fundamental job of NEDs is to see that the company is properly run, but not to run the company'.

References

Cranfield School of Management, *The Female FTSE*, November 2005

DTI, *Building better boards*, December 2004

> *Review of the Role and Effectiveness of Non-executive Directors*. The Higgs Report, January 2003

Patrick Dunne, *Directors' Dilemmas*, 2nd rev. edn, London: Kogan Page, 2005

Patrick Dunne, *Running Board Meetings*, 3rd rev. edn, London: Kogan Page, 2007

The Independent Chairman and Non-executive Director Survey, Independent
   Remuneration Solutions, 2006

T. McNulty, J. Roberts and P. Styles, *Creating Accountability within the Board: The
   Work of the Effective Non-executive Director: A Report for the Review of the
   Role and Effectiveness of the Non-executive Director*, London: Department of
   Trade and Industry, 2002

Glynis D. Morris and Patrick Dunne, *Tolley's Non-executive Director's Handbook*,
   London: Lexis Nexis Tolley, 2003

4

The role of the Company Secretary

DAVID JACKSON

Introduction

It is the question that you always slightly dread being asked at a dinner party: 'What do you do?' You say that you are a Company Secretary. The questioner normally nods, says something like 'how interesting' and moves the conversation on. The slightly more inquisitive may add, 'and what does that mean?' You say something inadequate about being involved with working with the board of a company and being a lawyer in business and, generally, working in the field of corporate governance. Having asked the second question, the inquirer never has the courage of the good non-executive director to ask the 'third question' and therefore promptly changes the subject.

In today's world, the role of the Company Secretary has no one meaning and covers a multitude of tasks and responsibilities. That said, the role lies at the heart of the governance systems of quoted companies and is receiving ever greater focus.

No matter what other responsibilities the Company Secretary has, his task is to serve and advise his board. This core role alone is becoming more challenging as the work of the board and its committees expands to meet the demands of developing corporate governance systems. I shall examine the evolution of the role of the Company Secretary of a quoted company together with the evolution of the work of the board. I shall pose two questions:

- Has the Company Secretary moved his or her focus to address issues concerned with the executive management of the company, in a compliance capacity, or is he focusing on the governance systems of the board which can affect board performance?
- What will Company Secretaries be doing in five years' time?

All this against the background of current governance policy in the UK and the developments associated with the Companies Act 2006, which notably allows private companies to dispense with the office of Company Secretary. As the office is to be preserved in quoted companies, the legislators must have clear expectations of the role that the holder of that office should play!

The background

How has the office of Company Secretary developed over recent time?

A major step forward occurred with the 1948 Companies Act when, for the first time, the Company Secretary was defined as an officer of the company and made legally liable for complying with the terms of the Act. The first recognition by the Courts of the increasing importance of the role came in a Court of Appeal decision in 1971 when Lord Justice Salmon described the Company Secretary as 'the Chief Administrative Officer of the company'.

Development of the role is also evidenced by the establishment of the Institute of Chartered Secretaries and Administrators (ICSA). The initial object of the Institute was the development of the profession of Company Secretary and the creation of high standards for that profession. As the position of the Company Secretary became established in law, and as membership of the ICSA increased, the aim of the ICSA has expanded to support the reputation of Chartered Secretaries as practitioners of good governance.

Lord Shepherd, as Chairman of Grand Metropolitan, was asked in the 1990s to give his view of the role of the Company Secretary. He gave this response:

- The Secretary should contribute to the general management of the company given his 'bird's eye view'.
- The Secretary should be the confidante and adviser to the Directors, a sounding board for the Chairman and indeed for the other Directors.
- The Secretary should be able to monitor the effects of change and to communicate in a simple and user-friendly manner.
- The Secretary should ensure that the board sticks by its values and that the values of the Board should be communicated within the wider company as a whole.
- The Secretary should be able to deal with and assess people.
- Finally the Secretary should ensure that the obligations of the company to both shareholders and stakeholders are met.

This, to my mind, is consistent with the idea of the Company Secretary being the Chief Administrative Officer: the trusted adviser and the 'conscience of the company'.

The twenty-first-century Company Secretary can be required to do all of the above. He may also be the General Counsel, charged with looking after a broad range of legal issues and supervising the legal department. He may be responsible for pensions, human resources, property, regulation and compliance. The variety of tasks that the modern Company Secretary can be asked to fulfil often depends upon the nature of the business of the company, the distribution of other roles among the executive team and the character, personality and skills of the Company Secretary himself.

Lord Shepherd's description of the role marks the Company Secretary out as the board's man but with an ability to contribute to general management. It is the case that, with few exceptions, the Company Secretary has become part of the executive team that manages the company. This may occur through him performing executive functions, giving legal advice or acting as secretary to the executive committee.

These executive functions of the Company Secretary are not new. When Lord Salmon in 1971 saw the Company Secretary as 'the Chief Administrative Officer of the company', there was an expectation that this figure would carry out executive or management functions together with his statutory role.

Before the advent of the combined roles of General Counsel and Company Secretary, the Company Secretary was at the centre of the administration of the company. Many had trained to become a Company Secretary as a separate profession. They would have been encouraged to have a broad experience of business and would have been the link between the board and those administrative functions outside the finance function. The role lay at the very heart of the organisation, with all the power and influence that was associated with such a position. Governance was not seen as a separate and distinct function.

In 1986 I joined Matthew Hall plc as its first full-time in-house legal adviser, working with the Chief Executive and Finance Director on mergers and acquisitions and the control of some broader litigation within the group of companies. The Company Secretary was all powerful. He jealously guarded his relationship with the Chairman and the board. The board had two non-executive directors, former executive directors of the company, and I believe one other 'independent' director. The company's share price was carefully monitored and relations with the institutional investors normally took place through a series of brokers' lunches. The annual general meeting was an important day in the company. It was held in the company's offices, indeed in the boardroom. The board table was removed and probably around forty chairs were set out. The board and advisers attended together with, if we were lucky or unlucky, about twenty shareholders.

The AGM was over in approximately fifteen minutes, again twenty if we were unlucky. The shareholders departed and the board and advisers retired to the executive dining room for a rather good lunch. In those days, a show of hands was certainly the best way of dealing with the votes on the resolutions, and counting the poll votes would certainly have been seen as an unnecessary expense.

The AGM was run by the Company Secretary. The Chairman was non-executive and separate from the CEO. So separate that when the Chairman decided that the company would prosper better as part of another group it was basically his decision to move the company on.

The company operated through four subsidiary companies each with its own Company Secretary, and each fairly autonomous. The role of the Company Secretary as the Chief Administrative Officer was totally appropriate as that required by the board and the broader organisation.

The advent of corporate governance

So what has changed? Since the 1980s the pivotal role of the Company Secretary has been diluted and replaced by the General Counsel/Secretary who derives authority not from the Chairman but from the Chief Executive. Over the past thirty years, companies have changed, as have their needs. A broad range of tasks that could be carried out by the Company Secretary, or those reporting to him, have now become specialisations in their own right. The nature of the unitary board has also changed. The board was previously executive-based and non-executive directors were not selected for their independence. They were frequently recruited from the ranks of advisers to the company or may have been retired executives. This was a time when non-executive directors were famously described by 'Tiny' Rowland as having less use than 'baubles on a Christmas tree'.

Separately there have been, since Cadbury, a number of influences which have altered the dynamics in companies. The authority of Company Secretary has been reinforced through the various codes of corporate governance. It was the report of the Cadbury Committee that recommended that the Company Secretary should only be dismissed with the agreement of the full board of directors. It was the Higgs Report that established the Company Secretary's central role of advising the board on corporate governance.

Higgs also recommended that the Company Secretary:

- should support the Chairman in assessing the information required by the board, and
- act as secretary to the board and its committees to ensure good communications.

In no particular order, the major changes have been:

- an increase in law and regulation
- a trend towards larger boards with a majority of non-executive directors who are independent
- the dilution of the Company Secretary's role as a number of his functional responsibilities moved elsewhere, and the development of the double-header role of General Counsel and Company Secretary.

But first and foremost has been an increased focus on the role of the board in governing, as distinct from managing, the company. The various scandals which led to the Cadbury Committee and its report were the stimulus for a clear definition of governance and the need for checks and balances on boards, especially in the area of financial control.

To try and draw some preliminary conclusions: the role of the Company Secretary in the twenty-first-century and its influence have clearly evolved. From being the Chief Administrative Officer of the company, his power and influence have been diluted. Where he has the additional role of General Counsel, quite often he will regard the legal role as being the main priority, leaving company secretarial duties to a trusted number two.

This leads to the main question: what is the role of the Company Secretary in twenty-first-century quoted companies? Has the role been reinvigorated by the focus on corporate governance? Is there now a greater role to support the board and, in particular, the Chairman and the independent non-executive directors? Or is all that we have seen in terms of advances in corporate governance really yet another law (and fairly thick at that) or regulation which has turned the Company Secretary into an executive compliance officer?

Role of the board

Strategic versus compliance

The Company Secretary today can only play the role that he is allowed or required to play by the Chairman or by the board as a whole. The Company Secretary who believes that his role is broader than compliance needs either to find a Chairman who believes in the value of good governance or will have to persuade the Chairman and the board that they, as a team, will add more value if they govern the company well. It may well be the case that some boards do not fully understand their role at the head of the governance system of a company.

So what do boards do?

At the time when Derek Higgs published his report on the effectiveness of non-executive directors and made recommendations for extensive revision to the Combined Code, it is my belief that there was more focus by Chairmen on the proposed changes to the Code and less on the report itself. This may have been caused by a mistaken view that the role of the Chairman was being diminished and that of the senior independent director was being increased. This was unfortunate as the benefits of the report were in danger of being lost in focusing on this one contentious issue. Summit meetings were necessary to resolve differences between Chairmen and shareholders over the role of the Chairman before a revised Code could be published. Sir Bryan Nicholson describes what happened in chapter 6.

The report and its underlying analysis posed the question of how boards should act and how non-executive directors could become more effective. The report encouraged boards to stand back and take a hard look at how they operated and what they did. There was encouragement for boards to be clear as to what are the distinct roles of the Chairman, Chief Executive and non-executive directors. The Code provided companies with an opportunity to establish a framework of governance which was fit for the company's specific purpose. Companies were asked to be transparent through a comply-or-explain regime.

The revisions to the Combined Code transformed it from a governance framework based on relatively light and high-level principles to a more prescriptive regime which, although still principles based, required disclosure against

71

a more detailed framework. For companies that were prepared to show where they differed from the norm this was not a huge problem. For the rest it was seen as increased regulation with which they had to comply.

We are now faced with commentators and academics who pose the question of whether boards are still focused on strategic issues or now are more focused on compliance. The revised Code has disrupted the work of some boards and made them unsure what they ought to be spending their time on. Has the revised Combined Code actually changed what boards do?

I recall being at a dinner with a Chairman of a FTSE 100 company and some other Company Secretaries discussing the role of the board. One of the Company Secretaries was explaining how much time it was taking him to draft his first corporate governance statement under the revised Combined Code and was outlining some of the challenges that he was facing. The Chairman became somewhat irascible and made a comment along the lines of 'There you are – we are talking about corporate governance again. Let's spend another 10 minutes on this and then we will get on to what boards really do.' Clearly his Company Secretary was going to have his work cut out in getting him to see corporate governance as anything other than a prescriptive list of requirements that are boxes that have to be ticked. As I pointed out to that Chairman, if boards don't do governance, then what do they do?

Conversations with a number of Company Secretaries may offer some explanation. It would seem that, in response to the revised Code, Company Secretaries have started putting governance onto the board's agenda to such an extent that these governance items may be in danger of dominating the agenda. One consequence is that governance issues result in increased monitoring of management by the board. Seen this way, the issue of strategic boards versus monitoring boards may be understood. It may well be that, as a consequence of the revised Code, boards have changed their agendas and become confused about their own role and purpose.

In trying to offer some guidance to boards as to how non-executive directors could be more effective, Derek Higgs advocated that boards should spend some time determining what they do and how they intend to govern the company. This may provide the answer to the strategy versus monitoring debate. Boards are not in fact thinking about what they do, and are simply adding what they view as the compliance requirements of the Combined Code onto what they have always been doing in the past.

It is all too easy for boards, particularly where the non-executive directors are executive directors in other companies, to take on an executive function. The whole point of having a board of directors is for it to 'govern' the company. It is impossible for a board, meeting relatively infrequently, to manage the company on a day-to-day basis. The board therefore needs to be able to establish a system of governance which allows the directors collectively to discharge their obligations to the shareholders as owners of the company. As John Carver has written, 'Boards are not management one step up but shareholder ownership one step down.'

In essence the board has three basic tasks:

- to hire and fire the Chief Executive
- to understand and to accept, after challenge, the Chief Executive's strategy
- to monitor and assess the performance of the Chief Executive and his team, and seek assurance that the strategy is being delivered, with any risks to the company being properly identified and themselves monitored.

As can be seen from these three unique tasks, the debate about the need to differentiate between strategic boards and compliance-driven boards is really a fallacy. A board which is properly governing the company will need to carry out both these activities, and carry them out effectively.

It is all too easy in today's climate of greater regulation for boards to think narrowly about what they do and to try and fit their activities within what they see as a compliance-driven framework.

Reputation oversight

Following a major incident or an accident resulting in serious economic or human loss, questions are likely to be asked about what part the board played. Boards are increasingly realising they must maintain general oversight of the company's reputation. This is a consequence of the rapid speed of modern communications and also a lack of understanding among commentators of the company's role in society and how that role should be discharged. When accidents do happen, it is sometimes wrongly assumed that the directors themselves could have averted them. Directors do not, and should not, micromanage and, as companies grow and become more international, this is becoming quite impractical as well as being entirely inappropriate. Nevertheless, when accidents happen, non-executive directors can become frustrated as they may feel they are relatively powerless to discharge their perceived responsibilities, as there are few levers for them to pull.

The principal way for the board to exercise oversight is through its review of the company's systems of internal control. The board delegates day-to-day operational control to management but retains the responsibility for ensuring that the systems of control are effective. It is when these systems fail that incidents that can damage the company's reputation are more likely to occur. Risk management should also seek to identify possible causes of damage to reputation and these should be on the board's radar.

The board needs to satisfy itself there are mechanisms in place so that it can pick up signals from within the company where there may be discontent or misdemeanours that could threaten the company's reputation. Most important among these mechanisms is an effective whistle-blowing procedure. The effectiveness of the mechanisms that might avert incidents needs to be the board's priority, rather than trying to manage the results of those incidents when the board does best to support the management in handling an incident. The board will wish to ensure management responds in a timely and appropriate manner. There may be occasions where the board has to act itself, such as the Shell example with the board investigating the reserves issue. The Company Secretary needs to make sure in such cases that the investigation is properly conducted and that good external advice is obtained. US boards are more likely to outsource the investigation of major incidents to external professionals.

Governance systems

In trying to be helpful to boards, a number of organisations have developed guidelines or codes and these have been adopted by many boards which want to be seen to be complying with best practice. It is not the case, however, that all these guidelines actually represent best practice. All too often they are adopted lock, stock and barrel by boards in the mistaken belief that they will demonstrate that they have all the right processes which will lead to good corporate governance.

For example, there are now guidelines on the powers which should be reserved for the board. These often require the board to make decisions on mergers, acquisitions and capital expenditure above a certain amount. This naturally draws the board into some form of executive action. By following best practice, the board may find that its focus and its work is dominated by decisions of an executive or management nature when it should be standing back and, having appointed an excellent Chief Executive and matching team, allowing them to look after these matters.

In my days at PowerGen the board pretty much operated in this executive capacity. There were interesting dynamics around the board table. The board had an excellent Chairman and a group of high-quality non-executive directors. The executive directors had mostly come from Government-owned utilities. While being fully supported by the non-executive directors, the executives were perceived as sometimes being too zealous in their pursuit of business opportunities that would not necessarily help to grow the bottom line. Issues most often arose over capital projects. Every project in a new country was seen to be a strategic move into that market. The need to submit bid documents never fitted easily with the timing of the board meeting, and matters were often delegated to special committees of executive and non-executive directors to clear bids on specific projects. Quite often the cases for these projects arrived relatively late and it was not easy for the non-executive directors to get themselves up to speed prior to making important decisions.

There was an understandable risk aversion on the part of the non-executive directors in these circumstances. They were operating in an industry which was effectively being invented as it was privatised and one that was developing rapidly.

Clearly, they were there to ensure that the interests of the shareholders were protected, but often that meant ensuring that the company and the executive team remained within fairly tight boundaries that had been prescribed by the prospectus. At the end of the day, if investors wanted to invest in some of the more interesting opportunities brought forward by the executive, they could have done so off their own back rather than doing it through the company. In these circumstances, the non-executive directors had no option but to involve themselves in such executive decisions. In a more mature organisation, they might have stood back and let the executive team deal with these matters within carefully prescribed boundaries. Was the board governing or managing in these circumstances? Given the environment of the recent privatisation, the board was probably behaving in the best interests of the shareholders, at least in the early days. As time went on though, behaviours changed. This is an example of a board not standing back and thinking what it ought to be doing and what role it ought to be playing.

Boards should first determine what they want the business to achieve. There should be a common understanding of the business purpose among the board members and shared by the Chief Executive. The direction of the business or its purpose should fully reflect what the shareholders also believe the company is going to do. There then needs to be a very clear discussion over what role the Chairman will play, what role the Chief Executive will play, how the non-executive directors will make their contribution, both through the main board and through its various committees. The governance of the company and the role the board plays should be appropriate to the particular company. The role of the non-executive directors, in particular, will vary in companies at different stages of their evolution. In a small, fast-moving company the non-executive directors could be required to be hands-on. They may be selected for their special skills or talents and indeed may take on a role similar to in-house consultants. They may be seen by the executive directors as additional members of the team. Processes will need to be devised to ensure the various monitoring functions which the non-executive directors are expected to undertake on behalf of the shareholders can still be carried out.

At the other end of the scale, in a global complex organisation the contribution of the non-executive directors will be very different. They will need to operate at a much higher level within the organisation and will need to make sure that, on behalf of the shareholders, the executive team is delivering on the agreed purpose and strategy.

What is important in any company, whatever its size, is that the board fully articulates how it is going to operate, that it defines the various roles, and that it decides the extent to which it will comply with the Combined Code. The opportunity should be taken each year, through the board's corporate governance statement in its annual report, to explain to shareholders where the company's governance practice has diverged from the principles and provisions of the Combined Code, and to engage with shareholders appropriately to discuss and explain those divergences.

There are those who advocate the strength of the UK system of corporate governance and the adoption of the comply-or-explain principle as being an excellent example of 'one size not fitting all'. This is a reasonable and proper approach to take when compared with some of the more legally based systems found in the USA and elsewhere. If only more boards would take the opportunity to think outside the box and put in place the appropriate governance structures relevant to their own circumstances and their position in their industry. It is a sign of weakness that a number of boards default to complete compliance with the Combined Code and thereby accept that indeed one size should fit all.

From the board's perspective, there is no one system of governance which will fit all companies. The Chairman should lead discussions with the other directors as to the nature of governance in the organisation. The governance system should be kept under review for its effectiveness and relevance, and the board should be prepared to allow the system to evolve as the governance needs change. This does not mean that governance should become an issue for debate at every board meeting. The opportunity should be taken, at the time when the board's performance as a whole is evaluated, to seek the views of all the directors on the board's governance system.

At the end of the day, the governance system which a board will describe is really just that: a system or a process represented by words on paper. The regulators, and those who place requirements on companies to have such systems, are putting their faith in the fact that once systems exist they will operate effectively. Determining the system of governance is only the first step. Operating the system at board and committee level, and ensuring that appropriate behaviours occur, is the next major challenge.

So what of the Company Secretary in all of this?

The Company Secretary

On reflection, I have been particularly fortunate in the experience that I have had as a Company Secretary. I have worked under two very different regimes: at PowerGen, I was General Counsel and Company Secretary reporting, latterly, to a combined Chairman and Chief Executive. I was a member of the executive committee. It was all too easy to see oneself in an executive role trying to determine with the executive team just how we were going to get certain decisions through the board.

At BP, the environment is different. I am the Company Secretary of only one company, BP plc, and I have no executive responsibilities other than certain limited functions related to the operation of the share register, the annual report and the annual general meeting. I am not the General Counsel and I report solely to the Chairman. My role is clearly focused on supporting the board and on ensuring that BP's governance system operates at the highest level and that every opportunity is taken to try and improve the performance of that system. What is not different is the personal relationship I have with the Chairman. Again, I have a very independent Chairman but I believe our relationship is based on trust and reliability. The breadth of the role of Company Secretary is critically dependent on the quality of the personal relationship he builds with his Chairman. The role of Company Secretary at BP is more akin to that of Chief of Staff or Head of the Chairman's Office. It is seen not as merely a compliance role or that of a servant to the board, but rather as that of a board adviser, particularly to the Chairman and non-executive directors. The Company Secretary is also the agent for the non-executive directors in ensuring their rights to put items onto the board agenda or raise issues that concern them are respected.

These very different regimes highlight the challenges for the Company Secretary today.

When clarity of roles is not a key issue, governance may be seen as a higher form of management with all the attendant consequences. At BP, it is all about clarity. Clarity as to the role of the board as opposed to that of the executive; clarity around the role of the Chairman compared with the Chief Executive; clarity over the expectations of the non-executive directors and of the board committees, and clarity over who will support this system of governance and what resource is going to be put behind that person. The Company Secretary ensures the board processes run smoothly and the governance system is rigorously applied. Board business needs to be handled efficiently and the committees need to be serviced. At BP, the Company Secretary also ensures that the self-evaluation of the board and its committees is carried out effectively, and that the induction of newly appointed directors takes place.

The Company Secretary is important for the nominations committee in ensuring that recruitment and appointment procedures for all board positions are followed. The board carries out regular reviews to identify what skills are needed on the board flowing from the agreed business strategy. The time needed to find appropriate non-executive directors and bring them onto the board can be very long. A Company Secretary who enjoys the confidence of the board will be a key participant in the recruitment process.

At BP, board evaluation is done in-house but the process is rigorous. Although a full evaluation is not carried out every year, an annual check is done to ensure that the recommendations from previous evaluations are being followed up. The Company Secretary assists the Chairman in carrying out the evaluation and writes the report for the board to discuss. Similar evaluations are made for most board committees. Those who advise the committees or who appear before them are all spoken to.

I posed a number of questions. What is the role of the Company Secretary in twenty-first-century quoted companies? Has the role been reinvigorated by the focus on corporate governance? Is there now a greater role to support the board, in particular the Chairman and non-executive directors? Is all that we have seen in terms of advances in corporate governance really another layer of regulation that has turned the Company Secretary into a compliance officer?

These questions need to be seen against the developments in the governance framework that I have endeavoured to describe above. Boards are responding to the challenges of the revised Combined Code. Questions are being asked about the role of the board. Is it there to deal with strategy or is it a corporate policeman fixed with a monitoring role? The fact that many boards see governance only as compliance may be as a result of the piecemeal way in which governance in the UK has evolved. The focus on committees and codes has come about because of the need to repair something that has gone wrong and to ensure that bad conduct or behaviour is not repeated.

There has been little effort, despite much academic work on both sides of the Atlantic, to come up with a conceptual framework of governance. Boards of directors are assumed to know what is their purpose and what are their individual tasks because they are directors. It is not clear that there is appetite in the boardroom for some of the conceptual thinking that underpins a framework of governance for UK companies. This may be a result of the fact that it is not yet proved that well-governed companies create more value for their shareholders. What is clear is that badly governed companies certainly destroy value.

Because boards are themselves only now coming to terms with the new regime, and because the Company Secretary's role is critically dependent on the views of the Chairman, there will be no one universal job description for the Company Secretary. What is clear is that the Company Secretary is going to have to spend more time addressing how he is going to support the board in adding value and becoming high-performing. This may be a challenge for those Company Secretaries who are also General Counsel. As described earlier, those who wear two hats frequently delegate the secretarial responsibilities. This is arguably acceptable when they amount only to administrative tasks. Not so easy when there are real governance issues to be dealt with. No matter what view a board takes on governance, it is likely that non-executive directors will have greater expectations of the services required from the Company Secretary, particularly when they serve on other boards that approach governance in a different way.

It is unlikely that there will be an early move away from combining the roles of Company Secretary and General Counsel. Companies may not wish, having become used to one lawyer both giving the executive legal advice and also serving the Chairman, then to incur the additional cost of recruitment. Lawyers will always, quite reasonably, want to find a place in the boardroom. If 'double heading' is the only way to do this, it is unlikely that the Company Secretaries will vote for splitting the roles.

I believe that the advances that we have seen in governance have unfortunately resulted in changing the Company Secretary's office in many companies into a compliance rather than a true governance or board performance position.

Ask those Company Secretaries employed by a number of UK corporations in governance roles what they do, and all too often the tasks they perform are essentially related to compliance.

Should we be surprised by this? Not really. It is only in the last year or two that the governance environment has started to settle down. The events in the US which led to the Sarbanes-Oxley Act, and the ripple effect into the UK and Europe, were of seismic proportions. The turbulence created by Enron, WorldCom and the other major failures, coupled with the robust US response, was bound to lead both to those companies wishing to avoid US-style regulation washing up on these shores, and to a desire to deal with whatever regulation came along and to move on.

The challenges

I believe that the enhanced focus on governance and performance presents a major challenge to the Company Secretary but also an opportunity. Whatever the views of Chairmen now, the role of the board will come under increasing scrutiny in the coming years. There is an increasing interest in what business does and in what is the role of corporations in society. This interest will be heightened by the new Companies Act, which has, as one of its key themes, the implementation of the concept of enlightened shareholder value through provisions codifying the duties of directors. The possibility of more shareholder resolutions and derivative actions will also concentrate directors' minds and require rigorous documentation procedures to maintain proper audit trails.

Shareholders will, over time, become more demanding in their engagement with companies, and more searching in their desire to understand companies' explanations for non-compliance with governance provisions. Boards will find that shareholders will come to realise that the governance systems that have been put in place to comply with the Combined Code are just systems. There will be a greater focus on board behaviour and performance which will be seen, initially, through greater scrutiny of board evaluation reports.

Boards will need to rise and meet these challenges. The Company Secretary will need to move into this space. It will not be a very different role from that described by Lord Shepherd, but there will be a greater focus on understanding what the board does and how the governance system of the company really operates. While the role might have changed from that of Chief Administrative Officer, as tasks have been transferred to other functions in the organisation, the focus on governance is seeing the re-emergence of the Company Secretary as a key official rather than a mere bureaucrat or servant of the board.

The role will need to be seen as one that adds value. While the 'double-headed' model of Company Secretary and General Counsel is unlikely to disappear, boards will wish to have advice from an independent person who is focused on ensuring that the board is delivering on its unique tasks, rather than having to work with a member of the executive team. Given the right kind of relationship with his Chairman, the Company Secretary can act as the Chairman's chief of staff and help him to run an effective board.

UK boards have now mostly developed corporate governance frameworks that comply with the Combined Code. Where they do not comply they are explaining their reasons. The focus now is on board performance. Are boards effective? Are the non-executive directors adding value? The Company Secretary truly has a part to play here but his role needs to be redefined. This is what I foresee will be the main change over the next five years, though it has already started in larger companies. Governance must not be viewed as an end in itself or it risks being reduced to box-ticking, and the Company Secretary will be seen as a bureaucrat whose job it is to see that all the right boxes are ticked. The more important task for boards is to decide how they will operate within the corporate governance framework they have constructed. The chosen way of operating will determine if they are high-performing and effective. This is the area in which the Company Secretary will increasingly be expected to contribute in support of his Chairman.

Investors will be monitoring board performance more closely and they will receive more information to help them. Although the Operating and Financial Review was abandoned, the enhanced Business Review, sitting within the Directors' Report in the annual report, will give investors more non-financial information than they have ever had before. The Company Secretary is likely to regain from the communications specialists his authority for preparing much of the annual report and accounts. It will be more important than before, once the Business Review is a feature, to ensure that the board's messages and communications are consistent. The Company Secretary is well placed to safeguard consistency and ensure appropriate transparency.

This greater transparency and disclosure will result in investors asking more questions about the board's affairs. It will cause boards to review the bright lines between the authorities and responsibilities of Chairman and Chief Executive on the one hand, and between executive and non-executive directors on the other. This has been a key part of the development of the corporate governance approach in BP. This need for clarity is especially important for companies operating in the USA, where regulators look to pierce the corporate veil. Governance systems need to take this sort of threat into account as companies become more global.

The Company Secretary will help to ensure the board does only what the board needs to do: focusing on articulating the board's values, approving and monitoring strategy, oversight of management, and determining board and senior management succession. The board should resist getting involved in business operations and making decisions that should be taken by the executive.

The opportunity is there. Company Secretaries can again play the pivotal role that they performed in the past. Governance and board performance lie at the heart of all that they should be focusing on in the future. It's up to them to walk into that space.

5
The role of the shareholder

PETER MONTAGNON

Recent history – growing pressure on shareholders to act responsibly

It is generally recognised nowadays that Britain plays a pioneering role in corporate governance, but this focus and leadership is relatively new. It goes back to the Cadbury Code of 1992, which set out basic principles of board behaviour and how shareholders should respond. Cadbury has now undergone several mutations and evolved into the Combined Code. Through the code system, the UK has developed the famous comply-or-explain concept. This is the key to the UK approach to maintaining high standards of governance. Instead of prescriptive regulation, it relies on consensus around standards, followed by disclosure coupled with peer and shareholder pressure, to drive incremental change in behaviour. In recent years, the focus on the role of shareholders in pushing for high standards has grown significantly.

The UK's lead in governance lies probably in the timing of its corporate scandals. The Cadbury Code was a response to the Maxwell and Polly Peck scandals of that period. The code system, introduced by the UK as a result, helped protect UK companies and their shareholders from the impact of subsequent excess at the height of the stock market bubble at the end of the 1990s. Of course, the market was not entirely free of shock: witness, the crises at Marconi and Cable & Wireless. Still, the UK did at that stage have some considered responses. Hence, for example, its approach to governance questions relating to audit was much less extreme than that of the US in the wake of Enron.

Yet the impact of the UK's own model and the worldwide wave of scandals that followed the bursting of the bubble was to focus still more attention on shareholders and their role. Another factor – the election of a Labour Government in May 1997 – also played an important part. New Labour wanted to address excess in the behaviour of management, but it did not want to do so through the introduction of restrictive regulation or legislation. It felt that it was more appropriate to harness the power of the market and make institutional investors use their power of ownership to promote effective leadership at the top of companies. It therefore focused heavily on the operation of the investment chain with a series of reports by Paul Myners, Ron Sandler and Sir Derek Higgs.

In 2000, the problems encountered by Tomkins, a large conglomerate, reinforced the government's argument. These were associated with a weak board structure, poor internal controls and financial excess. Legitimate questions were asked about why shareholders had done so little to intervene and address the issues before they became critical. Similarly, it was hard for institutional shareholders to escape some responsibility for the collapse of Marconi. Institutions had been actively urging the company to spend its cash on high-technology expansion to take account of the bubble in that sector. They had shown little concern to ensure that appropriate checks and balances accompanied the decision-making.

A particular public concern around this time was executive remuneration, which had been growing rapidly as the stock market bubble advanced. This was partly a reflection of the overall buoyancy of the market and partly a leaching across the Atlantic of the extraordinary excess in the US. For New Labour, remuneration was a particularly delicate issue. On the one hand, the very high rewards reaped by executives were offensive to traditional socialists. On the other, New Labour wanted to be business-friendly and not impose any formal pay policy for executives. Once again, putting the responsibility firmly in the hands of institutions was the obvious alternative. The public and press would blame shareholders if things got out of hand.

The political pressure became all the greater after the stock market bubble burst and public opinion became increasingly concerned about so-called 'payment for failure'. The government's eventual response was the Directors' Remuneration Report Regulations of 2002. These require listed companies to produce an enhanced remuneration report on which shareholders are given an advisory vote. This was a substantial change. Not only was there to be more disclosure including a table showing relative performance but, for the first time, shareholders obtained a vote covering all aspects of remuneration. Previous voting had been confined to schemes involving the issue of shares to directors or dilutive share schemes, including those for the benefit of all employees.

Subsequently the government came under strong pressure from the Trades Union Congress and other left-wing supporters to take specific action to curb payment for failure. This is an extremely difficult area. Although there is universal agreement that executives who have caused a collapse in value should not walk away from their jobs with compensation, it is almost impossible to provide for such constraint in law. Not only is failure indefinable in legal terms, there was a clear risk that any legislation passed in Britain could be successfully challenged in the European courts. In the event the government backed away. It was helped in doing so by a guidance paper on the subject published by the Association of British Insurers and the National Association of Pension Funds and by recognition from the Confederation of British Industry of the need for voluntary action. All three organisations acknowledged that the key to addressing the problem lay in careful drafting of the service contract at the time the executive was hired. This has led to a change in practice. For example, contract lengths now rarely exceed one year.

Even though the government did not legislate to outlaw rewards for failure, it did undertake a series of measures to place additional responsibilities on shareholders. The Directors' Remuneration Report Regulations, as noted above, introduced a vote on remuneration. The Myners Report on Institutional Investment in 2001 called for legislation to require institutions to take an activist stance along the lines of the US Erisa legislation on pension funds. The Higgs Report of 2002 was focused mainly on boards and their operation, but its proposals were generally seen as prescriptive and shareholders were to play an important role in policing them.

Finally, the Government introduced legislation in 2004 requiring companies to publish an Operating and Financial Review setting out the board's view of material issues affecting its future, including environmental and social issues. Though this was designed to respond to pressure from environmental and other stakeholder groups, the thrust of the legislation was to place an onus on institutional investors to take these issues into account and engage with companies on them. The Operating and Financial Review was subsequently withdrawn because, in the view of the Treasury, the benefits were outweighed by the audit costs. However, companies will still be obliged under European law to produce a Business Review and the pressure on shareholders to become involved in consideration of all material issues affecting the company remains.

Overall, therefore, since the Cadbury Report there has been growing pressure, both market and political, on shareholders to take a more active interest in governance. This has been backed up with press comment. The media does now generally expect institutional shareholders to act as responsible owners. Indeed for many institutions, the willingness to do so has become a reputational issue in its own right.

Governance as an alternative to regulation

Where the contribution of shareholders creates an effective chain of accountability, governance can be harnessed to perform a role that otherwise requires regulation. In the US there is no prospect of companies being made effectively accountable to their owners, because shareholders lack the ultimate weapon of being able to dismiss boards. The result is that, when crisis strikes, the US has no option but to resort to more stringent regulation, regardless of the heavy compliance and administrative costs involved.

The UK's code-based concept of comply-or-explain makes for a striking contrast. It enables companies to deviate from accepted norms of best practice provided they can persuade their shareholders that it is in their interest to do so. This is much less brittle than regulation and almost certainly better for value creation because of the different objectives of regulators and investors. While both wish to avoid crises that spark loss of value, regulators have less natural interest in the creation of value. Their natural desire is to sleep easy in their beds at night, secure in the knowledge that they will not be wakened by scandal in the morning. Investors on the other hand want companies they own to be successful. They do not want to hobble the entrepreneurial spirit. In considering when to allow exceptions to conventional best practice, they will therefore strike a much more subtle balance than regulators.

The response of the corporate sector to the growing role of shareholders has, however, been mixed. At times, it has seemed as though the relationship was confrontational. This was particularly true of the debate around the Higgs Report on corporate governance. Many investing institutions welcomed the basic thrust of its message: particularly the increased responsibility for the senior independent director, the emphasis on the need for non-executive director independence, and the suggestions that individuals should not chair two large companies or move from being Chief Executive to Chairman of the same company. Companies, however, saw these provisions as an invitation to shareholders to interfere. Criticism was levelled, sometimes vociferously, against shareholders who were accused of using their voting power uncritically to enforce an inappropriate set of new rules. Executives felt their freedom of action and their ability to deploy their entrepreneurial skills would suffer.

This mood was exacerbated by a number of arguments over executive remuneration. Advisory services that help shareholders with their voting decisions were accused of whipping up opposition to boards. This was particularly true of PIRC, the Pensions Information Research Consultancy, which has a reputation among shareholder bodies for taking a strong political line. Companies complained that shareholders had gone overboard. They said different groups were setting different standards, which were both more demanding than the Code itself and incompatible with each other. A series of high-profile meetings between company chairmen and senior investors did little to calm the mood. The climate of suspicion only really began to abate once the new Code was finally in place and companies found that there was no pronounced tendency of shareholders to vote against management.

In the end it was predictable that the mood of confrontation should abate. In some jurisdictions tension between companies and institutional shareholders is seen as the norm. This is arguably the case in the US, where the absence of a shareholder right to dismiss the board makes it hard to align the interests of shareholders and management. Such confrontation is less frequently the case in the UK where, as mentioned above, shareholders can dismiss the management. Shareholder views are therefore normally taken into account in major decisions and the relationship is more naturally collaborative. Many British institutions do take an active role in corporate governance, but their purpose in doing so is to secure value over the longer term rather than to hobble the management. This reflects the traditional importance of equity investment by long-term institutions, particularly pension funds and insurance companies. The purpose of corporate governance for these investors is not to introduce and enforce an arbitrary set of bureaucratic rules, but to ensure as far as possible that company boards are structured and run in such a way as to take robust strategic decisions and manage risk. Once they understand this, and are reassured that shareholders will usually apply corporate governance concepts flexibly, boards generally become better disposed to shareholder views.

Of course, there will always be specific situations where companies and shareholders confront considerable differences, but the relatively close alignment of interests between many boards and a large portion of the institutional investment community means the relationship is not a naturally confrontational one. The hostile mood that prevailed when the Higgs Report was being debated should be seen as the exception rather than the norm. The key to a successful contribution by shareholders should be seen not in the degree to which they wrest control of the boardroom from the directors, but more in the degree to which they provide an effective check and balance, which reduces risk, enhances the quality of decision-making and helps create sustainable value.

The overall result of this philosophy has been that British companies generally enjoy relatively high standards of governance. Thanks to the Code approach, the incidence of individuals combining the role of Chairman and Chief Executive is now rare; most companies have fully independent audit committees; and it has been possible to introduce a generally high standard of internal controls through the recommendations contained in the Turnbull guidance. None of this has required prescriptive legislation. Indeed it has been possible to avoid potentially serious legislative difficulties such as a requirement for a legal definition of independence in a non-executive director. This is all thanks to the fact that, having been empowered to dismiss boards, shareholders do a job which in other countries might be tackled by regulators. Though there are certainly some exceptions, the weight of the evidence from the generally rising standard of corporate governance is that shareholders are generally effective and that their interventions involve less compliance cost than those of regulators.

Where shareholders make a difference

One reason why the UK has been able to harness shareholder power to develop high standards of corporate governance has been the ownership structure of British companies. Traditionally there has been a heavy institutional presence on UK company registers and this presence is normally widely dispersed. This is different from other countries, especially in continental Europe where a single large holder may dominate the register. The comply-or-explain approach works less well in these cases because the block holder is normally very close to the management and will therefore be less effective in acting as a check and balance.

Moreover two types of institution, insurance companies and pension funds, have traditionally been large holders of equities. Again, this is not necessarily replicated in other jurisdictions where funded pensions are less common and/or insurance companies have been more heavily invested in bonds. A feature of equity investment by UK insurers and pension funds is that it is long term in nature. Though holdings may be adjusted at the margin, these institutions have typically had a long-term commitment to the equity market. This gives them a reason for being concerned with corporate governance. They believe it reduces risk over the longer term and helps companies deliver high-quality sustainable earnings. Moreover, both insurance companies and pension funds are effectively owners, unlike mutual fund managers who are merely agents.

Yet if the dispersed ownership by long-term institutions, which are prepared to act as owners, helps create a situation where companies can be made effectively accountable to shareholders, there are also limits to the degree to which this can be a substitute for regulation. One important aspect of company law is that it does make companies accountable to their shareholders, for example by giving them the right to appoint and dismiss boards, by ensuring some basic rights such as that to subscribe for new capital in proportion to existing holdings (pre-emption), by ensuring that companies put key issues to a vote and by ensuring that shareholders are properly informed. Shareholders cannot exercise their rights of ownership unless a suitable framework allows them to do so. Nor can they substitute for the law or regulation in every single case. The requirement for audit, for example, needs to be set out in the law. Shareholders have a role in ensuring that the governance of the audit process is appropriate and that the audit committee is suitably independent, but they cannot design and enforce audit requirements themselves.

So what are the areas where shareholder power can work as well as, or better than, regulation to maintain high standards of corporate governance?

Certainly one of these must be board structure. It is quite rare in the UK for shareholders to promote individuals as candidates for a particular board. This normally only happens after a company has run into trouble. Even then, there is a reluctance to usurp the nomination committee's right to make the actual selection. In 2004, shareholders were clear in their rejection of the choice of Sir Ian Prosser as Chairman of Sainsbury, the supermarket chain, which had been steadily losing ground to rivals, notably Tesco. As a former Chairman of Bass, the brewing and hotel concern, Sir Ian had a strong experience in leading a retail-facing company. However, City institutions made it plain that they did not feel he had the right touch to guide the company out of the troubles it was then facing. Sir Ian gracefully withdrew and, though the nomination committee subsequently consulted shareholders, the subsequent choice of Philip Hampton was the committee's own. Shareholders in these circumstances are more likely to indicate the type of skills they feel are needed Sir Philip Hampton's previous roles as finance director of several leading companies, including BT and the Lloyds TSB banking group, meant he had City experience that complemented the retail skills of Justin King, Sainsbury's Chief Executive.

Similarly, Michael Green was forced to withdraw in 2003 from the chairmanship of the new ITV television company as a result of shareholder desire for a properly independent chairman. It was widely felt in the City that the combination of Mr Green as Chairman and Charles Allen as Chief Executive would not work. They had each been in charge of one of the companies that had united to form the merged ITV and were used to running their own show. However, while there was general agreement that the board needed to change, there was none around the need to push for a particular replacement candidate. In the event the chosen candidate, Sir Peter Burt, a former banker, was once again a figure familiar with the City.

So, even in these quite extreme cases, the shareholders' role is to ensure proper process leading to the selection of a candidate who meets the right sort of criteria rather than to undertake the selection themselves. Normally it is possible to leave the selection up to the nomination committee precisely because the shareholders have the long-stop possibility of veto in the event of a bad decision. This concentrates the minds of the nomination committee in a way that allows shareholders to let boards be largely responsible for their own renewal. This is important for a board that is supposed to function as a unit with collective responsibility for decision-making and risk management.

By extension this approach works for the composition of the board as a whole. Shareholders do seek to satisfy themselves that there is an appropriate balance of executive and non-executive directors; that the non-executive directors are sufficiently independent; that committees, whose responsibility covers areas such as remuneration and audit, are properly constituted and independent. Shareholders are keen to see the appointment of a senior independent director who can be an additional point to turn to in trouble, especially when the concern is about the Chairman. They are increasingly wary of situations where the Chief Executive goes on to become Chairman of the same company, and they want to be sure that directors who are supposed to be independent really are independent in practice.

Ideally, problems should be averted before they arise through consultation between companies and their shareholders. There are now fewer cases of Chief Executives becoming Chairmen. This is partly because companies are aware of shareholder concerns and therefore reject the idea at the outset. Sometimes initial, private soundings may have deterred companies from proceeding. Even when the company believes it has a good case, there will normally be an extensive discussion with shareholders so that both sides understand each other's views. The Association of British Insurers (ABI) held ground-breaking discussions with Barclays over its decision to appoint Matt Barrett, its former Chief Executive, as Chairman in 2004. This helped Barclays to produce, and then subsequently flesh out, a full explanation of its thinking. It may also have influenced the bank's decision to look outside for its subsequent Chairman, Marcus Agius, from the Lazard investment banking concern, in 2004. Similarly HSBC went out of its way to consult shareholders about its decision to appoint its Chief Executive, Stephen Green, as Chairman in 2006.

Executives and other directors have sometimes grumbled about the need for such discussions but, generally speaking, the powers granted to shareholders, and the way they have exercised them, have led to an improvement in board structure and practice, with fewer situations where unfettered power is concentrated in the hands of one person. As mentioned already, it is now rare to find the roles of Chairman and Chief Executive combined. In recent years there has also been a new focus on board evaluation. One important factor in achieving this has been the development of consultation between boards and shareholders on key issues. This has grown considerably since the introduction of the new Combined Code.

Shareholders also play an important role in remuneration policy. In this area too, consultation has grown considerably since the introduction of the new Directors' Remuneration Report. The ABI now receives over 200 requests a year from companies seeking shareholder views on remuneration policy. In many cases these consultations produce changes which help avert a row before the proposals are formalised and put to a vote.

Companies are now obliged to offer shareholders an advisory vote on their remuneration report, which covers all aspects of remuneration ranging from base salary through to pensions, bonuses and share incentives. As before, a separate binding vote is required on share incentive schemes that are dilutive and/or involve the issue of shares to directors. The press watches votes on remuneration closely, and companies are concerned about the loss of reputation that may flow from evidence of widespread opposition to their remuneration policy. Moreover, a public dispute over remuneration can seriously demotivate directors at the centre of the disagreement. For these reasons, companies increasingly seek dialogue with shareholders in order to sort out problems before they arise. Nowadays, this dialogue extends beyond the design of share-based incentive schemes into new areas such as pensions, which has become a focus of attention and change in the wake of new tax arrangements.

The introduction of the Directors' Remuneration Report Regulations has created a dilemma for shareholders. For the first time they are able to pronounce on absolute amounts paid to executives. Indeed, they are obliged to do so through the vote. Many are, however, deeply unsure of their ability to determine the 'going rate' for a particular executive role. They believe this is an issue that ought to be left to the market, while their own focus has always been principally on the structure of the remuneration package. What matters to shareholders is that rewards reflect performance and that they align the interests of the management with those of shareholders.

There are three reasons why shareholders have become involved with remuneration. First, a conflict of interest arises when boards have the task of deciding the remuneration of directors who sit on these same boards. As owners, shareholders have an obligation to help mitigate this conflict. Second, remuneration creates incentives that will determine the approach taken by the management in driving the company forward. Shareholders have a strong interest in what happens. Finally, there is a general need to preserve the integrity of the system. If a lack of discipline and oversight allows companies to bestow lavish rewards on mediocrity and failure, it will no longer be possible to reward success. This will damage entrepreneurialism and inhibit wealth creation.

The efforts of shareholders over the years have met with some success, particularly with regard to the structure of remuneration. It was always possible for the UK to avoid the extremes witnessed in the US at the height of the bubble. Shareholder voting rights on incentive schemes enabled them to limit dilution (the limit of 10 per cent set out in the ABI's guidelines is widely respected). Moreover, thanks also to different taxation arrangements, it has been possible for shareholders to insist that awards of options only vest after medium-term performance conditions have been met. In other words, directors only actually receive the benefits after the performance has been delivered and in proportion to their actual achievements. By contrast, in the US, directors have been able to cash-in their options immediately. This leads to a short-term focus on the share price. Directors have an interest in ramping it up in order to maximise this benefit. There is also evidence that some US boards have awarded options to directors ahead of positive news which is likely to drive up the share price, or backdated them to a time when the share price was low. This, of course, further accentuates the gain and the transfer of value away from shareholders.

Shareholders in the UK have also managed to exercise some detailed influence on the design of share schemes. When options first became fashionable, it was normal for them to be allocated sporadically in large amounts. This created a particular risk for the executives, who could lose the entire benefit if the company failed to meet performance hurdles. Nowadays, it is normal for grants to be made annually so that executives have a continuing incentive to meet performance targets and will not lose all their benefit if targets are not met in one crucial year. Following this change, it has also been possible virtually to eliminate the practice of retesting, which allows executives to have a second chance to meet performance targets if they fail the first time. Shareholders always saw a retesting provision as seriously weakening the link with performance. Shareholder influence has also encouraged remuneration structures that limit the amount of reward for median performance and increase it for outstanding results. Finally, shareholders have taken a strong line on severance pay, as set out in the joint paper by the Association of British Insurers and the National Association of Pension Funds mentioned above. There is now more discipline in this area, and a growing tendency to make sure that severance is paid in instalments that stop when the executive concerned finds a new job rather than in one irretrievable lump sum.

Shareholders have been less successful, however, in restraining overall amounts of remuneration. This is partly because they do not wish to become involved in setting a going rate, as mentioned, but also because there are strong forces at work which drive executive remuneration continually higher. One of these is the ratchet effect that follows from the increased level of disclosure. No executive wants to be paid less than others in his or her peer group. Another is the activity of remuneration consultants who generate fee-income from helping companies revise their remuneration policy, a process which almost invariably leads to increases. There is a real risk that, without more discipline, there will be a public backlash which will lead to more political interference in remuneration.

There is a limit, however, to what shareholders can do here. The responsibility for setting absolute amounts must lie with the directors who sit on the remuneration committee. They are the ones who can determine the amount that is actually needed to provide pay that is genuinely competitive. They understand better than shareholders the conditions and competitive pressures facing the industry, and can therefore adjudicate more effectively on benchmarks proposed by consultants. They are also the ones who should say 'no' to excessive demands. Shareholders cannot do this without being involved in micro-management.

As mentioned above, another area where shareholders wield a potentially important indirect influence is internal controls. This is not because of any involvement in the work of audit committees, but is more to do with the obligation facing listed companies to confirm that boards have examined the effectiveness of their internal controls. The realisation by directors that shareholders can 'dismiss' them if they fail to live up to their obligations in this respect clearly concentrates minds. The result is a constructive approach to risk management, which has been achieved at far lower compliance cost than the equivalent regulation under the Sarbanes-Oxley Act in the US.

Similarly, the Association of British Insurers in 2002 launched a short set of guidelines calling on boards to disclose in their annual report that they had considered the risks inherent in the way their company managed social, ethical and environmental issues and to confirm that these risks were being managed. This was a purely voluntary requirement promoted by a group of leading shareholders, but the fact that companies started to make the statement, and boards began to consider the risks more conscientiously, has certainly had an impact on behaviour. A couple of years after the guidelines were first introduced, nearly 100 companies confirmed that they had included management of environmental, social and ethical risks in their general risk-management policies.

Finally, shareholders have a significant say in important strategic questions. This is not just a matter of companies listening to fund managers and analysts about the direction their business is taking. UK governance arrangements give shareholders a direct say on large transactions, which will alter the shape of a company. This goes beyond their right to vote on whether or not to accept a bid, which is common in other jurisdictions. The UK Listing Rules also give them a right to vote when a company wishes to make a substantial purchase or disposal of assets. This right is regarded as highly important. It is not the case that shareholders frequently use it to block company actions, but more that the need for a vote imposes a discipline on boards to consider in advance whether they will be able to carry their shareholders with them in any decision. At the very least, this should mean that the decisions taken by boards are more closely aligned with the interests of shareholders than would otherwise be the case.

And of course, when shareholders participate in pivotal decisions, the sense of ownership is much more real.

What happens in practice

As understanding of governance has grown over the years, so the shareholder community has sought to codify its own best practice. Part of the drive to do so reflects a belief that good governance does add to value and that collective pursuit of governance principles will therefore raise the general quality of investment returns over the longer term. Part responds to government and corporate pressure on institutions to show that their considerable power is being used responsibly and with consideration for both beneficiaries and the companies in which they invest. This came together in 2002 in the form of a statement of principles by the Institutional Shareholders Committee (ISC) which groups the main investor bodies: the Association of British Insurers, the Association of Investment Companies, the Investment Management Association and the National Association of Pension Funds.

The ISC statement[1] was revised in September 2005 but its main points remained intact. It sets out best practice for institutional shareholders and/or their agents in relation to their responsibilities in respect of investee companies. It commits them to:

- set out clearly their policy on how they will discharge these responsibilities
- monitor the performance of investee companies and establish a dialogue with them where necessary
- intervene where appropriate
- evaluate the impact of their engagement
- report back to their clients or to beneficial owners.

The statement makes clear that its exhortation to institutions to engage with companies constitutes not an obligation to micro-manage their affairs, but rather that they should institute procedures to ensure that shareholders derive value from their investments by dealing effectively with concerns over underperformance. Institutions should disclose their engagement policies to the public, preferably on their websites. The statement should cover arrangements for monitoring companies, strategy on intervention, an indication of the type of circumstances when action would be taken, and the institution's policy on voting. Institutions should also disclose their policies for addressing and minimising conflicts of interest.

The ISC statement suggests a number of areas where intervention may be necessary. These include when there are concerns about:

---

[1] For text see the Guidelines Section of the ABI's Institutional Voting Information Service website: www.ivis.co.uk.

- the company's strategy or operational performance
- its acquisition strategy
- independent directors failing to hold management properly to account
- internal controls failing
- inadequate succession planning
- unjustified failure to comply with the Combined Code
- remuneration policy
- the company's approach to corporate social responsibility.

Where no constructive response is received, a range of additional approaches may be considered, up to the requisitioning of an extraordinary general meeting to change the board. There is, however, a particular emphasis on considered voting. The statement states that institutional shareholders and their agents should vote all shares held directly or on behalf of clients wherever practicable to do so. They should not automatically support the board but, where concerns have driven them to oppose or abstain on a resolution, they should inform the company in advance of their intention and the reasons why.

As with the Combined Code, the statement represents an ideal and, as with companies' responses to the Combined Code, it is clear that not all large institutions comply with every aspect of the statement. However, the statement and the support accorded to it by member bodies of the ISC has undoubtedly helped raise awareness of the importance of good governance and raise the standards applied by institutions in practice. Evidence of this is provided by surveys carried out by the Investment Management Association, which are considered in greater detail below. It is also clear that dialogue between companies and institutions on governance matters has increased considerably in recent years.

Some companies hold regular meetings for their non-executive directors with shareholders at which any governance issue can be raised. Many institutions include their governance experts at meetings with companies. At the collective level both the ABI and the NAPF have been active in facilitating discussion. In 2003, the NAPF revived its case committee system, whereby members can propose an engagement with companies where problems are perceived to have arisen. The NAPF process is strictly private, but it is known that the organisation instituted dialogue with BSkyB at the time of the appointment of James Murdoch, son of Chairman Rupert, as Chief Executive. The NAPF also held a series of meetings with Shell after it revealed in 2004 that it had overstated its reserves. The ABI procedures are less formal than those of the NAPF, but the organisation also held a series of meetings with both companies. In the course of any year, it will facilitate discussions between institutions and around ten companies on governance subjects distinct from remuneration. Sometimes this helps both sides understand how to apply the Combined Code, as in the case of the discussions between ABI members and Barclays over the appointment of its Chief Executive Matt Barrett to be Chairman. Sometimes the dialogue helps create support for a succession process, as with the discussions leading up to the appointment of a new Chief Executive at Morrison, the supermarket concern, in 2006. Another large company, which was facing a simultaneous succession of both its Chairman and Chief Executive, canvassed the ABI and other shareholders well in advance of taking a decision to extend the tenure of the Chairman so that he could oversee the transition of Chief Executive.

The key lever that shareholders control is their ability to vote at general meetings. For this reason, large institutions usually seek to vote actively and are concerned that the voting system works properly. The average voting turnout at UK general meetings is around 55 per cent and has been moving gently upwards in recent years. Given the extent of overseas and short-term ownership of UK equities by hedge funds and other non-traditional institutions, this suggests that long-term institutions such as pension funds and insurance companies generally use their voting power as the ISC statement urges them to do.

However, serious concern developed in 2003 over whether the voting system was working properly when a number of shareholders and companies reported that votes appeared to have gone astray. One problem was that voting instructions had been delivered late by a courier. Another was that a large intermediary in the voting chain had failed to carry out instructions. In response, the ISC led the revitalisation of a technical cross-industry group, the Shareholder Voting Working Group, under the chairmanship of Paul Myners to consider ways of improving the system. This group included senior practitioners from the investment industry, registrars, custodians and companies.

Myners produced a series of reports which developed the principle that those at the ownership end of the investment chain need to drive and control the voting process so as to ensure that it works properly on their behalf. His report also pushed strongly for the use of electronic voting systems by companies and shareholders in the belief that this would reduce errors that result from the transmission of paper instructions up and down the sometimes complex voting chain. It also made a point of urging investors to recall stock that had been loaned when they wished to vote. The result has been an improvement in the reliability of the voting process, although there remains no guarantee of its robustness and further work will be required with custodians and others involved in the investment chain to improve the effectiveness of the system.

The international dimension

While much of the focus on shareholder activity has concentrated on the UK, international developments have also come to the fore as institutions have diversified their portfolios. This is a more difficult area because UK institutions will normally comprise only a small minority of holdings in foreign companies in contrast to the large collective stakes they tend to enjoy at home. At a practical level, however, they can and do occasionally seek to make their influence felt by striking alliances with other shareholders. This was the case, for example, with a 2004 resolution at Nestle, the Swiss food-processing multinational, by which the Chief Executive was also to assume the role of Chairman. A number of UK institutions became involved in a coalition, promoted by a Swiss corporate governance group, which was urging shareholders to vote against the resolution. Similarly, institutions from a number of countries worked together to persuade Shell to reform its corporate governance after its admission that it had overstated its reserves.

Institutional shareholders have also been active in the policy debate, especially with regard to European Directives. In 2005, the European Commission launched a Directive on Shareholder Rights aimed at facilitating cross-border voting by shareholders at general meetings. Among other provisions, the proposed Directive allowed for voting in absentia and established a right for shareholders to appoint proxies to speak and vote on their behalf at meetings. The Directive also set minimum notice periods for general meetings so that shareholders would have sufficient time to prepare and register their votes. In a popular move with investors, it also formally outlawed the practice of shareblocking whereby shareholders who wished to vote were unable to trade their shares during the notice of meeting period. The Directive attracted support from shareholder bodies including the Association of British Insurers in the UK and the International Corporate Governance Network.

At the same time Charles McCreevy, the Commissioner responsible for company law matters, made a series of public statements promoting the concept of one-share-one-vote. This reflected disappointment in the Commission at the way in which member states had chosen to opt out of a key requirement in the Takeovers Directive which provided for voting distortions (such as multiple voting rights and voting ceilings) to be overridden at key moments in a bid. The Commissioner's remarks were highly controversial, especially in countries such as Sweden, the Netherlands and France, where managements have traditionally been protected by limits on the ability of minority shareholders to register a vote proportional to their share of the capital. In 2006 the Commission commissioned a study on the issue, however, indicating that it was likely to remain a subject of discussion. The study found no economic evidence of a causal link between deviations from the so-called 'proportionality principle' and the economic performance of companies. In October 2007, Commissioner McCreevy announced that he had decided there was no need for action at EU level but urged shareholders to use their voting rights to push for more transparency on the need for and use of the so-called 'control enhancing mechanisms' such as one-share-one-vote.

Coupled with concern in a number of European countries about the behaviour of short-term shareholders, this means that the role of the shareholder has become a subject of hot political debate. In the aftermath of Deutsche Boerse's abortive bid for the London Stock Exchange, which resulted in the resignation of both its Chairman and Chief Executive in 2005, a leading German politician described hedge funds that had opposed the deal as 'locusts'. In the European Parliament debate on the Shareholder Rights Directive, Michel

Rocard, the former French prime minister, described certain types of share-holders as delinquent. European corporate chiefs, as well as politicians, were increasingly concerned that some short-term shareholders were acquiring voting rights through derivative positions and other financial devices which meant they had obtained control without paying for economic ownership. On the other side of the debate, investors and liberally minded economists and politicians were expressing anxiety about economic nationalism which was leading European companies to exploit weaknesses in legislation such as the Takeovers Directive to fend off foreign bids. A clear example of this was the determined opposition by Arcelor, the Luxemburg-incorporated steel concern, to a bid launched by Mittal, which is controlled by an Indian entrepreneur.

If Arcelor and other similar transactions encouraged shareholders to defend their legal rights of ownership, the course of the debate also made it clear that a claim to rights needed to be met by a recognition of responsibility. An important step forward in this regard came in 2006 with publication by the International Corporate Governance Network of a draft Statement of Principles on the Responsibilities of Institutional Shareholders.[2]

The ICGN statement was designed to build on and replace an earlier statement which had focused on the responsibility of shareholders to the companies in which they had invested. While the new statement retained this aspect of responsibility, it also focused on the internal governance of institutions, and in particular on the need for them to have governance arrangements that enabled them to deliver on their overriding obligation to act in the interest of their beneficiaries. The requirement for a responsible approach thus extended in two directions: to the beneficiaries whose savings the institutions were deploying, and to the companies in which the funds were invested.

Where responsibilities towards investee companies are concerned, the ICGN statement covers similar ground to the ISC statement. It argues that high standards of corporate governance will help companies deliver sustainable value over time, and urges that governance activity should become an integral part of the investment process. Shareholder rights should always be applied with the objective of value creation and not in a formulaic, box-ticking way. Shareholders should act in a proactive way to address governance concerns and have consistent policies for engagement with companies, which should include a clearly defined approach to situations when dialogue is failing. They should vote in a considered way and on the basis of a policy which is disclosed to both beneficiaries and companies in which they hold stakes.

The section on internal governance is mainly addressed to those bodies such as pension fund trustee boards which represent the interests of the beneficial

---

[2] The ICGN is a network of over 400 members from over thirty-five countries with an interest in corporate governance. As investors its members control some $10 trillion of assets. Further details on the orgnisation and the text of its statement on shareholder responsibilities can be found on its website: www.icgn.org.

owners, but it also sets standards for other intermediaries, particularly asset managers. It confirms that the overarching responsibility is to act at all times in the interest of beneficiaries. This means addressing four main principles:

- transparency, which enables beneficiaries to satisfy themselves that their funds are being handled appropriately
- disclosure and management of conflicts of interest
- expertise, which enables institutions to make sound decisions on beneficiaries' behalf
- oversight structures that are suitably balanced so that decisions are taken in the interests of beneficiaries.

The need to deal with conflicts of interest is regarded as particularly important. The statement acknowledges that these will arise from time to time – for example, if the plan sponsor is also influential as a trustee of the relevant scheme, or if an asset manager faces a controversial vote on the affairs of a company from whose pension fund it has separately obtained a fund management mandate. However institutions must have a clear policy for disclosing and managing such conflicts. It follows also that they need to have an internal governance structure and ensure that they are in a position to deliver on the overarching requirement to act in the interests of beneficiaries.

The way in which individuals are appointed to serve on the governing body should be disclosed as well as the criteria that are applied to such appointments. A most important factor will be the behaviour of those who sit on the governing body. It is essential that the oversight structure provides for independent decision-making so that investment and voting decisions are taken in the interest of the beneficiaries and do not reflect other objectives of those involved.

The structure of such bodies will vary from market to market and may be determined by regulation or legislation. Whatever the structure, it is important that every individual who participates acts in an independent manner and in line with the overarching objective of safeguarding the interests of beneficiaries. Such expectations should be set out clearly in the constitution of the governing body.

Independent decision-making is easier to achieve if the structure of the governing body is balanced with all relevant interests represented. In particular it is not desirable that the plan sponsor or employer dominates the governing body. Where this is the case, consideration should be given to the representation of individuals accountable to beneficiaries even if this is not mandatory.

In another new step, the ICGN statement emphasises the serious conflict of interest which may also arise where the plan sponsor is a government or other public authority which may take voting and investment decisions that reflect their public policy objectives rather than the interests of the beneficiaries. Where this is the case, there is an additional need to ensure a majority of independent participants on the governing body.

Progress to date

Perhaps the most authoritative statement of how UK institutions have responded to their increased responsibilities comes from the regular survey carried out by the Investment Management Association. The latest of these covers the situation at mid-2006 and was published in June 2007.[3] This covered thirty-three fund managers responsible for 68 per cent of the equities managed in the UK. It showed a steady trend towards more openness in the governance process and towards integration of governance activity in the investment process.

Highlights of the findings were that twenty-six out of the thirty-three managers surveyed had made their policies on engagement public compared with only fourteen three years earlier. All managers surveyed reported to clients on their voting activity or posted their voting record on their website on a regular basis. Altogether, fifteen institutions disclosed their voting decisions publicly on their website compared with just two when the first survey was carried out in 2003. As at June 2006, the fund managers surveyed employed 217 people working full time on engagement, an increase of more than 25 per cent in three years. The twenty-seven managers who provided details cast over 185,000 votes at over 17,000 annual meetings in the year to end June 2006.

What is also gratifying in the light of the ICGN statement is that twenty-six of the managers surveyed provided statements on the management of conflicts of interest. This is an increase from twenty-three recorded in the previous year. Also, eighteen out of those surveyed said voting decisions on controversial issues were taken at senior level whereas fourteen others portfolio managers are actively involved. A further sign that governance is being integrated with the investment process came from the finding that, in the majority of cases, corporate governance specialists sit in on company meetings with the portfolio managers and analysts when there is a relevant issue to be addressed.

The challenges ahead

The need to join up the governance and the investment process has, however, still some way to go. In some institutions there is still a sense that this is merely an overlay on the investment process. There are still problems in some houses integrating governance with the investment process. There is still a need to raise the quality of dialogue between shareholders and companies to ensure that it is properly informed, and there is still a need to move away from a short-term focus on the company's financial results and share price performance. When these are favourable, fund managers may be reluctant to address governance

---

[3] Survey of fund managers' engagement with companies, published by the Investment Management Association: www.investmentuk.org.

issues even though these may contain the seeds of future value destruction. As part of the communications process between companies and shareholders, some shareholders need to do more to explain unfavourable voting decisions to companies in advance. Here, sheer pressure of work often means it is difficult to live up to a commitment to communicate such decisions in a timely way.

Communication also needs to be better coordinated on both sides of the relationship. While there is a lot more dialogue between companies and shareholders these days, it still tends to be compartmentalised. Thus the Chief Executive and Chief Financial Officer talk to analysts and fund managers about financial results. This rarely involves discussion about governance matters. Corporate governance specialists talk to the independent Chairman or relevant directors, such as the remuneration committee chairman, but these conversations rarely involve executives. On the company side, the relations with analysts and fund managers are handled by the Investor Relations Department, while on the governance side the Company Secretary handles relations with institutions. Finally, those responsible for socially responsible investment may be having lengthy discussions with corporate responsibility executives in the companies. There is too little interface between these parties, either within investment institutions and companies or across the divide. The result is a fragmented relationship.

A particular need is to fold the approach to corporate responsibility more effectively into the overall relationship. While specialised investors in this area are sometimes seen as reflecting the interests of particular stakeholders rather than the company as a whole, there is also recognition among mainstream investors that the way in which companies approach social responsibility may have a material impact on their franchise and thus on their business prospects. Corporate responsibility issues therefore belong in the area of risk management. Where they are germane to the business, they are a legitimate subject for all shareholders to address. The challenge, however, is to ensure that they are addressed in the right way. The development of narrative reporting offers an important opportunity because it should help focus attention on factors affecting the company in the long term and therefore allow corporate responsibility issues to be debated in an appropriate context.

Finally, the market itself is changing. The share of UK companies held by traditional long-only investors has fallen, partly as a result of regulatory pressures on pension funds and insurance companies, partly because of the overall tendency of markets to globalise, and partly because of new investment techniques involving the use of derivatives, which may involve the separation of control from economic ownership. The result is that control may have shifted to overseas investors or to hedge funds with a shorter-term time horizon who are less predictable and with whom it is harder for companies to build up a significant relationship.

What will be the contribution of hedge funds to the process remains to be seen. Some of them are very well informed about companies in which they take stakes and can engage very effectively with the management. Some of them recognise, too, that corporate governance is connected to value. Thus one hedge fund, Knight Vinke Asset Management, played an important role in helping Shell restructure in the wake of its reserves scandal and benefited as a result from the return of a 'governance premium' once the restructuring was complete. The influence is thus not all negative, but companies sometimes say they are confused about who to talk to, and the way in which some investors hold their stakes through derivatives such as contracts for difference means companies may not be sure exactly who owns them. In these circumstances, there is clearly an advantage in maintaining a good relationship with known long-term holders who will provide a form of anchor.

Another factor is the influence of the bond markets, in which investment has grown substantially, particularly at critical moments in a company's history. Shareholders have ultimately, for example, had very little say in the affairs of a debt-ridden company such as Eurotunnel.

In short, just as the traditional institutions have begun to get better at exercising the responsibilities of ownership, their influence is diminishing as a result of changing market structures. Finding a way of ensuring that shareholders can continue to exert a positive influence on companies in these new circumstances is the biggest challenge of all.

6

The role of the regulator

SIR BRYAN NICHOLSON

Introduction

In this chapter I will briefly explain the rationale for the market-based approach to promoting good governance and why I believe the comply-or-explain approach to be the most effective means of achieving this objective, before going on to set out what I see as the proper role for the regulator and governments in encouraging the uptake of good practice. I will then illustrate how this role works in practice using two examples from my period as chairman of the Financial Reporting Council (FRC): the revisions to the Combined Code made in 2003 following the Higgs and Smith reports on non-executive directors and audit committees respectively, and the review of the Turnbull guidance on internal controls in the wake of the US Sarbanes-Oxley Act in 2004–5. The FRC is the body designated by the Government, with the support of the business, investor and professional communities, to be responsible for corporate governance. Finally, I will consider some of the challenges to the success of the market-based approach.

The market-based approach to promoting good governance

To set the context for a discussion of the market-based approach to promoting good governance I can do no better than start with two quotes. The first is the opening paragraph from the 1992 Cadbury Report, which put in place the basic elements of the framework that is still used in the UK, and the second is the first principle in the Combined Code on Corporate Governance:

> The country's economy depends on the drive and efficiency of its companies. Thus the effectiveness with which their boards discharge their responsibilities determines Britain's competitive position. They must be free to drive their companies forward, but exercise that freedom within a framework of effective accountability. This is the essence of any system of good corporate governance.[1]

---

[1] *Report of the Committee on the Financial Aspects of Corporate Governance* (The Cadbury Report), December 1992.

The board's role is to provide entrepreneurial leadership of the company within a framework of prudent and effective controls which enables risk to be assessed and managed.[2]

As these quotes make clear, accountability to the shareholders, while very important, is not the only objective of good governance. Good governance is a tool that can improve the board's ability to manage the company effectively. For example, the board is more likely to come to better decisions if it has amongst its members the right mix of skills, experience and independent thinking, and if the strategy put forward by the executive management has been rigorously tested. The company will be better prepared for what the future might bring if it has a clear understanding of the risks and opportunities it faces and systems in place to manage them effectively. These are not accountability issues – they are good business sense.

A regulatory framework that aims to improve standards of corporate governance is more likely to succeed, and be accepted by those that it regulates, if it recognises that governance should support, not constrain, the entrepreneurial leadership of the company. This, of course, works to the benefit of the shareholder as well if it improves the long-term value of the company and their investment.

This in turn requires a degree of flexibility in the way companies adopt and adapt governance practices. To use an overworked phrase, there is no 'one size fits all'. The Combined Code is specifically designed to allow the necessary flexibility for it to be used effectively across all listed companies.

To be effective, rather than simply accountable, good governance needs to be implemented in a way that fits the culture and organisation of the individual company. These vary enormously from company to company depending on factors such as company size and stage of development, the sector in which the company operates and the complexity of the business model. When the FRC reviewed the implementation of the Turnbull guidance on internal control in 2005, it found a clear correlation between a company's perception of the benefits that had been delivered and the extent to which it had integrated the guidance into its normal business processes and systems.[3]

If the test of good governance is whether it is effective in improving the management of the business, who judges its effectiveness? In my view it has to be the intended beneficiaries – the shareholders. They share with the board the objective of creating wealth and achieving sustainable shareholder value; and where they take an active interest they will have a good understanding of the company, and are able to take an informed view on the appropriateness of the company's governance practices.

[2] *The Combined Code on Corporate Governance*, Financial Reporting Council, July 2003 (also as updated June 2006).

[3] *Review of the Turnbull Guidance of Internal Control: Proposals for Updating the Guidance'*, Financial Reporting Council, June 2005.

This was why the Cadbury Report emphasised the importance of transparency through disclosure to shareholders, and introduced the concept of comply-or-explain. While the content of the Code and the regulatory framework that supports it have evolved, this remains the basis of the UK's corporate governance system for listed companies and has been increasingly adopted in other jurisdictions over recent years. Many other non-listed entities also use adopted versions of the Combined Code as the basis for their governance.

The Cadbury Code set out a selection of good practices and standards of behaviour that companies were encouraged to consider and, if appropriate, to adopt. If they felt the recommendations of the Code were not appropriate in their particular situation, they were encouraged to explain their reasoning for non-adoption to their shareholders.

The same approach was continued when the Hampel review of the Cadbury Code took place in the mid-1990s. Under the auspices of the FRC, a top-level group of people from the business, investor and other communities was set up under Sir Ronnie Hampel, then Chairman of ICI, to review the working of the Cadbury Code and to suggest any changes that might be thought desirable. It published its findings in 1998 and with it came into being an updated Code.[4] That Code also included the recommendations of the Greenbury Report on remuneration,[5] which had been published in 1995. Thus, for the first time it was called 'the Combined Code on Corporate Governance'. That name has stuck and the shorthand of it, the Combined Code, is now universally recognised.

The 1998 Combined Code was strengthened as compared to Cadbury by making it an obligation on companies to disclose how they were applying the Combined Code by making comply-or-explain a requirement of the Listing Rules of the London Stock Exchange. The 1998 Combined Code added to the highly visible 'provisions' of the Code (those elements subject to comply-or-explain) the practice of stating 'principles' which companies should follow when implementing the Code. These principles set out some basic tenets of good governance such as objectivity and transparency. They are not prescriptive. Companies can decide how best to implement them in their own particular circumstances, but they must pay regard to them and tell their shareholders how they are implementing them. Later, the 2003 Combined Code divided principles into 'main principles' and 'supporting principles', but the same process of reporting to shareholders on implementation continued.

In this way enforcement takes place at two levels. The Financial Services Authority (FSA) is now the body responsible for enforcing the Listing Rules. It ensures that companies are disclosing their corporate governance practices in their annual report and accounts by reference to the Combined Code. However, neither the FSA nor the FRC, which is responsible for the content of the Combined Code, makes a judgement on how the company has applied the

---

[4] *Committee on Corporate Governance: Final Report* (The Hampel Report), January 1998.
[5] *Directors' Remuneration: Report of a Study Group Chaired by Sir Richard Greenbury*, July 1995.

Code – for example, whether the company should have complied rather than explained (or indeed whether the explanation given was adequate), or whether the explanation of how the principles and supporting principles have been implemented is acceptable. That is clearly the duty of the shareholders.

Advantages of the market-based approach and comply-or-explain

I believe this model has a number of advantages over more traditional forms of regulation as a means of raising standards of corporate governance among listed companies.

First and foremost is its inherent flexibility, which makes it both better able to deal with differing company circumstances, and easier to update as views on corporate governance evolve. It is not possible to draft legislation that could anticipate all the different methods of applying the main principles and supporting principles in the Combined Code, or identify all the various factors that might affect a company's choice of governance practices; at best it could offer a choice of routes to compliance. Even when attempts are made to produce genuinely principles-based legislation, which sets only the outcome to be achieved not the means by which it must be achieved, there is almost inevitably a demand for greater clarity on the part of the regulator and/or the regulated which leads to more detailed rules, or of guidance which acquires the status of rules. Some might suggest that the rules and standards produced by the United States Securities and Exchange Commission (SEC) and the Public Companies Accounting Oversight Board (PCAOB) in relation to Section 404 of the US Sarbanes-Oxley Act were an example of this phenomenon.

The flexibility of the market-based approach is reinforced by the fact that the enforcement responsibility rests with the shareholders, not a regulator. Our experience with the Combined Code is that shareholders are often willing to take a pragmatic approach about how to apply best practice in a way that is in the best interests of the company. They can accept non-compliance on a particular issue if they are persuaded that there is good reason and can see that in overall terms the governance is good.

It is neither sensible nor desirable to ask a regulator to enforce a comply-or-explain regime beyond ensuring that the necessary disclosures are being made. A regulator cannot apply the same degree of flexibility. Regulators do not and cannot have sufficient understanding of the individual company to judge what is or is not appropriate for that company. There would be an understandable expectation of consistency from those being regulated that would make it very difficult for the regulator to endorse exceptions except in clearly defined circumstances. Shareholders do not have this inhibition.

This is a view shared by the European Corporate Governance Forum in its report on the operation of comply-or-explain issued in 2006. The Forum is an expert group set up by the European Commission in 2004 to examine best practice in corporate governance in EU Member States. As well as endorsing the comply-or-explain approach in its 2006 report it commented that 'regulatory authorities should limit their role to checking the existence of the statement, and to reacting to blatant misrepresentation of facts. They should not try and second-guess the judgement of the board or the value of its explanations. This is a matter for the company's shareholders.'[6]

One example of this would be the assessment of whether a non-executive director should be considered to be independent of the company or not. How this is done is still a source of considerable debate in the UK. When the Combined Code was revised in 2003, it set out for the first time some examples of circumstances which could potentially affect an individual's ability to take an objective position, while making it clear that companies were nonetheless entitled to classify an individual as an independent non-executive director if they considered that the potential conflict of interest was being managed and had not affected the individual's independence of mind.

Some companies consider that in practice this has led to a presumption on the part of investors that such individuals are unable to manage any conflict of interest; some investors feel that companies are somewhat opaque in their explanations as to why they consider individual directors to be independent notwithstanding the existence of such interests. But both sides agree that it would be wholly undesirable for the concept of independence to be defined in regulation. It was interesting to observe that when European Commission proposals for mandatory audit committees, which would include at least one member defined as independent, were being negotiated, opposition in the UK was led jointly by the CBI and the Association of British Insurers, one of the leading investor bodies.

Because of the need for legislation to be consistent and enforceable, such legislation could not countenance that an individual could be considered to be independent while another individual in exactly the same situation was not. Comply-or-explain does not have that problem; it allows a pragmatic judgement to be made case by case.

For example, the Combined Code includes a criterion relating to length of tenure, which requires the board to explain why it believes an individual remains independent when he has served on the board for more than nine years. If the Government had decided in 2005 to make regulations that stated that no non-executive director could serve for more than nine years, 10 per cent of all non-executive directors in FTSE 350 companies would immediately have had to step down.[7] This would have meant a great amount of experience and expertise being lost and would be completely contrary to the objective of improving standards of governance. The fact that boards overwhelmingly rotate their members in nine years or less, and therefore by their actions implicitly

---

[6] *Statement on the Comply-or-Explain Principle*, European Corporate Governance Forum, February 2006.

[7] 'Board Structure and Non-executive Directors' fees', Deloitte, September 2005.

accept that a maximum of nine years is appropriate for most members, does not mean that there should be a hard and fast rule. What there should be is an explanation to shareholders why any particular individual is being asked to serve beyond nine years.

I believe the other main advantage of the code-based approach is that it is more likely to lead to ongoing improvements in governance, for a number of interrelated reasons:

- It is better able to adapt to changes in attitudes and business culture. What is seen as good practice in one era may be viewed differently in the next, and aspects of governance that were not previously seen as significant may become so. It is easier to update a comply-or-explain code to reflect the market than it is to update legislation.
- It can be more aspirational than legislation. Legislation tends to be written in terms of the minimum necessary requirements. That is entirely right; to do otherwise would be to risk imposing unjustified or disproportionate burdens on those being regulated. However, to quote from the Cadbury Report, 'Statutory measures would impose a minimum standard and there would be a greater risk of boards complying with the letter, rather than with the spirit, of their requirements.'[8] On the other hand a comply-or-explain code can, and does, set out market leading practices and encourage the rest to aspire to the standards of the best, while recognising that it may take time for all companies to get there, or for certain concepts to be accepted or for good practice to emerge.
- It can encourage good practice relating to softer issues for which it would be inappropriate to prescribe minimum requirements in law. For example, the Combined Code contains provisions relating to the induction and training of non-executive directors. It would be hard to imagine regulations setting out a minimum number of days of training a year for all directors.
- By asking shareholders to act as the enforcers it encourages them to engage with the companies in which they invest and to take their responsibilities as owners seriously.

One example of how the Combined Code and its predecessors have encouraged and reflected changes in governance practice is the separation of the roles of Chairman and Chief Executive. When first recommended in the Cadbury Code in 1992 this was considered controversial, and the two roles were combined in many companies. Now it is almost received wisdom in the UK that it is desirable for them to be separated, and by 2007, 94 per cent of FTSE 350 companies had done so.[9] Research into the views of the Chairmen of these companies carried out in 2005 found that 'most of the Chairmen we interviewed believed that

---

[8] Cadbury Report.

[9] FTSE 350 Corporate Governance Review', Grant Thornton, December 2007.

the post-Cadbury trend towards separating the roles of Chairman and Chief Executive had been beneficial, and made for better governance'.[10]

Another more recent example is the provision added to the Combined Code in 2003 recommending that the board carry out an annual evaluation of its performance. At the time there was criticism of this provision from some company Chairmen who saw it as an attempt to tell them how to run their board. Subsequent feedback from those who have gone through the process is now almost uniformly positive, with many companies finding that the evaluation had lead to improvements in the board's processes and made an important contribution to succession planning. This was backed up by the results of a survey of Company Secretaries which found that nearly 80 per cent thought that evaluation would lead to improvements in board performance.[11] There continues to be some criticism that the Combined Code is too prescriptive in recommending a full annual evaluation, but under comply-or-explain companies can choose to vary the frequency or scope of the evaluations they carry out.

The final argument in favour of the comply-or-explain approach is that it seems to work. The EU Corporate Governance Forum considered that 'the experience of countries which have implemented this approach for several years shows that it does lead to a movement of convergence towards better governance practices',[12] and this is borne out by experience in the UK. When the FRC reviewed the implementation of the Combined Code in 2005 it was the overwhelming view of both investors and companies that there has been an overall improvement in the standards of corporate governance since it came into force. An NAPF survey published in August 2007 found that 79 per cent of pension funds considered corporate governance standards had improved further since 2005.[13]

However, the comply-or-explain approach is not working perfectly and there are threats and challenges to its continued success, to which I will return later in this chapter.

The role of governments and regulators

While comply-or-explain and the market-based approach to raising standards are preferable to prescriptive regulation, they nonetheless have to be backed up by a supportive regulatory framework. Government and regulators should not act as a substitute for the market, but they do have an important role to play in making sure that the market works effectively.

---

[10] Sir Geoffrey Owen and Tom Kirchmaier (London School of Economics), 'The Changing Role of the Chairman: Impact of Corporate Governance Reform in the UK 1995–2005', The Chairmen's Forum, 2006.

[11] 'Evaluating the Code: Is board Performance Evaluation Working?', Edis-Bates Associates, October 2005.

[12] See note 3. [13] 'Pension Funds' Engagement with Companies', NAPF, August 2007.

Specifically, if shareholders are to be given the role of enforcing governance standards, they need to be given the tools to carry out that role. This means ensuring they have sufficient information to make a judgement about the company's governance practices, and sufficient powers to influence the behaviour of the board.

Without these rights one relies solely on companies acting in their enlightened self-interest. While this can be a significant factor, it may not always be sufficient. The Cadbury Report, the Greenbury Report on directors' remuneration and the Hampel review of Cadbury were all business-led initiatives aimed in part at staving off the threat of possible legislation.

In the UK, the main disclosure requirement remains the obligation under the Listing Rules for companies to report on how they are applying the Combined Code. In recent years, additional requirements have been added through the Directors' Remuneration Report Regulations 2002 and the introduction, following the implementation of the EU Accounts Modernisation Directive, of a requirement to produce a Business Review.

The Directors' Remuneration Report Regulations 2002 are an interesting example. They were introduced as the Government's response to public concerns about levels of remuneration and so-called rewards for failure, and in part replace provisions previously in the Combined Code. Views will no doubt differ on the merits of the regulations, but they are not in themselves inconsistent with the market-based approach in that they set out what information the company is expected to disclose and then give the shareholders an advisory vote on the remuneration package. It seems likely that the existence of a successful model in the Combined Code based on disclosure and shareholder enforcement would have been one factor in the Government's decision to regulate in this way rather than intervene more directly by, for example, setting a cap on remuneration.

Shareholder rights are an essential precondition of the comply-or-explain system, and one reason why it has generally been able to operate successfully in the UK. Shareholders need to be able properly to hold boards to account for their decisions. Even if these rights are not often used in anger, the knowledge of their existence can have a significant influence on a board's behaviour. In their absence, legislators and regulators may of necessity be driven down a more prescriptive path.

It is interesting to contrast the rights of shareholders in the UK with those in the US, where shareholders typically have many fewer rights. For example, in the UK the company must ask the shareholders' views on such things as acquisitions, related party transactions and rights issues. In the US most decisions are reserved to the board. The business judgement rule allows directors to make significant decisions on their own that directly affect shareholders' interests, and not be liable.

In the UK, shareholders vote on the election of individual directors; in the US they typically can only vote for the slate, although there are beginning to be signs of movement on this front. In the UK, shareholders can put forward motions to the AGM and force the board to call an extraordinary general meeting if they have the support of a certain percentage of the company's overall share capital. In the US, thresholds for putting motions to the AGM are lower but, unlike in the UK, companies have wide discretion to exclude proposals.

The US and the UK have fundamentally different approaches to corporate governance regulation. In the UK, under comply-or-explain, the real enforcement authority is the company's shareholders. In the US, there is absolutely no question that it is the SEC that takes that role. Moves by the SEC to make it easier for shareholders to nominate independent candidates for director election were strongly resisted by US corporates. It seems clear from this reaction that the shareholder-led approach we have in the UK would not command the same broad support among the business community in the US.

Once this regulatory framework is in place, can the regulator gracefully step aside and leave it entirely to the market? I don't believe so. For the market-based approach to succeed it needs the active endorsement of all market participants, and the regulator can help achieve this by:

- developing consensus with the market about what constitutes best practice
- encouraging the uptake of good practice by companies, recognising that comply-or-explain allows for exceptions
- encouraging constructive dialogue between boards and investors, and responsible ownership on the part of shareholders.

Historically this is the role that has been played by the Financial Reporting Council in the UK since the late 1990s. It was seen as the most appropriate body to act as midwife to the Hampel review of the Cadbury Report. Subsequently, in 2002, the government made it more formally clear that it saw the FRC as the body responsible for UK corporate governance. Thus, under my chairmanship, it commissioned the Smith Report on the role of audit committees[14] in 2002, and was asked by the government to incorporate recommendations from that report and the 2003 Higgs Report on the role of non-executive directors[15] into an updated Combined Code which was published in 2003. As part of its responsibility for corporate governance, the FRC is responsible for keeping the operation of the Combined Code under review and proposing amendments where appropriate. This led to limited amendments to the Combined Code in 2006 following a public review.

The status and structure of the FRC has undoubtedly contributed to its ability to play the role of standard-setter and consensus-builder. Its governing body, the Board, contains representatives of listed companies and institutional investors as well as other stakeholders. These interests are also represented on

---

[14] *Audit Committees: Combined Code Guidance* (The Smith Report), January 2003.

[15] *Review of the Role and Effectiveness of Non-executive Directors* (The Higgs Report), January 2003.

the Corporate Governance Committee, which is a sub-group of the Board which directly oversees the Combined Code.

Although currently part-funded by central government, the FRC is classified as an independent regulator. For some of its other activities, such as enforcement of accounting standards and the oversight of the accountancy profession, it has direct statutory responsibilities set out in legislation. This is not the case in the area of corporate governance.

That has imposed an important discipline on the FRC in the way the Combined Code has developed, because it does not have a free hand to force through changes to the Combined Code, even if it were minded to do so. If the Combined Code has been effective, it is because, by and large, it has the consent of the market. If the FRC wishes to make changes, it needs to carry the market with it. Failure to do so, for example by putting forward proposals that appear either to companies or to investors to be unbalanced in favour of the other party, would cause it to lose credibility and possibly invite government intervention.

This is not to say that the role of the FRC as regulator is to preserve the status quo. As noted earlier, the view of what constitutes good practice develops over time, and governance codes need to reflect those developments. But, if they are to be effective, they need to develop in a way that enjoys broad support from boards and shareholders.

How does the regulator carry out this role in practice?

Case study 1: Revising the Combined Code after the Higgs and Smith Reports in 2003

In 2002, in the aftermath of the WorldCom and Enron scandals, the Government decided to commission a review primarily to examine the role of non-executive directors and to make recommendations. Apart from concern originating from the US scandals about the role of non-executive directors, the Government also believed that better governance of listed companies would improve the underlying performance of UK companies and increase UK competitiveness. Also, the government had a generally pro-business stance, but needed to show its concern that companies should be well-constituted and broadly accountable bodies.

The Government invited Derek Higgs, a senior and well-known director and City figure, to carry out the review. As the work progressed, his review broadened into a much wider review of corporate governance such that the Higgs Report amounted to a full-scale review of the then Combined Code, with a recommended updating of that Code backed by much supporting material.

The difference, however, from the Cadbury and Hampel exercises was that the review was carried out by a single individual rather than a representative group. Without doubt, that led to some of the difficulties which followed the publication of the Higgs Report and which would most likely have been avoided had Sir Derek had a representative group working with him. The reason is that any revision of the Combined Code is likely to be difficult and potentially controversial, and it is much easier to carry the various constituencies and reach consensus if they have all had senior figures representing them on the reviewing group. Apart from anything else, this provides solid cover for the Chairman who, if pressed on one point or another, can point to the support of senior figures from all sides. Also, other members in the peer group of each constituency are likely to follow the lead of individuals they respect and who will obviously have consulted with them personally as the work progressed. While a single writer can still talk to everyone, that single writer would not have this advantage.

At the point of publication of the Higgs Report in January 2003, the immediate press reporting was quite favourable, but rapidly turned hostile when company Chairmen particularly took exception to some of its content and tone. The media noise level and the hostility to certain particular points by company Chairmen obscured the fact that there was a significant measure of consensus regarding most of the substantive content of the report. Matters were not helped by the fact that the FRC, which I then chaired, announced that it would proceed to implementation of the report into a new Combined Code accepting in a period of consultation only changes stemming from 'fatal flaws' – a technical term which assumed the deal was done and the drafting only needed to be examined to see if any obvious flaws had been overlooked.

It rapidly became clear that the FRC's position on fatal flaws only was untenable and, as Chairman, I had to make it clear that all inputs would be properly considered and that the recommendations in the Higgs Report were open to alteration. Looking back, Sir Derek and I were perhaps too sanguine that the assurances Sir Derek thought he had been given by various representative bodies would actually deliver those constituencies in practice.

The FRC, therefore, converted its limited consultation announced in January immediately after the publication of the Higgs Report into a wider consultation. The FRC set up a sub-group of its Council with seven members representing different interests with a commitment to consultation with all the various representative bodies[16] with a view to having redrafted proposals ready for approval by the FRC Council at its July meeting.

As Chairman of the Council and of the sub-group, I led the work of the sub-group, the widespread consultations and the actual redrafting. The four main issues of concern raised and how they were dealt with were as follows.

1. The Higgs draft was seen as being overly prescriptive with too many provisions requiring comply-or-explain (roughly double the number in the then

---

[16] The representative bodies consulted were the CBI, the Institute of Directors, the Quoted Companies Alliance, the Association of British Insurers, the National Association of Pension Funds, the Investment Management Association, the Association of Investment Trust Companies, the British Bankers' Association and the London Investment Banking Association.

existing Combined Code). This led to concern about a drift to 'comply-or-else', considerable amounts of explanation being potentially required, and a worry that there would be too much box-ticking. This was dealt with mainly by some consolidation of the number of provisions, but also by moving some provisions into the category of principles, and the dividing of principles into main principles and supporting principles.

Provisions are subject to comply-or-explain, but main principles and supporting principles are not. Companies do have to explain to their shareholders how they are implementing the main principles and supporting principles, but the choice of how to implement is theirs. It is then up to shareholders to come back to any company if they do not like the method of implementation. The presumption is, given that there are various effective ways suitable to the circumstances of each company of implementing the principles, that shareholders would only make representations to the company if there were really strong objections to the method of implementation chosen by the company.

This approach brought the number of provisions essentially back to where it was in the previous Combined Code while introducing in an acceptable form, through the principles, a range of proposals dealing principally with the professionalism of the board and based on good practice followed already by many well-managed companies. Additionally, through agreement between companies and investors, there was put in place in the Preamble to the new Combined Code agreed words about companies giving good explanations where they did not wish to comply with a provision, and shareholders listening to the explanation, giving careful responses and not indulging in box-ticking.

2. Company Chairmen were particularly concerned that the role of the Chairman appeared to have been downgraded in the way the Higgs Report was written. There was concern that the role of the senior independent director (the SID) had been elevated such that it encroached on the prerogatives of the Chairman, and that certain proposals relating to the role of the non-executive directors also placed a limitation on the role of the Chairman. There was specific objection to making it a provision that the Chairman should not chair the nominating committee, the argument being that it was a fundamental part of the Chairman's role to shape a good board. It was easy to deal with the issue as the investor side was quite content for that provision to be removed, so it went.

The question of the role of the Chairman was principally dealt with by rebalancing the drafting to make clear the key position of the Chairman on the board. For example, there was material in the Higgs Report regarding the role of the SID in chairing meetings of the non-executive directors and in communicating with shareholders which Chairmen felt usurped their role. How this was dealt with can be seen by comparing the wording in the Higgs Report's suggested revisions and the wording of the Combined Code. The Higgs version says 'the non-executive directors should meet regularly as a group without the executives present and at least once a year without the Chairman present. The meetings should be led by the senior independent director.' This became, in the new

Combined Code, 'The Chairman should hold meetings with the non-executive directors without the executives present. Led by the senior independent director, the non-executive directors should meet without the Chairman present at least annually to appraise the Chairman's performance . . . and on such other occasions as are deemed appropriate.' As can be seen, the drafting changes were more of nuance than substance, but they allayed the fears expressed by Chairmen.

Similar changes, acknowledging the prime role of the Chairman, were made in relation to meetings with shareholders.

3. Consultations showed that the provision requiring comply-or-explain if a non-executive director were to serve beyond six years was considered to be an unacceptably short period of time. Business and investment cycles vary quite widely. While a significant number of companies do rotate their boards on a six-yearly cycle, more judge this to be too short a rotation period for the needs of their company. What no one objected to was the concept of a proper evaluation of the performance of each director at the end of their three-year term before deciding whether the individual's contribution justified a second term. Also, there was sufficient consensus that a third term should require a particularly rigorous review of performance and also of the needs of the board for succession planning, balance of skills and so on. Thus the wording was altered to reflect this and the provision requiring comply-or-explain only comes in after nine years.

4. There was significant consultation with bodies representing the smaller listed companies, essentially below the FTSE 350. What emerged was that the smaller companies did not wish to be considered second-class citizens by having less demanding good governance practices than their larger brethren. It was felt that, with common sense from their investors (usually a narrower group than with the larger companies), it would be perfectly possible for them to operate, with one exception, to the same code as the larger companies.

The one exception was the provision that at least 50 per cent of the board, excluding the Chairman, should be independent non-executive directors. The objections to this provision for smaller companies were essentially based on two factors. First, many companies entering the main market have boards with founders who are still active and with key executives on their boards, and with a smaller relative number of non-executives, and boards are in general smaller than is the case with larger companies. The provision would be likely to cause a heavy disturbance factor. Second, apart from the disturbance factor, there was the practical issue of the sheer amount of non-executive director recruitment which would be required, and its potential unbalancing effect on smaller company boards, including forcing those boards to become larger than was necessary for the size of company. Accordingly, the provision regarding the number of independent non-executive directors was amended for companies below the FTSE 350 to be a provision that there should be at least two independent NEDs on their boards.

The number of substantive changes made to the Higgs draft was in practice quite limited, but there was significant redrafting in terms of tone in order to gain acceptance from the different constituencies. Looking back, it is clear that Sir Derek achieved consensus on a wide range of issues, but this was obscured by certain points proving contentious. There was also a great deal of extremely valuable material in the Higgs Report which got translated almost unchanged both into the Combined Code and into the back-up material published with the Code. Likewise, one of the key thrusts of the Higgs recommendations, increasing professionalism in the way boards are run, has been widely accepted.

One aspect of the 2003 Combined Code which is hardly ever referred to is that part of the Code dealing with the recommendations made by the Smith review of the role of audit committees. After Sir Derek had been commissioned by the Government to carry out his review, the Government realised in July 2002 that the question of the work of audit committees was not covered by the Higgs review, but clearly needed attention in the light of the WorldCom and Enron scandals and indeed, apart from those, because it made no sense to review corporate governance without looking at the role of the audit committee.

In this case, the Government asked the FRC to set up and carry through such a review. Sir Robert Smith, Chairman of The Weir Group, and by background a qualified accountant, was asked to carry out the review supported by a group representing the appropriate constituencies. His report proved non-contentious and carried general support. It was carried through essentially unchanged into the new Combined Code. Partly of course this must be attributed to the work of Sir Robert and his colleagues, but also it points up the value of such reviews being conducted by a chairman with the help of other senior colleagues for the reasons stated earlier. Also, it should be acknowledged that any review in this area, as with the Turnbull review, is much more technical and, therefore, much less likely to attract the sort of strong feelings expressed by those consulted about the Higgs Report.

Although the process of putting in place a new Combined Code took some months longer than originally anticipated, in the end the process of consultation drew consensus such that the FRC Council supported the new Combined Code unanimously at its meeting in July 2003. Simultaneously, all the relevant representative bodies declared their support for the new Combined Code. This has given it both credibility and teeth and, as covered in other chapters, the 2005 review of the Code showed good progress being made in its implementation and no major problems. Going forward, the FRC's decision to establish a standing committee of its members to keep the Code under review, and its public commitment to carrying out regular reviews, helped in its general acceptance. While no one either expects or wants lots of annual changes to the Combined Code, the existence of a mechanism for regular review is a reassurance to the market that the Combined Code will remain relevant and supported.

Case study 2: Revising the Turnbull guidance (2004–5)

One of the principles of the Combined Code is that listed companies should have in place an effective system of internal controls. The Turnbull guidance was published in 1999 to provide advice to companies on how to apply this principle.

Produced by a working group led by Nigel Turnbull, the then Finance Director of the Rank Organisation, the guidance was aimed at the board rather than at the internal auditors or risk management specialists within companies; and as with the Combined Code itself, the working group recognised that to be useful it should be capable of being adapted to fit the company's circumstances. The guidance was therefore pitched at a high level, setting out principles rather than detailed processes. In total the guidance ran to only twelve pages.

Following the Enron and WorldCom scandals, and the subsequent introduction of Section 404 of the Sarbanes-Oxley Act in the US, many other countries understandably felt it necessary to review their regulatory framework relating to internal controls. In several countries, including the Netherlands and Sweden, this led to the introduction of new requirements which, like Section 404, placed an obligation on the company to state whether its internal control system was effective.

In the UK we were in the fortunate position that we already had in the Turnbull guidance an established and effective approach to risk management and internal control. This meant that we were able to resist any immediate pressure to follow the US lead and take time for mature reflection, by reviewing whether the existing framework was working as intended, or needed amendment in any way. The impact of Section 404 was, of course, a relevant consideration for the review, but it did not set the agenda. I believe that the way in which the review was conducted is a good example of the market-led approach to regulation in action.

A working group was set up under the chairmanship of Douglas Flint, Group Finance Director of HSBC Holdings, and involving representatives from listed companies, the investment community and the accountancy profession. The group carried out first an extensive evidence-gathering exercise and consultation, as part of which they received comments from companies accounting for 56 per cent of the total market capitalisation of UK companies on the London Stock Exchange Main Market, and investors responsible for over £2,300 billion of assets under management. This gave them the confidence that they had a proper understanding of what the market wanted, and a clear mandate when drafting updated guidance, on which they then held a second consultation.

The most striking aspect of both consultations was that the views of companies and investors were very closely aligned on most of the main issues. While investors had some criticisms, for example about the level of disclosure in annual reports, all respondents wanted to retain the flexibility of the current guidance rather than introduce a greater degree of prescription, and there was little desire for substantial change. Investors told us that they considered the relative lack of prescription in the guidance was seen as an important factor in its success, as it had enabled companies to apply the guidance in the way that was most appropriate to their circumstances. As a result, only limited changes were made to the guidance. I take this to be a strong endorsement by the market of the UK approach to corporate governance. While the Government felt it appropriate to change the manner in which the accountancy and auditing profession was regulated when the WorldCom and Enron scandals erupted, it did not consider legislation on internal controls to be necessary, and was content for the market, via the FRC, to take the appropriate reviewing action.

There was very little support for introducing requirements similar to those under Section 404. This was partly because experience in the US had highlighted concerns about costs. But there was also a concern, from investors in particular, that requirements of that sort might lead to a mechanistic focus on compliance rather than substantive assessment and management of risk, undermining what was seen as one of the main strengths of the UK approach.

The support from the UK investment community was also important in attempting to influence the debate at an EU and international level. Proposed legislation is often justified as being necessary to protect investors. As a result of the review of the Turnbull guidance, we were able to demonstrate that, in the UK at least, investors did not consider any benefits they might gain from Section 404 type legislation to be worth giving up the value they obtained from the existing system.

While it was undoubtedly the costs associated with implementation of Section 404 in the US that led other jurisdictions to pause for thought, I believe our review helped to demonstrate that other models are available. This appears to have had some resonance even in the US. In May 2005 a Bill was introduced to both Houses of Congress that would have required the SEC and PCAOB to 'jointly conduct a study comparing and contrasting the principles-based Turnbull Guidance of Great Britain to the implementation of section 404 of the Sarbanes-Oxley Act of 2002'.

Challenges to comply-or-explain

The code-based approach to promoting good governance only succeeds if it enjoys the consent of the market. It requires both companies and investors to recognise their responsibilities and operate within the spirit of comply-or-explain. If either party fails to do so, the system breaks down. As much attention must be paid to the manner in which a code is implemented as to its contents.

As noted, one of the points that most concerned companies when the Combined Code was revised in 2003 was that any increase in the number of provisions might encourage box-ticking on the part of investors: a greater focus on checking compliance with the provisions rather than on the application of the principles of good governance. Even though the number of provisions in the

2003 Code is hardly changed from its predecessor, that concern remained. To avoid it becoming a serious issue for any company requires good explanation by the company and a proper consideration of such an explanation by investors.

In fact, when the FRC consulted companies on how the Combined Code was working in 2005 it appeared that their worst fears had not been realised. We were told that, for the larger companies at least, their major shareholders were generally willing to engage in discussions and to treat each explanation on its merits. These appeared to be borne out by surveys conducted by NAPF and the Investment Management Association which found that fund managers were committing more resources to engagement with companies.[17]

However there was criticism of perceived box-ticking on the part of some investment institutions, intermediaries such as rating agencies and the media, which tends to present cases where companies have chosen to explain rather than comply as 'a breach of City rules', when this is clearly not the case.

One could say that, as long as the company's main shareholders remain content, they should be big enough to ignore the box-tickers. But if a board believes it will be publicly criticised for non-compliance even when shareholders have accepted their explanation and are supportive, one can understand why they might think it easier simply to comply. Anecdotal evidence suggests that some companies are defaulting to compliance regardless of their circumstances rather than run the perceived risks of explaining. There is an ongoing challenge to ensure that comply-or-explain does not drift into 'compliance for compliance's sake'. There is a role for the regulator in educating the market and the media.

Having said that, it is not good enough for companies to lay any blame entirely on the attitude of investors. Companies cannot assume that any explanation will be acceptable, and should aim to demonstrate to their shareholders that they are applying the principles of the Combined Code through their chosen governance practices. The better they are able to do so, the more amenable shareholders will be to accepting the explanation.

Most of the Combined Code is followed by most companies, with explanations of non-compliance being the exception, and a diminishing number of exceptions being noted as companies adjusted voluntarily to the 2003 Combined Code. However, while most companies apply the Combined Code responsibly, there are a few that have clearly mistaken its light touch approach for a soft touch. A number of the annual reports that the FRC studied as part of its review gave boilerplate explanations which, in effect, gave no explanation at all. This can give the impression that they have simply not bothered applying the Code. Companies cannot expect to be given an easy ride in those circumstances, and need to understand that if such behaviour were to become widespread it could lead to pressure from investors for regulatory action if they felt that comply-or-explain was failing.

[17] See note 13.

One dog that has not barked to any serious extent since the new Combined Code was introduced in 2003 has been that of the position of smaller listed companies, which for the purposes of the Combined Code are defined as those outside the FTSE 350. Having (apart from the requirement for only two independent non-executive directors) otherwise wished to be treated the same as larger listed companies, the smaller companies, like their larger counterparts, have simply got on with implementing the new Combined Code. However, that does not mean that it has all been easy going. Clearly, larger companies are more resource-rich to deal with any implementation issues. Also, even with a requirement for only two independent non-executive directors, there has been, and still is, relatively quite a lot of recruitment required.

The research done so far has not thrown up great problems. Research carried out by Manifest on behalf of the FRC in 2005 found high rates of compliance with many provisions of the Code among smaller companies. However, there is some anecdotal evidence that comply-or-explain may not work as well for smaller companies as it does for larger companies, primarily because the investment institutions will target their own limited resources on those companies that are a significant component of their investment portfolio (in effect this means the FTSE 100 companies, which at the end of 2004 accounted for 80 per cent of the value of the London stock market[18]). This means that smaller companies are less able to have a constructive ongoing dialogue with their main shareholders. This may leave them feeling more exposed to pressure from the box-tickers and therefore more inclined to default to compliance.

Looking further ahead, one of the biggest challenges for comply-or-explain will be to cope with changes in the structure and composition of the London stock market. The assumption underlying comply-or-explain is that boards and shareholders are united by a common interest in the long-term health of the company and sustainable shareholder value, and that the nature of the dialogue between them will therefore be about what governance practices will best be able to deliver these objectives.

The London stock market today looks very different from 1992 when the Cadbury Committee first created the concept of comply-or-explain. At that time pension funds and insurance companies – who are traditionally seen as long-term investors – held over half the total equity in the London market. Their share has fallen consistently ever since, and by 2004 was less than one third of total equity. In recent years, we have seen a growth in hedge funds and other investors that are perceived as having a more short-term focus. A potentially more significant development has been that overseas investment in London has risen from 13 per cent in 1992 to 40 per cent in 2006.[19]

[18] 'Share Ownership: A Report on Ownership of Shares as at 31st December 2006', Office for National Statistics, June 2007.

[19] See note 11.

One possible implication of the changing investor base, and in particular of the increased number of overseas investors, is that investors' views on what constitutes good governance – and consequently what they expect of companies – may change. Some European companies have already had experience of this at the hands of US and UK investors. I do not necessarily see this as a cause for concern as long as the pressure for change comes from the market, not from regulators. As demonstrated earlier in this chapter, views on what constitutes good governance change over time, and as markets become truly global it is only to be expected that this will have an impact on corporate behaviour. The Combined Code and comply-or-explain should be flexible enough to adapt.

I would be more concerned if investors were to walk away from comply-or-explain, either because they did not see it as their role to encourage good governance in the companies in which they invest or because they imported expectations that only a prescriptive approach could deliver improvements in standards of governance. Either of these eventualities could put pressure on the Government or regulators to take action that might reduce the current flexibility and the attractiveness of the London market. Equally, the present benign position of the European Union could change.

Conclusion

The evidence is that market-based regulation works best in the UK. I would argue that it is the best system for any market-based economy. When combined with a comply-or-explain approach, it provides the necessary flexibility to suit all types of companies, and the adaptability to change as circumstances and attitudes to corporate governance change. The role of government should be to provide a supportive regulatory framework, but it should not legislate in detail. Sarbanes-Oxley is a classic example of the problems caused by overly specific legislation.

One area which is key to being able to allow market-based regulation to operate is that shareholders should have adequate rights. The EU is working on this and has in general so far followed in corporate governance a sensible approach very much along market-based lines. Forces arguing for more prescription should be resisted. If action is needed at EU level, it should underpin the comply-or-explain approach, for example by promoting shareholders' rights. The present approach brings the twin benefits of encouraging, not stifling, entrepreneurial drive by boards, while providing the transparency investors need to have, either to know how their investment is being handled (or take action if they do not like it), or to decide to invest in the first place. It remains fit for purpose.

7

Directors' duties

CHARLES MAYO

Perspective

Individual and collective board responsibility

There is an increasing link between individual success or failure as a director and the collective success or failure of the board of directors as a whole. The duties of directors, and the expectations others place upon them, have increased so considerably in scope and level that we have arguably reached a position where the effect of the law is to impose collective responsibility on all directors on the board, even where failure is directly attributable to only one or some of those directors.

The law has historically concentrated on the skill, care and diligence of an individual director, deciding that individual's responsibility by reference to his own honesty, culpability, competence, functions and qualifications and other factors personal to that individual director. However, there are now many instances where the failure of one or some directors could well indicate a collective failing by the board as a whole or, increasingly, where the board as a whole must take responsibility. This is likely to be the case increasingly in the future.

If this is correct, how has this happened and where has it come from? This chapter covers some significant developments which, when viewed as a whole, support the proposition about the increasing alignment of the individual and collective responsibility of directors.

But where does this proposition come from? It comes from a combination of the following factors.

- The demands and expectations of society and the extent to which it is seen as good business to take into account non-financial considerations, most notably the impact on the community, environment and employees.
- Increased regulation as a reaction to corporate collapses and scandals with the aim (misguided some would say) of restoring trust and confidence.
- Increasing transparency in the capital markets, where institutional investors are investing on a cross-border basis to a greater extent and generally becoming more active in exercising their votes and in managing their investments. Greater use of technology ensures that inside or price-sensitive information not only is made available on a very timely

119

basis but is also equally available to different types of investor, both institutional and retail.

- Additional responsibilities of directors which require the board to act collectively and effectively to facilitate the individual director's compliance with those new duties. Examples concern the responsibilities to comply with the Listing Rules, to certify disclosure of relevant audit information to auditors, to prepare true and fair accounts and to comply with the Takeover Rules.
- Significantly increased obligations on companies to report more extensively and more frequently. And it is not just in relation to financial reporting that very significant changes are underway. In some senses the reporting required now in relation to non-financial matters may be just as significant. Examples include reporting on principal risks and uncertainties, publishing forward-looking information, and publishing key performance indicators (KPIs) on environmental, human capital and other non-financial matters. In policy terms, there is a deliberate link between this additional reporting and the accountability of directors for the 'stewardship' of the company in the light of the concerns and expectations of society at large.

There is no single point in time at which one could specifically say the law moved from individual responsibility of directors to collective responsibility. It is a change that has been developing for some time. It would be a mistake to think of this change as very new or radical or even very different from the effect of the law at present. In many instances, codification of directors' duties and a plethora of governance standards and best-practice guidance reinforce and merely serve to highlight changes which are already implicit in the law.

The proposition that the law has now moved to collective responsibility of directors might seem bold. Some may question whether it is correct at all or in specific instances. Perhaps most importantly, from a director's standpoint, it does not matter whether the proposition is right or wrong because what is inevitably true is that the reputation and personal standing of a director can be seriously damaged where there has been a failure by any one or more directors on that board. So, from an individual director's point of view, there is much to be said for all directors approaching their responsibilities as directors, mindful not just of the standards required of themselves individually, but also of the need for all directors to perform collectively as an effective and successful board.

Enlightened shareholder value versus pluralism

The pressures and expectations of society and the community come to the forefront in the debate as to whether directors should be required to follow an approach based on 'enlightened shareholder value' (in which directors promote the success of the company for the benefits of its shareholders as a whole) or a pluralist approach (under which directors act in the multiple interests of the different stakeholders).

What happens when there is a clash of interests between the shareholders and the other stakeholders? Do the interests of the shareholders have priority? Does the duty to promote the success of the company create one duty or a set of potentially conflicting duties which directors are required to balance?

The Company Law Review steering group concluded: 'the present scheme of the law fails adequately to recognise that businesses normally best generate wealth where . . . managers . . . recognise the wider interests of the community in their activities'.[1]

More recently, it has been suggested that pressures from shareholders, or managerial perceptions of such pressures, have inhibited long-term investment in value-creating internal and external relationships, as well as in physical assets and other intangibles.

This concept (having regard to these external relationships) is often referred to in the literature as 'enlightened self-interest'. The steering group preferred the label enlightened shareholder value, because the concept is that of a broad and well-informed view being taken of what is required to enhance the value of the business by both directors and shareholders.

The steering group accepted the argument that exclusive focus on the short-term financial bottom line, in the erroneous belief that this equates to shareholder value, will often be incompatible with the cultivation of cooperative relationships, which are likely to involve short-term costs but to bring greater benefits in the longer term.

The background to the reasons why the steering group preferred the enlightened shareholder value approach is salient. Most importantly, their reasoning puts into context some of the heat and light which the codification of directors' duties under the Companies Act 2006 has generated. The modern realities of business require directors to take into account a very wide range of considerations in order to promote the success of their companies; however, not only do directors in well-run companies do so already but, some would argue strongly, the law is already such that they were already required to do so. The steering group wrote (eloquently) as follows:

> We consider the most appropriate formulation of directors' duties is to give effect to the enlightened shareholder value perspective. The argument is that these duties, as currently expressed, and as interpreted in practice, often tend to lead to an undue focus on the short term and the narrow interest of members at the expense of what is in a broader and a longer-term sense the best interest of the enterprise, and thus its value to them as ultimate controllers able to realise that value.

---

[1] Company Law Review Steering Group (1999), *Modern Company Law for a Competitive Economy: The Strategic Framework*, p. 36.

The key company law provision is for the fiduciary duties of directors. These require them honestly ('in good faith') to manage the undertaking for the benefit of the company. That benefit is defined by case law as the interest of members present and future. The duties of directors to exercise their powers for their proper purpose are also relevant. These, for example, prevent directors from using their powers to impede the exercise by members of their rights to dispose of their shares, such as by issuing new shares to allies to defeat a takeover bid.

It is in our view clear, as a matter of policy, that in many circumstances directors should adopt the broader and longer-term ('inclusive') view of their role. This is indeed now widely acknowledged. But we do not accept that there is anything in the present law of directors' duties which requires them to take an unduly narrow or short-term view of their functions. Indeed they are obliged honestly to take account of all the considerations which contribute to the success of the enterprise.

There is nevertheless considerable evidence that the effect of the law is not well recognised and understood. This may be in part because the relevant principles are not enacted, but have to be derived from quite extensive case law, developed over 250 years and rooted in the eighteenth century law of trusts.[2]

From the steering group's perspective, the fact that the law is widely misunderstood suggests that there was a strong case for making explicit its true character. The group maintained that the object of the law should be to ensure that directors recognised their obligation to have regard to the need, where appropriate, to build long-term and trusting relationships with employees, suppliers, customers and others, as appropriate, in order to secure the success of the enterprise over time.

But, it should be acknowledged that, even before the Companies Act 2006, the law already required directors to have regard to the interests of employees. Section 309 of the Companies Act 1985 requires that 'the matters to which' the directors of a company are to have regard in the performance of their functions include the interests of the company's employees in general, as well as the interests of its members.

The steering group recognised that section 309 is arguably a statutory declaration of an enlightened shareholder value duty, requiring that directors consider the interests of employees in reaching a view of what is in the best interests of the company.[3]

The Government determined to follow the enlightened shareholder value approach, since that approach is 'most likely to drive long-term company performance and maximise overall competitiveness and wealth and welfare for

[2] *Ibid.*, pp. 39–40.   [3] *Ibid.*, p. 41.

all'.[4] These are proud words perhaps, but fundamental to how directors see their responsibilities in the overall context.

Core duties

There was no comprehensive statement in statute of what are the duties of a director. Indeed, the duties vary according to the nature of the position or office that a director is regarded as holding. Legally, it was a very peculiar position. One judge said almost as much: 'Directors of a limited company . . . occupy a position peculiar to themselves. In some respects they resemble trustees, in others they do not. In some respects they resemble agents, in others they do not. In some respects they resemble managing partners, in others they do not.'[5] And the law on directors' duties was derived from voluminous and historical case law. There was a lot of law, a lot of it was old law and too much of it was inaccessible. The Companies Act 2006 attempts to codify existing directors' duties and so increase accessibility to the law. Whether it does so successfully has been a matter of considerable and continuing debate. What tends to get forgotten, in the heat of the debate, is that codification is being done for a very good reason: to make the law more modern and more accessible, thereby more useful and relevant to business needs.

The codification of directors' duties is not, however, a complete statement of all the duties of a director. For example, it does not include the duty to consider the interests of creditors. The statutory statement is also not intended to change existing common law and equitable principles. So, the Act specifies that 'regard should be had to the corresponding common law rules and equitable principles in interpreting applying of the general duties'. And the statutory statement also includes some deliberate changes of policy to the existing law. This means that there will be some uncertainty as to whether the new wording will have the same effect as the previous case law.

The duty to act within powers

> A director of a company must –
>
> (a) act in accordance with the company's constitution, and
> (b) only exercise powers for the purposes for which they are conferred.
>
> Section 171

The requirement for a director to act in accordance with the constitution is not new. Currently the overriding duty of a director is to act in the best interests of the company. But there is a separate, objective duty to act within the purposes for

[4] Companies Bill – White Paper, Ch. 3, *Enhancing Shareholder Engagement and a Long-Term Investment Culture*, p. 20.

[5] *Regal (Hastings) Ltd. v. Gulliver and others* [1942] 1 All ER 378; [1967] 2 AC 134 at p. 147.

which powers have been conferred. Mr Justice Jonathan Parker in *Regentcrest plc (in liquidation) v. Cohen*[6] decided:

> The position is different where a power conferred on a director is used for a collateral purpose. In such circumstances it matters not whether the director honestly believed that in exercising the power as he did he was acting in the interests of the company; the power having been exercised for an improper purpose, its exercise will be liable to be set aside.

Thus, under the old law, it could be said that directors had a duty to exercise their powers for a proper purpose. Under existing case law, a proper purpose is determined according to the construction of the particular power (either express or implied by the articles of association of the company). Typically, powers are drafted in general terms without express statements of the purposes for which they can be exercised. In the leading case[7] on the purposes for which a power can be exercised it was decided that if the exercise of a power is challenged, the court will 'examine the substantial purpose for which it was exercised . . . to reach a conclusion as to whether that purpose was proper or not. In doing so it will necessarily give credit to the bona fide opinion of the directors.' Despite the codification of directors' duties, there remains a lack of a defined scope for this duty. One is left to decide, as Lord Wilberforce described it, 'as to the side of a fairly broad line on which the case falls'. It will still involve issues such as how willing the court is to intervene in business decisions, and whether the directors acted to promote the success of the company, for the members as a whole, which in itself may require discussion of whether they have considered the statutory factors. Nonetheless, the duty is a separate one and requires the exercise of powers to be both in compliance with the company's constitution and for the purpose for which they were conferred.

The words 'for the purpose' for which they were conferred arguably suggests some lower standard than that which might apply if the standard were an objective one based on what is 'proper'. In fact, when this duty is read in conjunction with the duty to promote the success of the company and of the standards of skill and care, no lower standard should be presumed in relation to the duty of directors to act within their powers. While the duty is expressed as an individual one, a board of directors which authorised the exercise of a power which is clearly not in accordance with the company's constitution (for example, breach of a borrowing limit) could be vulnerable to liability.

From the board's point of view it is therefore important to focus not only on what considerations are important to a board's decision, but also on the purposes for which they are exercising their powers in making that decision. Good faith alone is not sufficient, nor are reasonable care, skill and diligence. Where the

---

[6] [2001] 2 BCLC 80 at p. 105.

[7] *Howard Smith Ltd. v. Ampol Petroleum Ltd. and others* [1974] AC 821 at p. 835, per Lord Wilberforce.

constitution contains an express statement of purpose for which a power can be used, this must be observed. Where there is no such express statement, the power must still be exercised properly and the board must always act within the company's constitution.

The duty to promote the success of the company

A director of a company must act in the way he considers, in good faith, would be most likely to promote the success of the company for the benefit of its members as a whole, and in doing so have regard (amongst other matters) to:

(a) the likely consequences of any decision in the long term,
(b) the interests of the company's employees,
(c) the need to foster the company's business relationships with suppliers, customers and others,
(d) the impact of the company's operations on the community and the environment,
(e) the desirability of the company maintaining a reputation for high standards of business conduct, and
(f) the need to act fairly as between members of the company.

(Where, or to the extent that, the purposes of the company consist of, or include, purposes other than the benefit of its members, the reference to promoting the success of the company for the benefit of its members should be treated as if it were to achieving those purposes.)   Section 172

So far as the old law was concerned, Mr Justice Jonathan Parker in *Regentcrest plc (in liquidation) v. Cohen* said:[8]

The duty imposed on directors to act bona fide in the interests of the company is a subjective one. The question is not whether, viewed objectively by the court, the particular act or omission which is challenged was in fact in the interests of the company; still less is the question whether the court, had it been in the position of the director at the relevant time, might have acted differently. Rather, the question is whether the director honestly believed that his act or omission was in the interests of the company. The issue is as to the director's state of mind. No doubt, where it is clear that the act or omission under challenge resulted in substantial detriment to the company, the director will have a harder task persuading the court that he honestly believed it to be in the company's interest; but that does not detract from the subjective nature of the test.

Section 172 codifies this primary duty while enshrining the enlightened shareholder value approach. The Government has therefore suggested that success will normally mean 'long-term increase in value'.[9]

---

[8] [2001] 2 BCLC 80 at p. 105.
[9] Lord Sainsbury of Turville, Second Reading debate, Hansard Col. 245, 11 January 2006.

It is important to appreciate that key elements remain in this new statement, such as:

- the word success replaces the former word 'interests' and is a more modern, plainer term
- the subjective test in meeting the duty '*he* considers' has been retained
- 'in good faith' has been retained
- 'for the benefit of members as a whole' has long been the old but rather inelegant and imprecise definition of the company.

The new statutory factors are ones which large private companies and public companies would commonly consider when reaching a decision, as well as considering other factors relevant to their deliberations which are not referred to in the new Act. Even under the old law, if these factors were not being considered, then it is likely that directors would have been in breach of their duties as they applied before the Act came into force. What the new Act does is to make much clearer the necessity of considering these factors (among others).

For smaller, private, owner-managed companies, the new law will have an impact where board procedures are, understandably, less formal and there is a less obvious distinction between the views of directors and shareholders. Directors of smaller and other companies who cannot demonstrate awareness of the need to consider these factors may find that any defence to a claim that they have breached their directors' duties is severely compromised.

The explanatory notes[10] to the Act make it clear that, in having regard to the factors listed in section 172, the duty to exercise reasonable care, skill and diligence (see below) will also apply. This means that, while directors must have regard to the relevant factors listed in section 172 in promoting the success of the company, it does not require a director to do more than act in good faith and to exercise reasonable care, skill and diligence.

Some argue that the introduction of the reference to the 'community and the environment' in section 172(1)(d) has increased the scope of directors' duties. The suggestion has been made that an activist could acquire shares and then through the new statutory derivative action procedures bring an action against a director claiming that they failed to 'have regard' to the impact of the company's operations on the community and the environment. However, section 170(1) of the Act confirms that directors' duties remain owed to the company and to no other person. The law has not changed in this regard. It is the company which must suffer loss as a consequence of the directors' failing to have regard to a particular matter (not a shareholder or even a group of shareholders). Shareholders may still only bring a derivative action for a breach of directors' duties in their capacity as shareholders and in no other capacity (for instance as the representative of a lobby group).

---

[10] See paragraph 328 of the Explanatory Notes to the Act.

It was a hot topic as to whether, within the codification, there is a single duty to promote the success of the company (and in promoting that success to have regard to the statutory factors) or whether there are in effect two distinct duties, namely to promote the success of the company and to have regard to the statutory factors (among others). The Government was adamant in Parliament that a single duty – an overriding duty to promote the success of the company – is intended and is the result of the wording. The Government went to considerable lengths to tailor the wording to achieve the effect it intended. Some might have preferred Government to have gone even further to have made this clearer and take the view that there will only be absolute certainty once there is a court decision. There seems, however, room for little doubt as to the approach a court would take and, from the director's point of view, it seems appropriate to proceed, as the Government intends, as if there is a single duty.

What is clear is that the Government intends directors to have regard to at least the six statutory factors. A director who gives no consideration at all to any of these factors will be vulnerable to claims for failing to meet the standard of skill, care and diligence required of that director. This is deliberate on the part of the Government and, viewed in the context of the approach in favour of enlightened shareholder value, not surprising. Nor should there be undue concern that this is some inherently new obligation on directors. It is not. It formalises what was perhaps latent or less obviously developing in the law. One may debate whether the degree of formality arising under the Companies Act 2006 inhibits business decisions, creates a duty of due process or necessitates directors to keep additional records to prove that they did consider these factors.

Where the Companies Act 2006 missed an opportunity was to make absolutely explicit that the weight and relevance of the factors to be considered by the directors in fulfilling their duty to promote the success of the company is a matter for their good-faith business judgement. Under current law, where a director is exercising what can properly be described as his or her business judgement, the courts are reluctant to intervene. It has been stated:

> No matter what profession it may be, the common law does not impose on those who practise it any liability for damage resulting from what in the result turn out to have been errors of judgement, unless the error was such as no reasonably well-informed and competent member of that profession could have made.[11]

The courts will intervene only where that business judgement can be shown to be one which no other director, in like circumstances, could properly have reached. There is frequently a range of business judgements that can properly be reached in any given situation. Only when a director takes a decision that is not within that range may he or she be liable for negligence.

---

[11] *Saif Ali v. Sydney Mitchell & Co.* [1980] AC 198 at p. 220, per Lord Diplock.

The principle that courts should be slow to substitute their own decision for that of the directors was expressed by Lord Wilberforce (giving the judgment of the Privy Council), in the following terms:

> Their Lordships accept that such a matter as the raising of finance is one of management, within the responsibility of the directors: they accept that it would be wrong for the court to substitute its opinion for that of the management, or indeed to question the correctness of the management's decision, on such a question, if bona fide arrived at. There is no appeal on merits from management decisions to courts of law: nor will courts of law assume to act as a kind of supervisory board over decisions within the powers of management honestly arrived at.[12]

The Company Law Review steering group itself concluded:

> The law recognises that it is essential for directors to have a discretion in the way they manage, and legal actions will not interfere with proper exercise of such business judgement.[13]

The Government was adamant that it is now implicit in the Companies Act 2006 that the weight and relevance of the various factors in a decision is for directors to decide (in other words directors meeting the minimum standards of skill, care and diligence can subjectively decide what is relevant – so called 'subjective relevance'). The Solicitor General said as much in Parliament:

> Under the duty to promote the success of the company, the weight to be given to any factor is a matter for the good faith judgement of the director. Importantly, his decision is not subject to a reasonableness test, and, as now, the courts will not be able to apply a reasonableness test to directors' business decisions.

From a business point of view, it seems a shame not to take the opportunity to make absolutely explicit what the Government regards as implicit. From a legal perspective, the certainty would have been better although, even without it, it seems clear that a court would interpret the law in this way. The codification and the wording that require the courts to give effect to the existing law give them, as at present, a broad flexibility and, in the future, the power to modernise and increase further the standards expected of directors in specific circumstances.

From the board's point of view, the new duty possibly results in a greater mutual reliance by one director on another. The reason is that the statutory factors highlight the need for a board to have directors, supported by management and advice, with sufficient knowledge, skill and experience to assess each of the statutory factors. While one director cannot abdicate his own responsibility for considering the statutory factors, it seems legitimate for a board to draw on

---

[12] *Howard Smith Ltd. v. Ampol Petroleum Ltd. and others* [1974] AC 821 at p. 832.
[13] Company Law Review Steering Group, *Modern Company Law*, p. 35.

individual directors (as well as management) for their particular input, for example in relation to the impact of actions on the community and the environment. Boards, of course, currently do so, but the existence of the statutory factors may cause some Chairmen and some boards to be more concerned to obtain specific input from individual directors on different aspects of the statutory factors.

The duty to exercise independent judgement

A director of a company must exercise independent judgement.
This duty is not infringed by his acting:

(a) in accordance with an agreement duly entered into by the company that restricts the future exercise of discretion by its directors, or
(b) in a way authorised by the company's constitution.

Section 173

This duty codifies the current principles of law under which directors must act in good faith and must exercise their powers independently without fettering their discretion or subordinating their powers to the will of others. This replicates the decision of the Court of Appeal in *Fulham Football Club Ltd v. Cabra Estates plc*[14] which drew a distinction between the fettering of future discretion and the making of a decision to bind themselves to do what was necessary to execute a contact which, at the time when the contract was negotiated, they genuinely believed to be in the interests of the company as a whole. The former is prohibited; the latter is permitted.

This codified duty now incorporates in a single concept the old law that a director should (a) act in good faith and (b) not fetter his judgement by undue delegation or as a consequence of a conflict of interest. While the codified wording attempts to unite these separate duties together, section 170 of the Act requires the codified duties to be interpreted and applied in the same way as the old law. Nonetheless, the codified wording is much clearer and therefore brings into much sharper focus the need to act independently.

The duty to act independently requires a director to act independently in his judgement. It may be that a conflict of interest exists between the personal interests of a director and the interests of the company, but assuming the procedures concerning disclosures and approval of conflicts of interests are followed (as discussed below) then a director is still acting independently even if he is in fact conflicted.

Section 173 enables directors still to act independently even if they delegate their functions to the extent set out in the company's constitution.

From the board's point of view, the Chairman is likely to become even more concerned to ensure that:

[14] [1994] 1 BCLC 363.

- executive directors take a broad view of their responsibilities as directors, and not limit their contribution to matters within their particular function or line management role
- non-executive directors who are not independent (for example if appointed by a substantial shareholder) take care to express their own views (rather than the views of their appointor)

as, in either case, the director in question may not be exercising sufficient independent judgement.

The duty to exercise reasonable care, skill and diligence

A director of a company must exercise reasonable care, skill and diligence. This means the care, skill and diligence that would be exercised by a reasonably diligent person with

(a) the general knowledge, skill and experience that may reasonably be expected of a person carrying out the functions carried out by the director in relation to the company, and

(b) the general knowledge, skill and experience that the director has.

Section 174

This codifies the current law and is consistent with the approach applicable to wrongful trading and the obligation of directors to disclose relevant audit information.

Even in 1881 it had been said that no longer is 'a director an ornament, but an essential component of corporate governance. Consequently, a director cannot protect himself behind a paper shield bearing the motto "dummy directors".'[15]

As regards the board, on the face of it no particular change in behaviour is required: the new standard reflects the standard of conduct required of all directors under the old law. Nonetheless a board will need to be concerned that it is not just having regard to the statutory factors (among others) in its decision-making process, but also is doing so with sufficient care, skill and diligence. This in turn highlights the importance of a board assessing how it will do so. To a large extent a board can help itself by, for example, having a method of operating under which:

- the company has environmental, community, employee, ethical conflicts policies which the board formally considers periodically
- the board keeps under review the principal risks and uncertainties affecting the company
- those members of management providing board papers and input to the board are themselves aware of the statutory factors and seek to have regard to them in their input to the board.

---

[15] *Williams v. Riley* 34 NJ Eq 398 at 401(Ch. 1881).

All are likely to be regarded as necessary (at least by a Main Market company) and are evidence of the taking of reasonable care. They demonstrate that decisions were informed by these steps, and the board can maintain they were not decisions which no reasonable board would have decided and which should therefore be treated as negligent. These steps may not prevent individual directors from taking a wrong decision but they help protect the board against liability for the acts and omissions of individual directors.

What is the appropriate test by which to judge the acts or omissions of directors? It is helpful to consider the test of negligence applied to professionals generally as well as the traditional formulation of the law in relation to directors. In the so-called Bolam test (so called, after the name of the court case)[16] the Judge decided that:

> where you get a situation which involves the use of some special skill or competence, then the test as to whether there has been negligence or not is not the test of the man on the top of a Clapham omnibus, because he has not got this special skill. The test is the standard of the ordinary skilled man exercising and professing to have that special skill.

Although the law on directors' duties of care and skill developed separately from the law on professional negligence, there seems little between the two tests as formulated in Bolam and now as applied to directors under the Companies Act 2006. It would be surprising if the common law standard of skill, care and diligence expected of professionals differed significantly from that expected of directors. In either case, liability arises when the professional or director takes action outside the range of possible actions that his or her peers would, in all the circumstances, have taken. Both the professional and the director can be wrong without being negligent. It indicates that the more the board can establish a framework to consider the statutory factors in its overall decision-making process with appropriate skill, the more it will avoid wrong decisions, let alone negligent ones.

The duty to avoid conflicts of interest

> A director of a company must avoid a situation in which he has, or can have, a direct or indirect interest that conflicts, or possibly may conflict, with the interests of the company.
>
> This applies in particular to the exploitation of any property, information or opportunity (and it is immaterial whether the company could take advantage of the property, information or opportunity).   Section 175

Under the old law, directors' conflicts were regulated under the common law principle known as the 'no-conflicts' rule. Its aim was to prevent a fiduciary from being swayed in any decision by considerations of any personal interest or

---

[16] *Bolam v. Friern Hospital Management Committee* [1957] 2 All ER 188; [1957] 1 WLR 582.

the interest of a third party. As made clear by Lord Russell in *Regal (Hastings) Ltd v. Gulliver*,[17] the 'no conflicts' rule applies regardless of bad faith, so the court will not examine the fairness of the transaction in substance. The rule is strict in that if a conflict existed that could have allowed the director to consider interests other than the company's there has been a breach of the duty.

It was clear, however, that the strict application of the rule could not go unqualified. Thus, a director could contract, or have an interest in a contract, if that interest had been properly disclosed to the company and the company had consented (by an ordinary resolution of the members in general meeting) to the director's participation. The old law allowed for a modification of the requirement for the members to approve any conflicts, by inclusion of a provision in the articles of association that the board can do so instead of the general meeting.

Under the old law it was clear from the case of *Re Bhullar Bros. Ltd*[18] that a conflict of interest can arise even if the company itself is not a party to the transaction in question. This was a case on the exploitation of a corporate opportunity that the company was incapable of taking advantage of. The director therefore took the opportunity for himself, believing that, as the company was incapable of contracting, there was no conflict of interest. It was decided that:

> It seems obvious that the opportunity to acquire the property would have been commercially attractive to the company . . . Whether the company could or would have taken that opportunity, had it been made aware of it, is not to the point . . . the anxiety which the appellants felt as to the propriety of purchasing the property . . . is, in my view, eloquent of the existence of a possible conflict of duty and interest.

And, under the old law, the 'no conflicts' rule extended to possible conflicts. Lord Cranworth had already decided in *Aberdeen Railway Company v. Blaikie*[19] that no fiduciary:

> shall be allowed to enter into engagements in which [the director] has, or can have, a personal interest conflicting, or which may possibly conflict, with the interests of those whom he is bound to protect.

As a result, it seems that the old law had reached a point where a director could be prohibited from entering into transactions in which he had, or could have, a personal interest which is conflicting, or which might possibly conflict, whether or not the company was a party to that transaction or capable of entering into that transaction.

The requirement for authorisation by independent directors is essentially codifying the current law as it operates in practice, with some additional

---

[17] [1942] 1 All ER 378; [1967] 2 AC 134.   [18] [2003] EWCA Civ 424; [2003] 2 BCLC 241.
[19] (1854) 1 Macq 461; (1854) 17 D (HL) 20.

flexibility for some private companies. Many companies incorporate in their articles of association the provisions of the old Table A, article 85 which allow directors to authorise another director to be interested in a transaction or arrangement in which the company is interested, or to hold multiple directorships, provided the director concerned has disclosed the nature and extent of any interest. The new law allows the independent (non-conflicted) directors to authorise the conflict if, for a private company, the company's constitution does not prohibit this and, in the case of a public company, if its constitution so allows.

A concern has been expressed that the effect of the new law is that multiple directorships will not be possible. This arises because the common law presently maintains a negative position, namely that a director can comply with the 'no conflicts' rules and therefore avoid any disadvantage to the company by declaring the extent of his interest to the company or board and by not participating in discussions or a vote on that particular matter. This is in contrast to the new law which involves a positive duty that the director must avoid all situations in which his interests will or may possibly conflict.

The Government has been clear that the duty is of general application and does not imply an obligation to avoid the conflict, if the situation cannot reasonably be regarded as likely to give rise to such a conflict. It argues that this avoids the impossible situation in which a director could be required to predict possible conflicts before he could know they would arise. As stated by the Solicitor General:

> If a person cannot possibly foresee a situation, it cannot be reasonably regarded as being likely to give rise to a conflict of interest. On the other hand, if they can foresee it, the directors or members of the company should be able to make an informed decision about whether it is an acceptable conflict.[20]

The Solicitor General usefully referred[21] to Lord Upjohn in *Re Bhullar Bros. Ltd*:

> The phrase 'possibly may conflict' requires consideration. In my view it means that the reasonable man looking at the relevant facts and circumstances of the particular case would think that there was a real sensible possibility of conflict.

This gives some reassurance as to potential, future conflicts. The ability to manage future conflicts therefore depends, in part, on whether they are foreseeable and the disclosure required when a transaction is proposed.

This, however, does not address the situation where a conflict of interest does actually arise. In the case of a multiple directorship, the circumstances

---

[20] The Solicitor General, Standing Committee Debate, *Company Law Reform Bill [Lords]*, Hansard Col. 615, 11 July 2006.

[21] *Ibid.*, Col. 614.

giving rise to the conflict may not necessarily be within the direct control of the director of one company, if the conflict arises because of decisions made by the board of the other company. Here, one has to assess both the ability of a director with an actual conflict to absent himself from board discussions and voting on that matter, and the duties of the conflicted director to disclose his interest. So far as the former aspect is concerned, the Government's views were expressed in Parliament by the Solicitor General who said:

> I was asked about people absenting themselves from a meeting. People will not be able to do that as of right. They cannot just walk out of a meeting without declaring that they have interests. If they have been authorised, in advance or at the time, to have a particular interest, there should be no difficulty with them merely absenting themselves from a particular directors' meeting. In the vast majority of cases, an appointment will be made on the basis that a director will be able to withdraw. He will have declared his interest and therefore should be able to do that.[22]

The effect of the view expressed by the Solicitor General is that directors will not be able to absent themselves 'as of right' but (in the vast majority of cases) will do so where the director has declared his interest and his appointment has been made on the basis that he is able to withdraw in relation to the conflicted matter. In both a private and a public company, it should be possible to construct the constitution of the company and the board procedures so that a director with a multiple directorship can disclose that other directorship on appointment, and obtain the authorisation of the independent directors to be able to withdraw from discussions and voting where there is a specific conflict (either an actual one or a reasonably likely one). A director may well be advised to obtain the equivalent authorisation from the board of which he is already a director before accepting the appointment as a director of another company. Hopefully, current sensible practice (which does enable directors to absent themselves on specific matters) will continue. If we go back to the purpose behind the 'no-conflicts' rule, it is to prevent the fiduciary from being swayed in any decision by considerations of any personal interest or the interest of a third party, so the practice of allowing multiple directorships and directors to absent themselves on specific conflicts should still enable a director to comply with this duty.

A board will want to review the company's constitution and, possibly, adopt a procedure to be followed for independent directors to clear conflicts which the constitution permits them to clear. They may also want to become more formulaic in their approach to board meetings, checking (and recording in the minutes that they have done so) that directors have disclosed actual or possible conflicts.

---

[22] *Ibid.*, Col. 613.

The duty not to accept benefits from third parties

> (1) A director of a company must not accept a benefit from a third party conferred by reason of:
>
> (a) his being a director, or
>
> (b) his doing (or not doing) anything as director.
>
> Section 176

Third parties mean anyone else other than the company, its holding company or its associated subsidiaries or anyone acting on their behalf. It is worth noting that the word 'subsidiary' is used in this exception and not 'subsidiary undertakings'. For this reason, directors should consider the reasonableness of receiving benefits from subsidiary undertakings such as certain joint ventures, limited liability partnerships and partnerships when considering any payments from such entities which may not be subsidiaries and should seek prior shareholder approval as necessary in such circumstances.

The purpose of separating the conflicts of interest between a director and the company (section 175) and those that may arise through acceptance of third party benefits in section 176 is that conflicts of interest between the independent director and the company may, in most circumstances, be approved by the independent directors, whereas (unless allowed by the constitution) only the shareholders may approve a director receiving benefits from third parties. It is possible to authorise the acceptance of third party benefits by directors of public companies by inserting appropriate authorisations in the company's constitution to allow independent directors to approve the benefit.

The duty to disclose interests in proposed transactions or arrangements

Under the old law (section 317, Companies Act 1985), a director was obliged to declare his interest immediately before a transaction in which he has an interest is entered into by that company. As already discussed, the law had reached the point where a potential situation could give rise to a conflict and thereby an obligation to disclose much earlier. Section 317 is replaced in the new Act by a duty to disclose and up-date disclosure of interests (direct or indirect) in any *proposed* transaction or arrangement with the company, and by a criminal offence of failing to declare or update a declaration of an interest (direct or indirect) in an *existing* matter to which the company is a party.

In relation to the duty to declare interests in *proposed* transactions or arrangements, the duty is to disclose 'the nature and extent of that interest' to the other directors. The declaration may be made at a meeting of the directors or by notice to the directors. If the declaration of interest proves to be, or becomes, inaccurate or incomplete, a further declaration must be made. The declaration of interest (or its update) must be made before the company enters into the transaction or arrangement. The duty does not require a declaration of interest of which the director is not aware or where the director is not aware of the transaction or arrangement in question. For this purpose, a director is treated as being aware of matters of which he ought reasonably to be aware.

A director does not need to declare an interest:

- if it cannot reasonably be regarded as likely to give rise to a conflict of interest; or
- if, or to the extent that, the other directors are already aware of it (and for this purpose the other directors are treated as aware of anything of which they ought reasonably to be aware); or
- if, or to the extent that, it concerns terms of his service contract that have been or are to be considered:
  by a meeting of the directors; or
  by a committee of the directors appointed for the purpose under the constitution.

It will be as well for boards to take a cautious and early view of whether and when a transaction is 'proposed'. A chairman might, for example, want formally to say to the board that a particular transaction or arrangement is now proposed and remind the directors to disclose their interests (including actual or possible conflicts) as necessary. A cautious view is to remind directors who will be absent from a board meeting also to notify their interests on the same basis.

Additional obligations

The additional obligations on directors discussed below have been selected because they illustrate circumstances where, either expressly or effectively, they require boards of directors to act collectively in order to meet those obligations.

The obligation to declare interests in existing transactions or arrangements

The new law creates a new offence requiring a declaration of interest in *existing* transactions or arrangements. Under this new offence (section 177 of the Companies Act 2006) where a director is in any way, directly or indirectly, interested in a transaction or arrangement that *has been entered into* by the company, he must declare the nature and extent of the interest to the other directors in the manner required. (The offence does not apply if the interest has already been declared in accordance with the director's duty to declare his interest in the proposed transaction or arrangement as described above.)

Where a declaration of interest in an existing transaction or arrangement is required, the declaration *must* be made at a meeting of the directors, by notice in writing or by general notice. If the declaration of interest proves to be, or becomes, inaccurate or complete, a further declaration must be made. The duty to make the declaration, or to update it, must be made as soon as is reasonably practicable. As with the duty of disclosure in relation to proposed transactions or arrangements, the director with the interest (the conflicted director) and the directors without the interest (the independent directors) are all treated as aware of matters of which they ought reasonably to be aware.

Although a director is not expected to disclose an interest of which he has no knowledge, or in relation to a transaction or arrangement of which he is not aware, to avoid any lapse of memory it is expressly provided that the test applied in relation to the knowledge of directors on this matter will be an objective test of reasonableness.

From the board's point of view, what the combination of this codification and new offence does is to demand extra vigilance. This is required by individual directors to identify, anticipate, disclose and update their disclosure of actual or reasonably foreseeable conflicts and to do so as soon as is reasonably practicable. It also requires some extra vigilance on the part of the independent directors. The independent directors will want, as at present, to be sure that individual directors do comply. They may, therefore, be concerned to ask formally not just whether directors have interests to disclose but whether they have any update to make of previous disclosures. Quite possibly, one effect will be to make independent directors more concerned to ensure formally that all other directors know of the proposed transaction or arrangement and therefore can make the appropriate disclosure or update. In this way, directors have greater certainty that they are meeting the standard of skill, care and diligence required, that their actual knowledge includes matters of which they ought reasonably to be aware and that they are acting within their powers (for example, where the quorum provisions specifically exclude a conflicted director). Views and emphasis might differ on whether this was what was already required under the old law but, even if it was, it is illustrative of how the codification process is surfacing requirements latent or less obvious to the business person under the old general case law.

The obligation to comply with the Listing, Disclosure and Transparency Rules

A director who is knowingly concerned with a breach of these Rules can be fined or otherwise sanctioned by the FSA. For ease of regulatory enforcement the focus is on the conduct of an individual director. Regulators prefer not to meet the defence that as everyone was responsible, no one person alone should be liable. In substance these Rules impose significant collective responsibility on the board. A listed company (such as a Main Market company with securities admitted to trading on the London Stock Exchange) and all its directors have continuing obligations to the FSA, in particular to notify information needed to enable shareholders and the public to appraise the company's position and avoid creating a false market.

To comply with these continuing obligations involves a high degree of collective responsibility on the part of the board. This is evidenced by the way the Listing Principles require a listed company to:

- take reasonable steps to enable its directors to understand their responsibilities and obligations as directors
- take reasonable steps to establish and maintain adequate procedures, systems and controls to enable it to comply with its obligations
- act with integrity towards holders and potential holders of its listed equity securities
- avoid the creation or continuation of a false market in such listed equity securities
- treat (broadly speaking) its shareholders equally.

The obligation to disclose and certify disclosure of relevant audit information to auditors

The CAICE Act requires the directors' report to contain a statement that, so far as each director is aware, there is no relevant audit information of which the auditors are unaware, and that the director has taken all the steps he should have taken to make himself aware of such information and to establish that the auditors are aware of it. This requirement for a new statement in the directors' report applies to all companies whose accounts have been subject to a statutory audit for that financial year.

For this purpose, a director takes all of the steps that he ought to have taken in order to make the statement if he has:

- made such enquiries of his fellow directors and of the company's auditors for that purpose, and
- taken such other steps (if any) as were required by his duty as a director of the company to exercise due care, skill and diligence.

The care, skill and diligence required of a director are consistent with the current common law duties of directors, such that the extent of the duty in the case of a particular director is:

- the knowledge, skill and experience that may be reasonably expected of the person carrying out the same functions as are carried out by the director in relation to the company, and
- (so far as they exceed what may reasonably be so expected) the knowledge, skill and experience that the director in fact has.

If the statement is not made at all, the existing offence in the Companies Act 1985 – failure to comply with the provisions as to the contents of directors' reports – will apply. If a statement is made but it is a false one, each individual director who knew the statement was false, or who was reckless as to whether it was false, and who did not take reasonable steps to prevent the report from being approved is guilty of an offence. A person found guilty on indictment will be liable to imprisonment for up to two years and/or an unlimited fine, and on summary conviction to up to twelve months' imprisonment and/or a fine up to the statutory maximum (£5000).

This requirement imposes high degrees of collective responsibility on a board and every director must:

- take '*all* the steps he ought to';
- make enquiries of every other director and the auditors;
- take such other steps as required by them duly to exercise due care, skill and diligence.

Reporting

Collective responsibility for financial and narrative reporting

The EU 'Accounts Amendment' Directive (2006/46) already has a requirement for board members to be collectively responsible, at least towards the company, for drawing up and publishing annual and consolidated accounts and reports and, as and when required and if produced separately, the company's corporate governance statement. These requirements are already contained in the Companies Act 2006.

In the UK, the collective responsibility for preparing these accounts is covered by provisions requiring the directors to sign and approve accounts, to prepare directors' reports and to file accounts. Failure to comply can result in criminal penalties or civil enforcement action.

The link between directors' duties and narrative reporting

When the directors' duties and additional obligations described above are considered in conjunction with changes to financial reporting and also to non-financial (narrative) reporting, the scale of the increased responsibilities of the board collectively becomes very apparent. From the Government's point of view there is intended to be a link between the directors' stewardship of a company and the obligation to make available reports to shareholders and other stakeholders, as to how that stewardship has been exercised. Some would regard this as a logical outcome of an enlightened shareholder value approach. Others would regard it as a form of creeping pluralism.

Business reviews

> The purpose of the business review is to inform members of the company and help them assess how the directors have performed their duty under section 172 (duty to promote the success of the company).
>
> Section 417(2)

The requirement for a business review in the directors' report was introduced in 2005 and reflects the EU Accounts Modernisation Directive. This Directive requires companies to provide 'a balanced and comprehensive analysis of the development and performance of the company's business . . . [which] shall include both financial and, where appropriate, non-financial key performance indicators . . . including information relating to environmental and employee matters'.[23] (It is important to appreciate that, even before the Accounts Modernisation Directive, directors' reports involved a forward-looking requirement to include 'an indication of likely future developments in the business'.) The overall effect is to extend significantly the scope of reporting required of the directors.

The business review must be a balanced and comprehensive analysis of:

- the development and performance of the business of the company and its subsidiary undertakings during the financial year, and
- the position of the company and its subsidiary undertakings at the end of that year, consistent with the size and complexity of the business.

The business review must also describe the principal risks and uncertainties facing the company and its subsidiary undertakings.

The business review must, to the extent necessary for an understanding of the development, performance or position of the business of the company and its subsidiary undertakings, also include:

- analysis using financial key performance indicators (KPIs), and
- where appropriate, analysis using other KPIs, including information relating to environmental and employee matters.

A medium-sized company does not need to include analysis of non-financial information, unless it is an ineligible company or a parent company required to prepare group accounts. However, the Government has stated (in its guidance on directors' reports) that these companies are strongly encouraged to report, where appropriate, on these issues voluntarily in recognition of the benefits these disclosures make.

For these purposes, KPIs mean factors by reference to which the development, performance or position of the business of a company and its subsidiary undertakings can be measured effectively. The business review must also, where appropriate, include references to, and additional explanations of, amounts included in the company's annual accounts.

A holding company which prepares group accounts must produce a group directors' report which includes those subsidiary undertakings which are consolidated in its group accounts. A group directors' report can, where appropriate, give greater emphasis to the matters that are significant to the company and those subsidiary undertakings included in the consolidation, taken as a whole.

---

[23] Directive 2003/51/EC *OJ* L 178, p. 18 of 17.7.2003.

Thus, the overall effect is to require the board to report on its stewardship to a high standard (a fair review) and in very broad terms (for example, through the use of KPIs).

Enhanced business reviews by quoted companies

For quoted companies even more will be required of their boards. The Companies Act 2006 requires the business review of quoted companies to include, to the extent necessary for an understanding of the development, performance or position of the company's business:

- forward-looking information: the main trends and factors likely to affect the future development, performance and position of the company's business, and
- social information: narrative reporting with information about (or a requirement to explain the omission of information about) environmental matters, employees, and social and community issues (including information about any policies in relation to these matters and their effectiveness).

The concept of narrative reporting needs to be seen in the light of a series of related developments, including disclosure of an operating and financial report in a prospectus, proposals to introduce further management commentary as part of International Accounting Standards and the implementation of the Transparency Directive, among others.

Where a directors' report does not comply with the statutory requirements as to its preparation and contents, every director of the company who

- knew that it did not comply or was reckless as to whether it did, and
- failed to take all reasonable steps to secure compliance with the provision in question

is guilty of an offence and potentially liable to an unlimited fine.

Transparency Rules

To consider now the impact of a quoted company's board's collective responsibility for reporting more frequently and more extensively to investors under the Disclosure and Transparency Rules, which implement in the UK the EU Transparency Directive. There is a sort of logic to the Transparency Directive. For the EU to operate as a single, effective capital market, it is logical that Main Market companies, and other companies whose securities are admitted to trading on a regulated market in the EU, should produce information which assists investors in the relevant market(s) to receive more information: more information on a timely basis, more information on a comparable basis and more information that is publicly available. So the Directive follows this logic, requiring these regulated companies to produce annual and half-yearly financial reports, and (unless they report quarterly) two other interim management statements each year. These reports and statements all have to be made public and the annual and half-yearly reports have to be accompanied by responsibility statements by the company and its directors.

The overall effect is rather like a goldfish bowl in which the activities of regulated companies seem visible from all angles. Regulated companies are required to publish financial reports or statements four times a year, together with any trading statements they regularly make, plus any other announcements under their continuing obligations relating to inside information.

In the UK, the new rules (described below) apply to all issuers whose shares are admitted to trading on a regulated market and whose home state is the UK. Issuers admitted to the Official List will therefore be caught, but AIM-only companies are not. Issuers with securities admitted to trading in an EU Member State other than the UK, but who have chosen the UK as their home Member State, are also caught. Issuers with shares admitted to the Official List also have to comply with their obligations under the Listing Rules.

Although the Transparency Directive had to be implemented by 20 January 2007, the FSA has applied it such that the rules only take effect for financial reporting periods starting on or after 20 January 2007. For example, if a company has 31 March as its year end, it had to produce its first interim management statement (see below) in 2007. But, if a company has 31 December as its year end, it will only have to produce its first interim management statement in 2008.

The responsibility statement is a new requirement and has to be given by the issuer and its directors. They must confirm that, to the best of their knowledge;

- the financial statements, prepared in accordance with the applicable set of accounting standards, give a true and fair view of the assets, liabilities, financial position and profit or loss of the issuer and the undertakings included in the consolidation, taken as a whole, and
- the management report includes a fair review of the development and performance of the business and the position of the issuer and the under-takings included in the consolidation taken as a whole, together with a description of the principal risks and uncertainties that they face.

As currently, UK listed companies will be obliged to publish an annual financial report (the annual report and accounts) in accordance with the require-ments of the Companies Act 1985 and the Listing Rules. As such, the annual financial report must include a directors' report which has to include the enhanced business review. The content of the management report replicates the content requirements in the Companies Act 1985 for the business review (which are derived from the Accounts Modernisation and other Directives). GB-incorporated companies will already be subject to these requirements under the Companies Act 1985.

The half-yearly report must include a condensed set of financial statements, an interim management report and a responsibility statement.

The interim management report must include at least:

- an indication of important events that have occurred in the first six months and their impact on the condensed financial statements, and
- a description of the principal risks and uncertainties for the remaining six months of the financial year.

As with the annual financial report, a responsibility statement has to be given by the issuer and its directors and they must confirm that to the best of their knowledge:

- the condensed financial statements, which have been prepared in accordance with the applicable set of accounting standards, give a true and fair view of the assets and liabilities, financial position and profit or loss of the issuer or the undertakings included in the consolidation as a whole, and
- the interim management report includes a fair review of the information required to be included about the important events in the first six months and their impact and the principal risks and uncertainties for next six months (as described above).

The FSA's proposals (which reflect the Directive) require equity issuers to make interim management statements which provide:

- an explanation of material events and transactions that have taken place during the relevant period and their impact on the financial position of the issuer and its controlled undertakings, and
- a general description of the financial position and performance of the issuer and its controlled undertakings during the relevant period.

A company which publishes quarterly financial reports does not have to produce an interim management statement as well.

A breach of the Transparency Rules (now incorporated with the previous Disclosure Rules as the Disclosure and Transparency Rules) is the same as a breach of the Listing Rules so that a company which contravenes any of the rules (and any director knowingly concerned in the breach) could be fined or otherwise sanctioned by the FSA.

Safe harbours

It is generally understood that the purpose for which accounts are prepared under the Companies Act 1985 and sent to members is to enable them to be informed in the exercise of their governance powers as shareholders. As such, directors are considered to owe a duty of care to members as a body, and not to individual shareholders or potential investors.

There is a concern that the Transparency Directive alters the current position by extending the duties of issuers and their directors in respect of the financial statements. This is because the requirement to make these reports public throughout the EU appears to support the argument that the audience for these reports is now the investing public at large, not merely existing shareholders. There is therefore a risk that the inclusion of a responsibility statement from the directors could be used by investors or members of the public to assert that the directors personally owe them a duty of care.

The Directive does provide, in its recitals, for each Member State to determine appropriate liability rules under its national law and to determine the extent of the liability. The issue has been whether the UK could implement the Directive in a way that limits the purpose of the reports (that the Directive requires to be published) to the same purpose as the law currently affords to them when published under the Companies Act.

This issue is addressed in the Companies Act 2006, which has introduced a new civil liability regime. A company will be liable to anyone, who acquired securities in reliance on information in a 'publication', for loss suffered in reliance on an untrue or misleading statement in that publication or any omission therefrom. A company will, however, only be liable if a person discharging managerial responsibilities (a PDMR, which includes the directors) knew that the statement was untrue or misleading or was reckless as to whether it was; or knew that the omission was a dishonest concealment of a material fact.

Issuers will therefore have civil liability for statements in reports published under the Disclosure and Transparency Rules only if they were untrue or misleading and were made in bad faith or recklessly, or involved the deliberate and dishonest concealment of material facts. In practice, an issuer is only likely to be liable if a director knew that a statement was wrong or misleading. The intention of the provisions is to restrict third party civil liability by limiting civil liability to this new offence.

Similarly, the Companies Act 2006 introduces a new statutory civil liability regime for directors for directors' and remuneration reports. Directors will be liable to companies for any loss suffered as a result of an untrue or misleading statement in one of these documents or an omission therefrom. A director will only be liable, however, if he knew that the statement was untrue or misleading or was reckless as to whether it was untrue or misleading or he knew that the omission was a dishonest concealment of a material fact.

So, there could be harbours of sorts but not necessarily 'safe' ones.

Shareholder derivative actions

Now, one must finally consider the effect of the changes made by the Companies Act 2006 on the ability of shareholders to bring shareholder derivative actions on behalf of the company against the directors. Generally the board of directors of a company or the shareholders acting collectively in general meeting decide whether to initiate litigation in the name of the company. This is problematic in the case where the wrongdoing director controls the company by owning the majority of the shares or having an influence over the other major shareholders. The wrongdoing director may then be able to suppress litigation even though the litigation would be in the company's best interests. As a result the common law created the shareholder derivative action. This can be brought by an aggrieved minority shareholder who brings the action in the name of the company against the directors for a wrong done to the company, with damages being awarded to the company. The common law attempted to find a balance between protecting the interests of minority shareholders and allowing the collective majority to take the decision whether to pursue litigation. The rule in *Foss v. Harbottle*[24] and various recent alterations in the law have created a set of complex rules for when a derivative action may be taken. The Companies Act 2006 puts the derivative action on a much more modern basis.

The Companies Act 2006 will enable a derivative claim to be brought, in a wider range of circumstances, for an actual or proposed act or omission involving negligence, breach of duty or breach of trust by a director of the company. Before the new Act, negligence would not have been classed as a fraud on the minority unless it could be shown that the majority profited as a result of negligence and the company suffered a loss.

Despite the extension of the grounds for bringing the derivative action, a broad discretion is given to the courts to decide whether to give permission to a member to continue with a derivative action. The court decides whether to dismiss the application or ask for more evidence and can make any consequential order it deems fit. Shareholder derivative actions are also discussed in the following chapter.

[24] (1843) 2 Hare 461; 67 ER 189.

8

What sanctions are necessary?

KEITH JOHNSTONE AND WILL CHALK

Introduction

Corporate governance deals with the 'processes by which organisations are directed, controlled and held to account and is underpinned by the principles of openness, integrity and accountability'.[1] This chapter will examine that system of accountability in relation to the mainstream requirements of the UK corporate governance environment. In particular, it will look at where and in what form the sanctions which underpin accountability exist and what sanctions are necessary for the regime as a whole to be a success.

Central to the reform debate in the 1990s was the question as to whether the traditional 'self-regulatory' approach should be followed or whether governance through legislation and regulation was more appropriate. Corporate Britain, for obvious reasons, favoured the former approach, concern focusing on the fact that governance by legislative or regulatory prescription would constrain innovation, hamper development and wealth creation and potentially result in judicial scrutiny of commercial decisions. In the opposite corner were increasingly vociferous groups of disaffected shareholders, creditors and the wider community who highlighted that the regime, as it existed then, lacked effective sanctions, not only to deter abuse but also to punish it when it did occur.

The way forward was to be a compromise: employing predominantly voluntary codes allowing companies to self-regulate, to grow and to develop without excessive interference but in certain areas using law and regulation to set the boundaries of behaviour, promote transparency and increase accountability.

Currently, views on the effectiveness of the regime remain polarised. Many commentators and interest groups assert that the regime is still weak and yet the view from the boardroom is an entirely different one. Even though the UK regulatory regime is still considered to have a light touch when compared to its US counterpart, listed companies complain that the weight of law and regulation emanating from Brussels and Whitehall is excessive. Directors will also say that the ever increasing potential for personal liability, and its consequences, are threatening to deter talented individuals from accepting directorships in quoted companies. Moreover, recent legislation, and in particular certain aspects of the Companies Act 2006 (2006 Act), threaten to raise the stakes even further.

---

[1] Per the International Federation of Accountants, 2001.

No regime of corporate governance can ever completely eradicate the possibility of governance failures and any attempt to do so is only likely to undermine capital markets and wealth creation. So, what sanctions are necessary to ensure sufficient but not excess accountability?

The Virtuous Circle of corporate governance

To be able to review our system of accountability, we need to define which 'rules' constitute the corporate governance landscape and what drives companies and boards to adopt appropriate governance standards. The Virtuous Circle is a rudimentary depiction of that landscape and of those drivers (see figure 8.1).

The Virtuous Circle is divided into four segments, with the overarching, high-level reasons for boards to comply with the principles of good governance described in the outer ring of each. Consequently, we believe there are four main drivers:

- law and regulation
- the Courts
- shareholder pressure
- good corporate citizenship.

Moving in from that, the next ring shows the main protagonists: those organisations and bodies which either develop the rules or guidelines and/or apply pressure on boards.

Finally, in the main section of each segment are the means through which pressure is applied.

Ultimately, pressure is applied on boards, hence their position at the centre of the Virtuous Circle and at the heart of the corporate governance regime. The objective of this pressure is good governance, which can be summarised as:

- compliance with law, regulation and best practice
- a balanced board making quality decisions
- focus on risk management strategies
- balanced, accessible and regular assessments of the company's position and prospects
- transparency of board remuneration
- good corporate citizenship.

Law and regulation in the Virtuous Circle

The law is the primary source of pressure on boards. Much of this emanates from the EU, particularly in the form of the Company Law Directives[2] and,

---

[2] In particular the Fourth (Directive 78/660/EEC), Seventh (83/349/EEC) and Eighth (Directive 84/253/EEC) Directives.

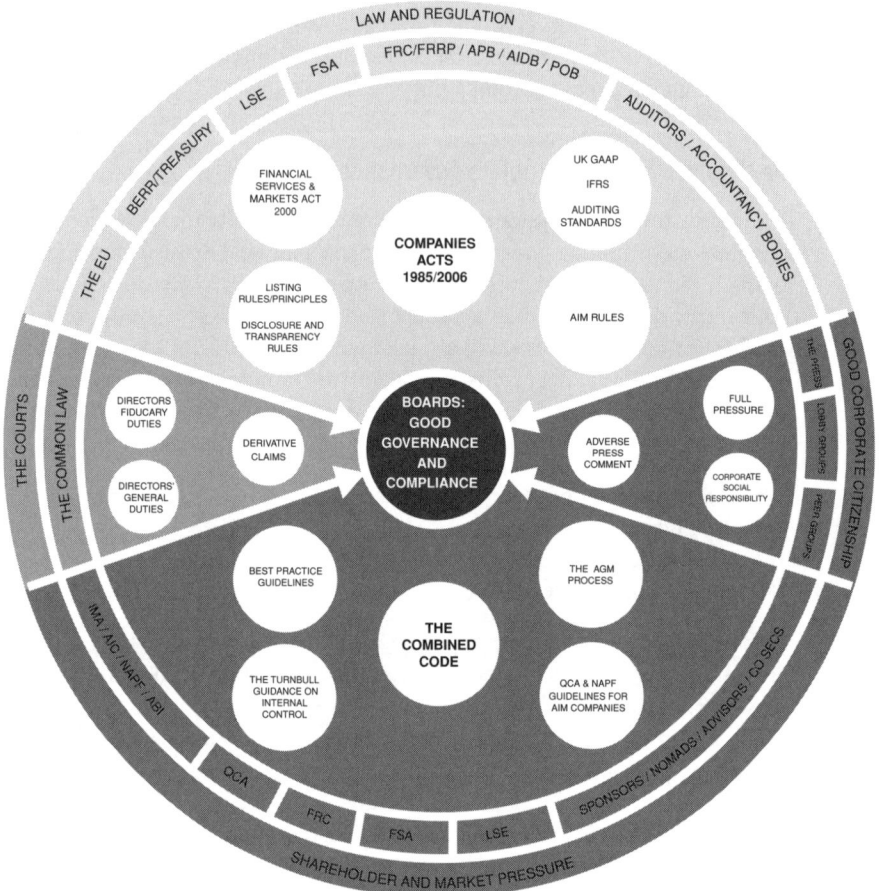

Figure 8.1 The Virtuous Circle of corporate governance

more recently, the Modernisation Directive[3] which contained the requirement for companies to produce a business review in annual reports. The Department for Business, Enterprise and Regulatory Reform (BERR) and the Treasury also play a major part here in promoting legislation in relation to companies and financial services respectively. In addition, the BERR investigates and enforces certain aspects of the regime and has the power to appoint investigators, whereas the Treasury has largely delegated these functions to the Financial Services Authority (FSA).

---

[3] Directive 2003/51/EC.

The intended outcomes of the Virtuous Circle of corporate governance:

BOARDS : GOOD GOVERNANCE AND COMPLIANCE

The purpose of the Virtuous Circle :

- Compliance with law, regulation and best practice

- A balanced board making quality decisions

- Focus on risk management strategies

- Balanced, accessible and regular assessments of the company's position and prospects

- Transparency of board remuneration

- Good corporate citizenship

KEY

ABI :	Association of British Insurers
AIC :	Association of Investment Companies
APB :	Auditing Practices Board, an operating body of the FRC
AIDB :	Accountancy Investigation and Discipline Board, an operating body of the FRC
CO SECS :	Company Secretaries
FRC :	Financial Reporting Council
FRRP :	Financial Reporting Review Panel, an operating body of the FRC
FSA :	Financial Services Authority
IMA :	Investment Managers Association
LSE :	London Stock Exchange (for AIM Listed companies)
NAPF :	National Association of Pension Funds
POB :	Public Oversight Board, an operating body of the FRC
QCA :	Quoted Companies Alliance

Figure 8.1 *(cont.)*

A small number of statutes are at the heart of the law and regulation segment in the Virtuous Circle:

- the Companies Act 1985 (1985 Act) as variously amended, most pertinently by the Directors' Remuneration Report Regulations 2002 (Remuneration Regulations) and the Companies (Audit, Investigations and Community Enterprise) Act 2004 (C(A,ICE) Act), and which is in the process of being further amended and superseded by the 2006 Act (taken together, the Companies Acts); and
- the Financial Services and Markets Act 2000 (FSMA).

Companies admitted to Official Listing and to trading on regulated markets also have regulatory obligations which derive from Part VI of FSMA, and which are contained in the Listing Rules and Disclosure and Transparency Rules (together,

149

Part 6 Rules). These rules are overlain by Listing Principles and enforced by the FSA. For companies listed on the Alternative Investment Market (AIM), as it is an 'exchange regulated market', pressure is applied through the AIM Rules for Companies (AIM Rules) enforced by the London Stock Exchange (LSE).

In terms of corporate reporting, centre stage in the Virtuous Circle are the Companies Acts requiring the production of annual accounts with prescribed contents. For companies admitted to regulated markets, these must now be produced on a consolidated basis in accordance with International Financial Reporting Standards (IFRS). Standards of corporate reporting are also upheld through the audit process and the scrutiny of independent auditors, who themselves are governed by auditing standards.

There are several other organisations surrounding boards in this segment of the Virtuous Circle compelling compliance, directly and indirectly, with the corporate reporting process. Most prominent among these are:

- the Financial Reporting Review Panel (FRRP) whose powers were significantly enhanced by the C(A,ICE) Act; the FRRP seeks to ensure that the provision of financial information by public and large private companies complies with Companies Acts; it has enforcement functions in relation to narrative reporting, not least in relation to directors' reports and, in due course, in relation to Business Reviews; it also monitors compliance with the accounting disclosure requirements of the Listing Rules;
- the Auditing Practices Board (APB), which sets auditing standards and gives guidance on the performance of external audits and other activities undertaken by auditors;
- the Audit Inspection Unit (AIU) of the Professional Oversight Board (POB), which was established following the Government's post-Enron review of the UK accountancy profession; under the regulatory framework established as a result of this review, the professional Accountancy Bodies (defined below), continue to register firms to conduct audit work, with their regulatory activities being overseen by the POB; the AIU assists the POB in this role by monitoring the quality of audits of all entities with listed securities and other entities in whose financial condition there is considered to be a 'major public interest'; AIU reports are sent to the senior management of the auditor in question as well as to the Accountancy Body with which the firm is registered, and consequently the AIU/POB acts as an indirect source of pressure on boards;
- the Accountancy Investigation and Discipline Board (AIDB), which acts as an independent investigative and disciplinary body for accountants in the UK; like the AIU/POB, the focus of the AIDB is on cases of public interest – for example, those pertaining to larger companies with sizeable shareholder bases which have been referred to them by Accountancy Bodies with whom an individual accountancy firm is registered; other cases will continue to be dealt with by the Accountancy Bodies;

- the Accountancy Bodies[4] which set and enforce standards of conduct[5] for their member firms by conducting investigations into complaints with regard to the conduct of their members.

The Courts in the Virtuous Circle

The potential for civil claims through the Courts against directors for breach of their common law fiduciary duties is part of the Virtuous Circle. However, owing largely to the fact that these duties are owed to the general body of shareholders taken as a whole, and are enforceable against the directors only by the company acting on their behalf, these duties have not historically played a prominent role.

Under the common law, an individual shareholder may bring a derivative claim against a director or board in his own name for the company's benefit and join the company as a party to the proceedings. Such actions are only available in a very narrow set of circumstances (usually when the conduct of directors is tainted by fraud) and the extent of the pressure they apply to boards or individual directors is, therefore, limited.

However, from 1 October 2007, the following aspects of the 2006 Act have been brought into force which may significantly alter that position:

- first, the codified statement of directors' duties which includes the duty to promote the success of the company whilst adhering to the principles of 'enlightened shareholder value' – these duties are those which the Government considered to be the most significant general duties existing in the common law;
- second, provisions which will place into statute for the first time this common law right of shareholders to bring a derivative claim on the company's behalf against directors as well as extending the grounds upon which shareholders may bring such a claim to include breach of trust, negligence and breach of directors' duty.

There are safeguards built into the 2006 Act to guard against vexatious claims being brought by 'activist' shareholders but, even so, the expectation is that the 2006 Act will increase the involvement of the Courts in applying pressure on boards (even though, strictly speaking, this will take place through the combination of the common law and legislation).

Individual shareholders do have the ability to bring a statutory claim under the Companies Acts to the extent that the company's affairs have been conducted in a manner which is unfairly prejudicial to the interests of its members generally

---

[4] Comprising, among others, the Institute of Chartered Accountants in England and Wales, the Institute of Chartered Accountants in Scotland, the Institute of Chartered Accountants in Ireland and the Association of Chartered Certified Accountants.

[5] For example, in the area of audit, compliance is required with the 'Audit Regulations and Guidance' and the 'Designated Professional Body Handbook'.

or some part of its membership. However, such actions are rare and can be discounted as a source of genuine pressure given the ease with which a company may defeat a claim. Accordingly, such claims do not appear in the Virtuous Circle.

The narrow segment in this part of the Virtuous Circle represents therefore the somewhat limited impact that this area has had to date on conditioning board behaviour. However, the provisions of the 2006 Act may significantly increase the importance of these influences on board behaviour in the near future.

Shareholder and market pressure in the Virtuous Circle

Shareholders and the esoteric concept of the market apply at least as much pressure on boards as law and regulation. The influences at work here have been summarised by the FRC: 'Companies and pension funds, supported by their professional advisers and encouraged by the investor community, have the primary responsibility for achieving high standards of reporting and governance.'[6]

The way in which this pressure is applied is primarily through voluntary codes of conduct associated with corporate governance in its purest form. Therefore, shareholder and market pressure is exerted through or by reference to:

- the Combined Code, which is seen as the cornerstone of the UK corporate governance regime for Officially Listed companies; the requirement to include a statement in the annual report and accounts as to whether a company has complied with the provisions of the Code or, to the extent it has not, the reasons why not, is embedded in the Listing Rules and, ultimately, the pressure for compliance comes from shareholders' reaction to company disclosures under this comply-or-explain principle;
- the Corporate Governance Guidelines for AIM Companies produced by the Quoted Companies Alliance (QCA) – companies listed on AIM are not formally required to comply with the Combined Code, although some choose to do so; consequently, the QCA has produced a code which it feels is more appropriate for companies listed on the junior market; more recently, the National Association of Pension Funds (NAPF) has produced a similar AIM focused corporate governance policy document;[7]
- the updated[8] Turnbull Guidance on Internal Control which deals with risk management issues;
- other guidance appended to the Combined Code which includes the Smith Guidance for Audit Committees as well as guidance for board chairmen and for non-executive directors;

---

[6] FRC Regulatory Strategy, May 2006, version 2.1, p. 5.

[7] NAPF: Corporate Governance Policy: Policy Voting Guidelines for AIM companies, March 2007.

[8] The FRC has published an updated version of the Turnbull Guidance which is effective for financial years beginning on or after 1 January 2006.

- Best Practice Guidelines issued by the institutional shareholder representative bodies, either collectively under the umbrella of the Institutional Shareholders' Committee (ISC) or individually by the following:
  - the Association of British Insurers (ABI)[9] which often publishes guidelines in conjunction with the National Association of Pension Funds (NAPF);[10] through IVIS,[11] members are provided with a monitoring service in respect of companies which comprise the UK FTSE All-Share Index and other companies on request; the service focuses on the Combined Code and ABI guidelines (and IVIS reports are colour-coded to help users identify 'non-compliant' or 'inconsistent' issues);
  - the NAPF;[12] through RREV[13] members are provided with research and voting recommendations, again covering all companies in the FTSE All-Share Index; those voting recommendations are based on NAPF's corporate governance policies;
  - the Investment Management Association (IMA) which is the trade body for the UK investment management industry – its members provide investment management services to institutional investors and private clients;
  - the Association of Investment Companies (AIC) which is the trade body of the investment industry and represents investment companies and their shareholders; the AIC also works closely with the management groups which administer the companies concerned;
- the AGM process and, in particular, by the constituent elements of the ISC and other bodies, such as the Pre-emption Group;[14] it is corporate reporting and the AGM process that also bring into play those organisations that provide voting services or act as intermediaries in the voting process for larger shareholders – including IVIS, RREV, PIRC, ISS and Manifest;[15]
- sponsors, nomads and other advisers – the part played and advice given by sponsors for Main Market listed companies, nomads for AIM

---

[9] For example, the ABI's guidelines on executive remuneration (December 2006).

[10] For example, Best Practice on Executive Contracts and Severance – A Joint Statement by the ABI and NAPF (December 2003).

[11] Institutional Voting Information Service.

[12] For example, the NAPF's 2004 Corporate Governance Policy (December 2003) which sets out good-practice principles and voting guidelines on a number of issues.

[13] Research, Recommendations and Electronic Voting – a joint venture between NAPF and ISS.

[14] The Pre-Emption Group provides guidance on the considerations to be taken into account when disapplying pre-emption rights. It is constituted by representatives of, among others, the Hundred Group, the ISC, LIBA and the Securities and Investment Institute.

[15] PIRC: Pensions and Investment Research Consultants. PIRC produces, among other things, Shareholder Voting Guidelines (February 2005); IVIS: Institutional Shareholder Service – a provider of 'global' research and proxy voting services; Manifest: Manifest Information Services Limited.

companies and other advisers, not least lawyers, in relation to both cannot be discounted;

- Company Secretaries – in addition, given the qualifications required to hold the position in a public company, the influence of Company Secretaries on boards should not be underestimated.

Good corporate citizenship in the Virtuous Circle

Good corporate citizenship encapsulates many concepts but the prime driver behind it is public opinion, which plays an important role in conditioning board behaviour. Hence it is properly included in the Virtuous Circle. Predominantly, the agents applying pressure in this area are:

- the press – in a decade marked by volatile equity markets where the merest hint of scandal can have an impact on share prices, adverse press comment plays a part in compelling compliance with governance best practice as well as exposing malpractice;
- lobby groups (including trade associations) – the pressure applied to many segments of the Main Market by, for instance, the environmental lobby and the weight of opinion generated by the debate surrounding globalisation and the need for corporate social responsibility underline the influences at work here;
- peer groups – the high degree of segment-based analysis undertaken in the market means that peer pressure (ensuring that companies are seen to be keeping up with the corporate governance standard-bearers in their segment) also plays a part in the Virtuous Circle.

The sanctions: law and regulation – policing the boundaries

Law and regulation set the boundaries of behaviour within which companies and their directors must operate and constitute one of the two key segments of the Virtuous Circle. Strong legal- and regulatory-based sanctions are necessary to ensure that these boundaries are secure, that companies and their officers are deterred from crossing them and that those that do are punished effectively and appropriately. Having secure boundaries should allow much of the rest of the corporate governance regime to be determined by voluntary and flexible codes of best practice, policed by shareholders. That, at least, is the theory.

Problems can arise in legislative responses to corporate scandals. The understandable, knee-jerk political reaction to the collapse of major corporations, such as Enron, is to legislate and demand immediate compliance with more rigid rules enforced by an objective and risk-averse organ of the state. However, the inflexible nature of such laws, coupled with the cost of compliance, has the potential to downgrade the attractiveness of a jurisdiction for business and investment.

Sanctions under the Companies Acts

Centre stage in this segment of the Virtuous Circle are the Companies Acts. A traditional view of sanctions for breaches of the Companies Acts would categorise them, in general terms, as follows:

- imprisonment of officers: for example, should a company wish to dis-apply rights of pre-emption in relation to a further issue of shares, it must seek the consent of shareholders and, in doing so, the directors must provide a statement setting out certain matters, including the reason for recommending the resolution be passed. To the extent that a director knowingly or recklessly permits the inclusion of any matter that is false or deceptive in that statement, he commits a criminal offence punishable by a twelve-month term of imprisonment if convicted on indictment;
- fines for companies and/or directors: for example, a director failing to disclose to the board a personal interest in a transaction or arrangement to which the company is already a party is liable to an unlimited fine if convicted on indictment;
- civil remedies and restitution: for example, a loan entered into between a company and a director which breaches the Companies Acts is voidable at the option of the company; as such the company will be able to rescind the transaction and recover any money or other asset with which it has parted; furthermore, the director involved is liable to account for any direct or indirect gain he has made from the transaction as well as being liable to indemnify the company for any loss it has suffered.

Sanctions and corporate reporting

Fundamental to an effective system of corporate governance are disclosure and transparency – hence their prominence in the Virtuous Circle. Directors of companies failing to keep 'sufficient' accounting records can be sentenced to up to two years' imprisonment if convicted on indictment. If annual accounts are approved which do not comply with the Companies Acts or, in the case of the consolidated accounts of listed companies, IFRS, then every director who is party to their approval and who knows they do not comply or is reckless as to whether they comply is liable to a fine.

Key disclosures in annual accounts, aside from the financial statements themselves, are contained in the directors' report (the requirements of which are also prescribed by the Companies Acts) and directors can be fined if directors' reports are non-compliant.

Ultimately, failure to deliver accounts to the Registrar of Companies within the permitted time limits renders directors liable to a fine, and in 2004/5 there were more than 2600 convictions for this offence.[16] Thus, the boundaries of

---

[16] DTI Report, Companies in 2004–5, published October 2005.

the corporate reporting regime seem to be secure – with strong sanctions based on the criminal law. However, more sophistication is required for the system of corporate reporting to work effectively.

The role of auditors

Arguably, a more sophisticated sanction securing compliance lies in the role of auditors. As the steering group which undertook the Company Law Review emphasised in its 2001 report: 'The auditor's role is fundamental in ensuring truth and comprehensiveness in reporting, and that management is properly accountable to shareholders and to external constituencies. The audit process also benefits these interests indirectly, by encouraging good corporate governance.'[17] The Hampel Report stated: 'The statutory role of the auditors is to provide the shareholders with independent and objective assurance on the reliability of the financial statements and of certain other information provided by the company. This is a vital role; it justifies the special position of the auditors under the Companies Act.'[18]

Audit reports must state whether accounts have been properly prepared in accordance with the requirements of the Companies Acts or IFRS and whether the information in directors' reports is consistent with those accounts. Auditors must also report to shareholders on the auditable part of the directors' remuneration report and state whether it has been properly prepared.

Auditors must investigate and then state whether the accounts give a true and fair view of the financial position of the company. No board wishes to have a qualified audit report and the compelling effect that the threat of such a qualification would have on conditioning board behaviour is obvious.

The presentation of the true and fair view means that an auditor's opinion is given on the substance of accounts, rather than their strict legal form, and that should make UK companies less susceptible to the problems unearthed in the Enron case. That said, the Government has heeded arguments that the introduction of IFRS has weakened this position such that, under the 2006 Act, directors will also be required to stand behind this statement.

This system of checks, balances and accountability is strengthened by the regulation of the audit profession through professional standards set by the APB, and scrutiny of individual audits through the POB, the AIDB and the individual Accountancy Bodies. Moreover, the FRRP has been given authority to review accounts of public and large private companies for compliance with the law and accounting standards and keep under review interim and final reports of listed issuers. By way of sanction, the FRRP may apply to the court to compel a company to revise defective accounts and the FRRP's remit now extends to the business review elements of directors' reports.

---

[17] Para 5.129, Company Law Review.
[18] Para 6.2, Report of the Committee on Corporate Governance, January 1998.

If one adds to this regime the changes made to address auditor conflicts of interest – namely the controls over provision of non-audit services and the requirement for audit partner rotation – one might conclude that the boundaries of the UK corporate reporting regime were effectively policed. Yet legislation has gone further still.

Plugging the 'expectations gap'

The Company Law Reform steering group stated in 2000 that, in relation to corporate reporting and the audit process, there was an *'expectations gap – that is the gap between what auditors can achieve and what users think they can achieve'*. The group said that

> The general public . . . often assumes that a primary task of the statutory audit is to expose fraud and other criminality. Governments and regulators also expect an increased contribution towards the detection of fraud. In reality auditors cannot be expected to detect a carefully planned and executed fraud' [and] Even among informed commentators there can be a reluctance to accept that corporate failure is an inevitable feature of the capitalist system and that the collapse of large companies will tend to expose accounting weakness and financial malpractice.[19]

A year later, the collapse of Enron precipitated UK legislation (the C(A,ICE) Act) aiming to plug this expectations gap, avert similar disasters in the UK and increase the reliability of, and confidence in, company accounts. First, auditors were given extended powers to require information and explanations from a wider group of people, including employees, and a criminal offence for failing to provide that information was introduced. Second, directors were obliged to include in accounts a statement that, so far as each of them was aware, there was no 'relevant information' of which the auditors were unaware, and that they had taken all the steps they should have to avail themselves of such information and ensure that the auditors knew of it as well. A director failing to do so risks possible imprisonment or a fine. This second limb is a potentially onerous obligation, and immediately begs the question of how far each director needs to go to satisfy himself that he has investigated and passed on all relevant information and the extent of the audit trail required to prove it.

The 2006 Act goes further still. Two new criminal offences are to be introduced for auditors where they knowingly or recklessly cause an audit report to include 'any matter that is misleading, false or deceptive' or knowingly or recklessly cause a report to omit a statement that is required by the Act. Each offence is punishable by a fine – the original proposal had been to allow a custodial sentence.

---

[19] Para 5.129, Modern Company Law for a Competitive Economy – Developing the Framework – March 2000, Company Law Reform Steering Group.

Has the legislature gone too far? One of the main aims behind company law reform and the promulgation of the 2006 Act was to remove 'unnecessary burdens to directors and [preserve] Britain's reputation as a favoured country in which to incorporate';[20] the BERR has claimed that the deregulatory aspects of the 2006 Act will save businesses as much as £250 million. The CBI's concern is that, notwithstanding the (new) ability of auditors to limit their liability, these new offences alone will wipe out the rest of the 2006 Act's cost savings. By making auditors even more cautious, thereby increasing the time spent performing audits, it is feared that the cost of producing accounts will spiral.

It is clear that legal requirements should only be imposed if the effect of those requirements is proportionate to the benefits accruing and, in relation to the recent requirements imposed on directors and auditors, this does not appear to be the case. One might wonder whether these measures are necessary at all given the checks, balances and sanctions attendant to the rest of the corporate reporting regime? If they are necessary, could the same result have been achieved by increased resources for both the POB and the FRRP?

Shareholders and legislative sanctions

Shareholders also have a prime role in the context of legislative sanctions. While a narrow view of accountability under the 1985 Act would focus on the limited ability of individual shareholders to bring claims, this ignores the impact on board behaviour of shareholder meetings and the AGM process generally. In any event, that narrow view must widen to bring into the picture the new category of statutory derivative claims introduced by the 2006 Act.

This importance of shareholders under the Companies Acts is also reflected in the corporate reporting regime – in particular, the requirement for public company accounts and, separately, the directors' remuneration report to be laid before shareholders for approval in general meeting. While the vote of members in relation to remuneration is indicative only, a vote not to approve either the accounts as a whole, or the remuneration report itself, would send a strident warning to a board of discontent and of likely shareholder reaction to other resolutions put to members, not least those in relation to the re-election of directors.

FSMA: sanctions in a regulatory context

For listed companies, regulation also plays a prominent role in the Virtuous Circle. Sanctions in relation to companies with an Official Listing derive from Part VI of FMSA and are enforced by the FSA. They can be divided into:

---

[20] Company Law Reform Bill – White Paper, March 2005.

- civil sanctions, including sanctions for listed companies, directors and other persons discharging managerial responsibilities (PDMRs);[21] and
- criminal sanctions for misleading the market.

Sanctions for listed companies, directors and PDMRs

Where breaches are 'minor in nature or degree, or the person may have taken immediate and full remedial action',[22] the FSA may issue a private warning. Such warnings are not classed as formal disciplinary action but are kept on record as part of an issuer's or an individual's compliance history.

On a day-to-day level, perhaps the most effective deterrent to breaching the rules is in the pro-active enforcement policies of the FSA. Best-practice letters are frequently sent to issuers in relation to conduct which does not breach the letter of a particular rule but where the conduct nevertheless shows room for improvement. The FSA also uses its periodic publication – *List!* – to disseminate informal guidance to companies and advisers on issues such as rule breaches that have come to its attention, particularly where a breach has occurred owing to a misapprehension as to the requirements of a rule. Further, the FSA also targets sensitive areas where they consider non-compliance to be a possibility. For example, when, in the run up to Christmas in 2004, the trade press reported slow trading and poor consumer demand on the high street, the FSA wrote to all listed retailers reminding them of the obligation to keep the market updated of their expectations as to company performance 'as soon as possible', and not simply to delay that announcement until their scheduled trading updates after Christmas.

For more serious breaches, the FSA may publish a statement of censure in relation to either a listed company and/or any person who was, at the time of the breach, a director of the listed company and knowingly concerned in it. This sanction is given teeth because of the effect of the statement on the reputation of the listed company or director sanctioned. Thus, Eurodis Electron plc was censured[23] for a breach of its disclosure obligations in failing to notify the market promptly of a marked deterioration in its working capital position. Sportsworld Media Group plc[24] was also censured for failing to update the market promptly of a change in its business performance and expectations as to its pre-tax profits. However, as is often the case, the companies concerned were in serious financial difficulties anyway (the latter being in receivership), and it is arguable in these circumstances that the effectiveness of the sanction is undermined, as neither the company nor its management has a reputation left to lose.

---

[21] There is no definition of 'persons discharging managerial responsibilities' in FSMA but informal guidance issued by the FSA suggests that this relates to a senior tier of management immediately below board level.

[22] Note that these factors, by themselves, will not determine the course of action taken by the FSA.

[23] See: www.fsa.gov.uk/pubs/final/eurodis.pdf.

[24] See: www.fsa.gov.uk/pubs/final/sportsworld – 29 mar04.pdf.

In relation to the relatively new power under FSMA to impose unlimited fines on companies and directors (or former directors), the FSA's general approach has not been to impose a tariff of financial penalties, but to look at all the circumstances of the breach and the person committing it, as well as the wider effects of the breach on the market. This is because the FSA maintains that there are few cases in which the circumstances are essentially the same and the FSA considers that, in general, the use of a tariff for particular kinds of breach would inhibit 'the flexible and proportionate approach it takes in this area'.[25]

The ability to impose financial penalties is a necessary and effective sanction, particularly in relation to directors knowingly concerned in any breach. In the Sportsworld case, while the company itself would have been fined were it not for the fact that it was in receivership, arguably the more effective sanction was the fine of £45,000 imposed on the former Chief Executive. Not only does this send a clear message to the market and other directors of the consequences of non-compliance, but it also punishes, without adversely affecting the position of shareholders, creditors and other stakeholders.

Suspensions and cancellations

The FSA has the power to suspend or cancel a company's listing but classes the ability to do so as a non-disciplinary measure. The FSA will consider a suspension in circumstances where the smooth operation of the market is temporarily jeopardised – for example, if a company has failed to publish financial information or is unable to assess accurately its financial position, or where the FSA considers that there are reasonable grounds to suspect non-compliance with the Disclosure and Transparency Rules generally. The power to cancel permanently a listing is available if the FSA is satisfied that there are 'special circumstances that preclude normal regular dealings in [a company's listed securities]'. Therefore, it is conceivable that, in extreme cases of persistent rule breach where market integrity is threatened, suspensions and cancellations could be used as a sanction of last resort.

Should they be used as a disciplinary measure more often? In our view, they should not. To use suspensions or delisting as a sanction penalises blameless shareholders, particularly when there are more effective sanctions at the FSA's disposal; it is only when the integrity of the market is consistently and seriously threatened that they should be contemplated. To do otherwise would be counterproductive as, ultimately, it runs the risk of damaging the reputation and competitiveness of the market as a whole.

The Listing Principles – facilitating the enforcement process

The FSA's fundamental review of the Listing regime in 2004/5 precipitated the introduction of seven overarching Listing Principles; these apply to companies with a primary listing of equity securities and are enforceable in the same way

---

[25] FSA Handbook, ENF 21.7.4.

as other provisions of the Part VI Rules. According to the Listing Rules, their purpose is to ensure that 'listed companies pay due regard to the fundamental role they play in maintaining market confidence and ensuring fair and orderly markets'.[26] The Principles were also introduced to address the FSA's perception that the way in which the Listing Rules and associated guidance were drafted before their amendment in 2005 encouraged 'issuers and their advisers to adopt a literal interpretation of each rule rather than promoting compliance with the overarching standards which the listing sourcebook . . . is designed to achieve'.[27] The FSA wanted a way to ensure compliance with not just the letter of the rules but also their spirit.

There was a great deal of concern surrounding the introduction of the Listing Principles, not least because they have been drafted in broad terms and, with certain exceptions, are not objectively verifiable. The Listing Principles are not a sanction in themselves, although they smooth the path for enforcement action to be taken. While, under each of the Principles, the onus is on the FSA to show that an issuer has been at fault, their introduction has undoubtedly strengthened the FSA's hand and they certainly play a part in the Virtuous Circle. Indeed, the FSA may discipline an issuer on the basis of the Principles alone, such as where an issuer has committed a number of breaches of detailed rules which individually may not merit disciplinary action, but the cumulative effect of which indicates a breach of a Listing Principle.

Sanctions for AIM listed companies

Sanctions for AIM listed companies are similar to those for companies with an Official Listing save for the fact that they derive not from statute but from the contract that exists between the LSE and the listed company (that is, in return for listing the securities of the company in question, the company agrees to abide by the rules of the LSE in the form of the AIM Rules).

The AIM Rules provide that companies may be fined and censured. Delisting is also considered to be a sanction under the AIM Rules as opposed to a device for the protection of the market. As for nomads, they may be censured and have their registration revoked in addition to (in contrast with Official List sponsors) being subjected to financial penalties.

Sanctions for sponsors and nomads

If the FSA considers that a sponsor has breached any provision of the Listing Rules it may publish a statement censuring the sponsor.

Perhaps more significantly, just as auditors add a level of sophistication to the regime of sanctions in the context of corporate reporting, the same may also be said in relation to the role of sponsors relative to the Part VI Rules (and, indeed, nomads in the context of the AIM Rules). In the extreme, the FSA may cancel a sponsor's accreditation if it considers that it has failed to meet certain

---

[26] LR 7.1.2G.   [27] FSA Consultation Paper CP203, October 2003, Chapter 4, para 4.2.

criteria which focus on a sponsor's competence. Where a sponsor has been appointed, it must 'guide the listed company . . . in understanding and meeting its responsibilities' under the Part VI Rules. This will be evidenced primarily by the conduct of the listed companies to which the sponsor gives advice. Consequently, the sponsor regime can be seen to act as a factor conditioning corporate conduct in the same way as more traditional sanctions.

Misleading statements and practices

The regulatory sanctions discussed so far are civil offences. FSMA also vests in the FSA the ability to bring criminal prosecutions in relation to insider dealing and, more importantly from a pure corporate governance perspective, for knowingly or recklessly issuing misleading statements. These sanctions are necessary to check real excesses of behaviour and deter others from jeopardising the integrity of the market. The first convictions secured by the FSA using these powers have sent a clear signal to the market. The former Chief Executive and Finance Director of AIT Group plc[28] were both imprisoned and forced to repay substantial sums to investors for recklessly misleading the market. They were also disqualified from acting as directors. This introduces the final sanction which plays a part in this segment of the Virtuous Circle.

Disqualification of directors

Directors may be disqualified under the Company Directors Disqualification Act 1986 (Disqualification Act). The aim of the Disqualification Act is to prevent those who are unfit to do so from taking part in the management of companies. Consequently, proceedings may be brought to disqualify directors on a number of grounds, including for conviction of an indictable offence in connection with the promotion, formation or management of a company, for persistent breaches of companies legislation or, on summary conviction, for breach of specified companies legislation including the obligation to file accounts. Disqualification may be pursuant to a Court-imposed Disqualification Order or, since April 2001, by way of an undertaking given by the director concerned so as to prevent the need for the matter to be dealt with through the Courts.

Depending on the grounds for the proceedings, disqualifications may be ordered for between two and fifteen years 'in particularly serious cases'[29] – as Lord Woolf said: 'The period of disqualification must reflect the gravity of the offence. It must contain deterrent elements. This is what sentencing is all about.'[30] In addition, breach of a Disqualification Order or undertaking is

---

[28] *R v. Rigby, Bailey and Rowley* [2005] EWCA Crim 3487.

[29] In *Re Sevenoaks* [1991] CH 164, periods of disqualification were divided into three brackets, a bottom bracket of two to five years where the case 'is not, relatively speaking, very serious', a middle bracket of six to ten years for 'serious cases not meriting the top bracket' and a top bracket of over ten years for 'particularly serious cases'.

[30] Westmid Packing [1998] 2 All ER 124.

a criminal offence carrying a maximum penalty of two years' imprisonment and/or a fine. Individual deterrence and general deterrence are relevant factors taken into account when determining the period of disqualification.

It is public protection, even more than deterrence, that goes to the heart of the need for Disqualification Orders. Given that it is rare for directors to be imprisoned for breaches of the Companies Acts or FSMA, it could be argued that fines alone are not sufficient to deter future serious misfeasance by others and, more importantly perhaps, the individual concerned in the particular breach. The Disqualification Act should add vital weight to the regime by allowing the public to be protected in the future, something which neither fines nor reputational damage can necessarily do.

Is disqualification an effective sanction in practice? In day-to-day business it is very unlikely that directors will think about, much less worry about, disqualification. Of some 1300 disqualifications in 2004/5, over 1100 of them were made following insolvency.[31] It seems that it is only when companies have reached their end game that disqualification on the grounds of unfitness really has a part to play. For this reason, disqualification does not appear in the Virtuous Circle.

The sanctions: the role of the Courts

The growing significance of the Courts

Directors who get it wrong may be subject to common law civil claims for breach of duty, tort (negligence or deceit), breach of trust and fraud. In practice, the most common claims are for breach of duty and the sanctions available under these claims are considered in this section.

Cases such as *Foss v. Harbottle*[32] have long established that a director owes his common law duties to the company and that it is the company which may bring any claims against him for a breach.

However, in exceptional circumstances, claims against directors for breach of duty can be brought by shareholders. These derivative claims, in fact, are actions brought by shareholders to enforce causes of action vested in the company rather than actions by shareholders in their own right. The case law establishes that, in the main, derivative claims can be brought only where the breach of duty constitutes a fraud or abuse of power to the benefit of the wrongdoers and the wrongdoers are in control of the company (such that a direct claim by the company cannot be brought in practice).

For some time, there have been concerns that derivative claims are not an effective remedy for wronged shareholders, on the basis that the principles governing such claims are defective in some aspects and uncertain in others.

---

[31] DTI Report, Companies in 2004–5, published October 2005.
[32] (1843) 2 Hare 461.

More recently, calls for a clearer statement of the law on derivative claims have increased while, at the same time, a string of high-profile breach of duty cases has fixed public attention on the circumstances in which directors should be brought to book for their actions. Against this background, the 2006 Act includes new provisions which clarify and extend the availability of derivative claims, and it is these provisions which merit such claims being included in the Virtuous Circle.

The 2006 Act endorses the *Foss v. Harbottle* principle while introducing a statutory basis for bringing shareholder claims against directors that replace the common law principles. Under the 2006 Act, a shareholder may bring a derivative claim against a director for breach of trust, negligence and breach of duty. However, the Courts have a general discretion to allow or prevent such a claim from proceeding at an early stage.

Consequences of breach of duty

The main potential consequences for a director who is guilty of a breach of duty are as follows:

- He can be personally liable to account to the company for any net financial benefits he has received as a result of the breach of duty, and such liability is unlimited. Financial benefits received by a director can be traced where, as a result of the breach of duty, they are held on constructive trust, and a director's assets may be frozen to assist in this. In certain cases, compound interest can be ordered to be paid on the relevant sums.
- He can be personally liable in damages for the net loss which the company suffers as a result of the breach of duty, and such liability is also unlimited. The measure of loss is usually related to restitution, so that the company is put back in the position it would have been in if the breach had not occurred.
- Actions taken by directors, such as an issue of shares, or arrangements made by them, such as entering into a contract on behalf of the company in breach of duty, may be declared void.
- If the director is an employee of the company, and the breach of duty involves some element of extreme behaviour, such as dishonesty, he can be summarily dismissed without compensation. In addition, shareholders can choose to take this action under the Companies Acts if directors choose not to.
- Actions giving rise to a breach of duty at common law often constitute specific statutory offences (particularly under the Companies Acts) involving criminal liability for the director, resulting in fines or imprisonment.
- In respect of potential or ongoing breaches of duty, it is open to a company to apply for an injunction, for example where customers of one company are being diverted to another which is owned by a director, and the director has brought the jurisdiction of the Disqualification Act into play.

The position of non-executive directors

Non-executive directors cannot necessarily claim a reduced level of duty or liability compared to executive directors. Again, it may be that there is some mitigation arising from their position, depending on the circumstances, but the comments of the Court in the *Equitable Life*[33] case emphasise that there is no general principle that a non-executive director should be treated any differently from his executive counterparts.

Protecting directors

The liability of a director for breach of duty may be the subject of an indemnity from the company and/or directors' and officers' insurance. Rules introduced in April 2005[34] extended the range of matters for which a director may be indemnified but, critically, a director cannot be covered for liability owed to the company itself. D & O insurance is, of course, commonplace (for listed companies it is expected under the Combined Code), but liability to the company is routinely excluded and, even where it is not, limitations apply.

Before the issue of personal liability rose up the corporate agenda, directors were often content not to have specific indemnities in place, but to rely on companies invoking a specific power to do so in their articles of association in the unlikely event this was necessary. However, given that indemnity provisions in articles of association are only commitments between the company and its members, it is possible that a director may not be able to invoke such an indemnity as and when he needs to. As a result, it is increasingly common to see stand-alone deeds of indemnity being put in place between companies and directors to give directors a right to indemnification.

The impact of the 2006 Act

The 2006 Act expressly confirms that the existing civil remedies for breach of directors' duties will continue to apply in respect of the codified duties. It is not clear how this will operate in practice in respect of those elements of the codified duties which are additional to or different from the existing common law duties. However, given the range and flexibility of the existing sanctions, it is suggested that greater difficulties will be met in assessing whether a director has breached the new codified duties than in assessing the nature of the sanctions which should be imposed if a breach is proved.

The new statutory basis for derivative claims has been the subject of much debate. While the principle of opening up a clearer route for shareholders to bring directors to account for their actions is generally applauded, concerns have been expressed in Parliament and, subsequently, by industry bodies, such

---

[33] [2003] EWHC 2263.
[34] Pursuant to the C(A,ICE) Act which amended the 1985 Act – see ss. 309A et seq.

as the Institute of Directors and the CBI, that the provisions of the 2006 Act will result in:

- derivative claims with low merits or malicious claims being brought to the detriment of the company and the shareholders as a whole;
- activist shareholders bringing derivative claims to achieve other purposes, such as to hamper takeovers or to pursue their own financial agenda.

Against this, it is argued that:

- under the 2006 Act, a claimant shareholder will be responsible for the costs of bringing an action, while any financial award resulting from a successful action will accrue to the company (this same situation applies to existing derivative claims at common law). This will operate to deter shareholders from bringing derivative claims unless they are merited;
- the Courts have a discretion to deny any derivative claim from proceeding and, in fact, the 2006 Act directs the Courts to refuse permission to bring a claim in certain circumstances (such as where the shareholder is considered to be acting in bad faith or a hypothetically impartial director would consider that continuing such a claim would not promote the success of the company).

It is likely that the new law will result in an increased number of claims being brought against directors. The overall impact may be to provide shareholders with improved access to the Courts in appropriate cases (and, in doing so, assist in the application of effective corporate governance), but there is a real danger that it may equally open the door to spurious claims that could not have been brought under the existing common law. The responsibility for what happens next lies with the Courts, and their decisions as to which cases are allowed to proceed and those which are refused will be keenly watched.

Adequacy of civil sanctions for breach of duty

It is generally accepted that a range of flexible and meaningful sanctions must be in place to deal adequately with the consequences of breaches of duty by directors. The question is whether the existing common law and the 2006 Act provide those sanctions.

Some would argue that the steady flow of actions against directors, many of them in respect of high-profile company failures, demonstrates that current sanctions are not sufficient to deter directors from engaging in bad governance or illegal practices. By contrast, others would argue that the increasing number of actions being taken against directors is not due to their being ignorant of, or complacent about, their duties, but is rather a consequence of the prevalent blame culture. And yet others might argue that the cases show a welcome increase in the policing of boardroom behaviour.

In recent years, some commentators have concluded that a greater emphasis on criminal rather than civil sanctions would improve compliance. Others have suggested the introduction of a business judgment rule to be applied by the Courts, similar to that which exists in the US, in assessing not only breach of duty but also the seriousness of that breach and therefore the severity of any sanction. Some have also proposed a codified statement of the sanctions available, similar to that contained in the 2006 Act in respect of directors' duties.

The 2006 Act does not take account of these suggestions – it specifically reaffirms the existing sanctions applicable under the common law. It is considered that, on balance, this is the correct approach. An analysis of the case law tends to support the view that the variety of sanctions available is adequate to compensate victims, punish guilty directors, act as a deterrent and generally foster compliance. In the current climate, it is clear that this area of the law plays an important, but not disproportionate, part in the Virtuous Circle.

The sanctions: shareholder and market pressure – power in the hands of the owners

Shareholders and their agents

In the Virtuous Circle, a further key segment is governed by shareholders or their agents through the form of codes and guidelines including, centrally, the Combined Code.

It is obvious that codes and guidelines are fundamentally different from law and regulation in both concept and effect. Nonetheless, it is an important distinction which has a profound effect on behaviour and approach. So, in the context of the Virtuous Circle and in contrasting the shareholder and market pressure segment with the law and regulation segment, the key question must be: do codes and guidelines work? Do they exert sufficient pressure on boards to guarantee sufficiently high standards of governance? Would it be more effective to have law or regulation instead?

It is suggested here that codes and guidelines do have a key role to play in the Virtuous Circle and, in some of the central areas of governance, are preferable to law and regulation. It is important to recognise that shareholders should have a central role to play in judging what is right for their company on governance issues. Ultimately, shareholders can impose sanctions on boards or individual directors if they wish to intervene because of concerns regarding their behaviour or decisions. Therefore, the argument in favour of codes and guidelines (and against law and regulation) in the central areas covered by the Combined Code is a powerful one.

The investment community in the UK, dominated as it is by insurance companies, pension funds and other institutional shareholders, has been at the

167

heart of the debate about corporate governance. They and their agents were prominent well before the 1992 Cadbury Report.[35]

Since 1992, it is clear that individual shareholders have become more active in upholding governance standards. As owners, it is also clear that they should claim a key role in ensuring that the companies in which they invest are governed to the standards which they consider to be appropriate and which ultimately help to support, in the widest sense, the efficiency and durability of capital markets.

The Virtuous Circle, as it now exists, also includes a number of agents for shareholders: representative bodies which, on behalf of their members, helped to contribute to the creation of the Combined Code and to a variety of best-practice guidelines. Those agents also help to police day-to-day compliance. The agents specifically mentioned in the Virtuous Circle include ABI, NAPF and IMA, which, together with the AIC, are the members of the Institutional Shareholders' Committee. That Committee has itself revised its statement regarding the responsibilities of institutional shareholders and their agents (see 'What sanctions apply under the codes and guidelines' below).

So, in this important segment of the Virtuous Circle, the presence of shareholders and their agents, bringing pressure on boards to comply with governance standards, is entirely appropriate.

Codes versus law and regulation

It is arguable that the issues covered, for instance, by the Combined Code should instead be covered by regulation in order to ensure compliance, as contrasted with the comply-or-explain principle of the Combined Code. Law and regulation would provide clear penalties for breaches by boards or individual directors and would thus underwrite compliance. So why not simply transfer all compliance issues within the Combined Code to law and regulation and ensure that companies comply?

The answer lies, in part, in the Cadbury Report, which laid the foundation for the Combined Code and provides authoritative support for the comply-or-explain approach.

> We believe that our approach, based on compliance with a voluntary code coupled with disclosure, will prove more effective than a statutory code. It is directed at establishing best practice, at encouraging pressure from shareholders to hasten its widespread adoption, and at allowing some flexibility in implementation. We recognise, however, that if companies do

---

[35] Sir Adrian Cadbury's Committee on the Financial Aspects of Corporate Governance (December 1992). Indeed, that 1992 Report acknowledges a number of 'relevant published statements' which include, for example, the Institutional Shareholders' Committee: 'The Role and Duties of Directors – A Statement of Best Practice' (April 1991) and PRONED: 'Code of Recommended Practice on Non-Executive Directors' (April 1987).

not back our recommendations, it is probable that legislation and external regulation will be sought to deal with some of the underlying problems which the report identifies. Statutory measures would impose a minimum standard and there would be a great risk of boards complying with the letter, rather than with the spirit, of their requirements.

The Combined Code itself is underpinned by the Listing Rules which, arguably, go some way towards regulation in that, ultimately, there are sanctions for non-compliance with the Listing Rules (see 'What sanctions apply under codes and guidelines' below). However, in real terms, the Combined Code (supported by the Listing Rules) upholds the approach, favoured by the Cadbury Committee, of a 'voluntary code coupled with disclosure'.

The comply-or-explain approach has the following advantages:

- (Crucially) flexibility enables the different circumstances of a broad range of companies to be accommodated, as long as the explanations for any non-compliance satisfy the shareholders.
- The focus is on shareholders and their agents to assess the explanations given by individual companies and respond if required. The Cadbury Committee took the view that it was appropriate for the issues covered by the Combined Code to be policed by shareholders rather than the regulators.
- The response of companies to a code is likely to be more constructive since there is a concern that companies will tend to 'comply with the letter, rather than with the spirit' of law or regulation.
- Arguably, the Combined Code imposes a lighter burden on companies than would be the case with law and regulation which, in a number of instances, would require audit trails of compliance, and indeed compliance would ultimately have to be an issue of relevance to external auditors.

Companies that do not comply with statutory or regulatory requirements face serious sanctions and, in addition, damage to their reputation through adverse press comment. So the reality is that boards will comply with legal or regulatory requirements to avoid such sanctions. The problem, however, is that because of the serious nature of those sanctions, legislation and regulation need to be precise, need to define the prescribed action or omission and normally operate on a one size fits all basis.

Over time, provisions may be moved from the Combined Code into law or regulation. The public outcry over excessive levels of remuneration ultimately led to the Remuneration Regulations. In addition, the effect of EU Directives and the process of harmonisation of company law across the EU will, eventually, create legislation on some issues currently covered by the Combined Code. However, the question arises: 'Is that progress?' Probably not. Take, for example, the European Commission's Directive on statutory audits of annual and consolidated accounts[36] (Audit Directive). Article 41 provides that each public interest entity (which includes UK listed companies) must have an audit committee and the Directive goes on to provide that: 'At least one member of the audit committee shall be independent and shall have competence in accounting and/or auditing.' Real concerns have been expressed about the consequences of Member States legislating to implement the provisions of this Directive. Among those concerns are issues about definition and the clear potential for loss of flexibility for companies owing to the fact that:

- A statutory definition of 'independence' would be required – effectively replacing (in the context of audit committees) the current Combined Code guideline on independence. That, in turn, will mean that boards may no longer be entitled to form a judgement abut the independence of a director, and shareholders would cease to be the arbiters of boards' decisions in that context.
- A statutory definition will also be required for 'competence in accounting and/or auditing'.

So the likely result will be less flexibility, with no ability for boards to present any alternative solution to shareholders, if a board considers that the regulation is not appropriate to its particular circumstances.

What sanctions apply under codes and guidelines?

As mentioned above, the Combined Code is underpinned by the Listing Rules. Even though it is not described as a disciplinary measure by the FSA, the ultimate sanction for non-compliance with any Listing Rule is, at least in theory, the FSA suspending or cancelling a company's listing. Much more relevant to the concept of enforcement of the Combined Code is shareholder power which, in various ways, can ensure compliance. In September 2005, the ISC revised the publication[37] in which it describes the circumstances where shareholders and/or agents might intervene and the actions which might be considered.

> Instances when institutional shareholders and/or agents may want to intervene include when they have concerns about:
>
> - the company's strategy;
> - the company's operational performance;
> - the company's acquisition/disposal strategy;
> - independent directors failing to hold executive management properly to account;
> - internal controls failing;

---

[36] Directive 2006/43/EC.

[37] 'The Responsibilities of Institutional Shareholders and Agents – Statement of Principles'.

- inadequate succession planning;
- an unjustifiable failure to comply with the Combined Code;
- inappropriate remuneration levels/inventive packages/severance packages; and
- the company's approach to corporate social responsibility.

If boards do not respond constructively when institutional shareholders and/or agents intervene, then institutional shareholders and/or agents will consider on a case-by-case basis whether to escalate their action, for example, by:

- holding additional meetings with management specifically to discuss concerns;
- expressing concern through the company's advisers;
- meeting with the Chairman, with senior independent director, or with all independent directors;
- intervening jointly with other institutions on particular issues;
- making a public statement in advance of the AGM or an EGM;
- submitting resolutions at shareholders' meetings; and
- requisitioning an EGM, possibly to change the board.

In addition, it is now best practice for companies to include vote-withheld boxes in proxy appointment forms. The revised Combined Code in 2006 included a new provision as follows:

> For each resolution, proxy appointment forms should provide shareholders with the option to direct their proxy to vote either for or against the resolution or to withhold their vote. The proxy form and any announcement of the results of a vote should make it clear that a 'vote withheld' is not a vote in law and will not be counted in the calculation of the proportion of the votes for and against the resolution.

In effect, a vote withheld is an indication of a shareholder's dissatisfaction on the issue and, in some cases, can be seen as a 'yellow card'.

The more extreme examples of the above sanctions are, of course, shareholders submitting resolutions at general meetings or requisitioning an extraordinary general meeting (EGM). English company law provides clear rights for shareholders in this context:

- shareholders can requisition a company (at the expense of the requisitionists) to give notice of a resolution to be moved at the next annual general meeting and to circulate a statement from the shareholders who make the requisition, for example, to consider an issue of non-compliance with a provision of the Combined Code or to seek to remove one or more members of the board;
- shareholders can requisition an EGM for similar purposes;

- a company may by ordinary resolution remove a director before the expiration of his period of office, notwithstanding anything in its articles of association or in any agreement between the company and the director concerned; this is a fundamental right of shareholders and, arguably, the best weapon they have.

Therefore, the combined effect of these provisions constitutes powerful sanctions for non-compliance with the Combined Code and other guidelines. They give shareholders the power to take action against the board or individual directors for any concerns or failures of the type referred to in the September 2005 statement from the ISC. This power has manifested itself in the following instances:

- the biggest revolt against a chief executive came in 2002, when abstentions and votes cast against John Ritblat of British Land plc totalled 31.5 per cent;
- the biggest protest vote against a chief executive was against James Murdoch, Chief Executive of BskyB, in 2003, when 17.29 per cent of votes were registered against him;
- the biggest revolt against an executive was the 36.9 per cent vote, including abstentions, against Brian Wallace, deputy Chief Executive of Ladbrokes.[38]

Proposals for reform

To address the concerns of those arguing that the existing sanctions are not sufficiently clear and accessible to ensure compliance with, for example, the Combined Code, it is worth considering adding further weapons to the armoury of shareholders in the more extreme situations.

One possibility would be to include, in company law, a requirement for boards to convene an EGM to address any complaint from a regulator about non-compliance with, for instance, the Part VI Rules; the purpose of such a meeting would be '*to consider whether any, and if so what, steps should be taken to deal with the situation*'.[39] Failure to convene a meeting could lead to directors being liable to fines.

Another possibility might be to extend the circumstances where individual directors might be disqualified, for example for a serious breach of the Part VI Rules. This might be more effective than a delisting and would, in one sense, provide a fairer result as it would target the perpetrator (the director or directors who are the culprits) as opposed to penalising shareholders.

Finally, as the arguments for good corporate governance are well established and the benefits that the Code has brought to Officially Listed companies are

---

[38] Source: *The Times*, 26 July 2006.

[39] This wording appears in section 142 1985 Act in relation to the duty of the directors to convene an EGM in the event of a serious loss of capital.

now widely accepted, serious consideration could be given to introducing a requirement for AIM companies to implement a similar code on a comply-or-explain basis; one which is tailored to companies listed on that market (and therefore along the lines of those published by the QCA and/or NAPF). Such a code should impose an obligation on AIM companies to focus on their own corporate governance regime.

The sanctions: good corporate citizenship – the power of public opinion

The power of public opinion is an effective, albeit smaller, part of the Virtuous Circle. It is constituted in general terms by the following factors.

Adverse press comment

While it is not possible to prove that adverse press coverage can bring pressure on boards or galvanise shareholders into action and intervention, the evidence is compelling. Over recent years, much of the UK press coverage on governance issues has focused on the remuneration of directors. For example:

- *'Pay at Vodafone: now we are talking telephone numbers'* (*Financial Times*, 21 July 2006) – Vodafone responds to pressure over controversial bonuses for directors by launching a special review of its remuneration policy;
- *'Four Berkeley directors to share £200m windfall'* (*The Daily Telegraph*, 19 March 2007) – concerns about a highly controversial management incentive scheme at housebuilder Berkeley Group were reopened after a near tripling in thirty months of the reward directors were on course to share under the unusual scheme.

In a paper entitled 'The corporate governance role of the media' by Alexander Dyck (Harvard Business School) and Luigi Zingales (University of Chicago), 'The role of the media in pressurising corporate managers and directors to behave in ways that are socially acceptable' is analysed and the authors comment as follows: 'The only definite conclusion we can draw at this point is that the media are important in shaping corporate policy and should not be ignored in any analysis of a country's corporate governance system.'

Peer pressure

It is even more difficult to prove that peer pressure should also be recognised as part of the Virtuous Circle. However, those who have experience of working with boards will recognise that, on occasions, peer pressure does work in this way. The pressure comes typically from non-executive directors who experience best practice as board members of other companies and then preach the gospel. If such a proposal is supported by several non-executive directors, it is difficult for a board to resist.

Also boards will frequently look carefully at what comparator companies are doing on various issues, particularly in the field of remuneration.

Corporate social responsibility

Companies and boards have generally seen wealth creation for shareholders as their principal objective. Over the years, legislation has widened that objective for the benefit of other stakeholders, including employees and creditors. In addition, the concept of corporate social responsibility (CSR) has emerged and, although this is not clearly defined from a legal point of view, companies are now reporting extensively on their CSR activities and agenda. Those CSR concepts are now undoubtedly part of the corporate governance landscape and, therefore, part of the Virtuous Circle; in fact, they are playing an ever increasing part in it. Redraw the Virtuous Circle in ten years' time and the size of this segment, reflecting its relative influence on board behaviour, is likely to have increased significantly, and will certainly have done so if the current response to institutional ethical investment policies and focus on the impact of corporate activity on the global environment continues. Again, what is noticeable here is the lack of traditional sanctions compelling behaviour. For this reason, the need for, and influence of, the sanctions brought in with the enhanced Business Review for listed companies is open to question, given the history of voluntary compliance.

Consequently, this segment identifies the main source of pressure on boards as the need to be good corporate citizens, and the conclusion must be that, even without legal sanctions, that pressure appears to be working.

Conclusion

Looking at the constituent elements of the Virtuous Circle and the drivers for boards to adopt appropriate governance standards, the balance of sanctions and the system of accountability underpinning corporate governance in the UK seems about right.

The two largest segments of the Virtuous Circle – law and regulation, and shareholder and market pressure – represent dynamics which produce a balanced and meaningful corporate governance regime and, at present, these are appropriately supplemented by the other elements of the Virtuous Circle, namely the Courts and common law, and public opinion demanding good corporate citizenship.

The boundaries between the two largest and most influential segments are also about right. Extremes of behaviour and the fundamental tenets of the corporate reporting regime are appropriately matched by clear legal principles and policed by strong criminal and civil sanctions. For the most part, the legislature has resisted the temptation to try to control through legislation boardroom behaviour which, to paraphrase from the Cadbury Report, would impose minimum standards allowing boards to comply with the letter and not the spirit of their requirements. This has allowed the middle ground in the Virtuous Circle to be populated by flexible codes of conduct which, on a day-to-day basis, allow shareholders (and key stakeholders) to be the arbiters of what does and does not constitute satisfactory compliance and behaviour.

However, this is not to say that the current system is perfect, that it could not be improved upon and, crucially, that there are not serious threats to it on the horizon.

There are potential problems associated with the implementation of the Audit Directive and, indeed, the 2006 Act appears to be paving the way for statutory provisions to replace Combined Code provisions by granting the FSA and the relevant Secretary of State a statutory power to produce corporate governance rules. It is this movement of voluntary codes into law and regulation that poses the greatest threat to the regime, as it moves us ever closer to the US model laid down by the 2002 Sarbanes-Oxley Act. This drift towards legislative measures has imposed on the US economy an estimated net cost of US$ 1.4 trillion[40] and has meant that, whereas in 2000 'nine out of 10 dollars raised by foreign companies through new stock offerings were done in New York . . . in 2005, the reverse was true: Nine out of 10 dollars were raised through new company listings in London or Luxembourg'.[41] The dangers of such a shift to legislation and regulation are very clear.

With the possible addition of the other sanctions proposed in the section 'Proposals for reform' (above), the comply-or-explain approach must surely be the way forward in relation to the mainstream areas of corporate governance. Clearly, to address those specific areas where excesses arise and where there are public interest concerns or a perceived need to protect wider stakeholders, the legislature may need to bring forward law or regulation. But the Combined Code has undoubtedly been a success in raising governance standards with a relatively light touch in those mainstream areas and 'if it ain't broke. . .'.

---

[40] American Enterprise Institute for Public Policy Research, 10 July 2006.

[41] Craig Karmin and Aaron Lucchetti, 'New York loses edge in snagging foreign listings', *Wall Street Journal*, 26 January 2006.

9

Regulatory trends and their impact on corporate governance

STILPON NESTOR

Introduction and overarching market trends

This chapter reviews recent regulatory developments in corporate governance, identifies emerging trends and offers thoughts as to the possible impact of these trends on the behaviour of market participants.[1] The second part of the chapter discusses key regulatory trends at EU level and their impact on the European corporate governance landscape. The third part turns to a discussion of US regulatory trends while the chapter closes with some brief concluding remarks. The analysis of EU and US trends is organised around the two most important governance principles: transparency and accountability of agents to principals.

Since the 1980s, privatisation and technological change have fuelled the development of equity markets around the world. In the context of these developments, institutional investors have become by far the dominant owners of securities in the largest equity markets in the world, as Figure 9.1 shows. There is a fundamental challenge for regulators from institutional dominance: in view of the changing ownership and control environment, they need to revisit regulatory assumptions about market failures and question some of the basic objectives of investor protection.

The US regulatory model for the financial markets, the 1930s blueprint for securities regulation worldwide, may be losing its relevance. The US model is predicated on a market dominated by small retail investors who cannot fend for themselves: insurmountable information asymmetries exacerbated by the high cost of collective action mean investors cannot effectively exercise voice. Their only power is to buy and sell securities. Hence, all they need is adequate, timely and reliable information, and a liquid market. All the rest is taken care of by professional managers who run the large, listed corporations.

As ownership of equity by institutional investors in US (and continental European) public markets has increased, these assumptions are no longer totally valid. The owners of a company are fewer and large enough to be able to shoulder the costs of being true owners. A Chairman of a large US company recently told me 'the critical mass of our shareholders is nowadays fifteen phone calls away'. Moreover, many institutions have limited exit opportunities. A large part of their

---

[1] The author would like to thank Cynthia Mike-Eze, analyst at Nestor Advisors, for background research for this chapter.

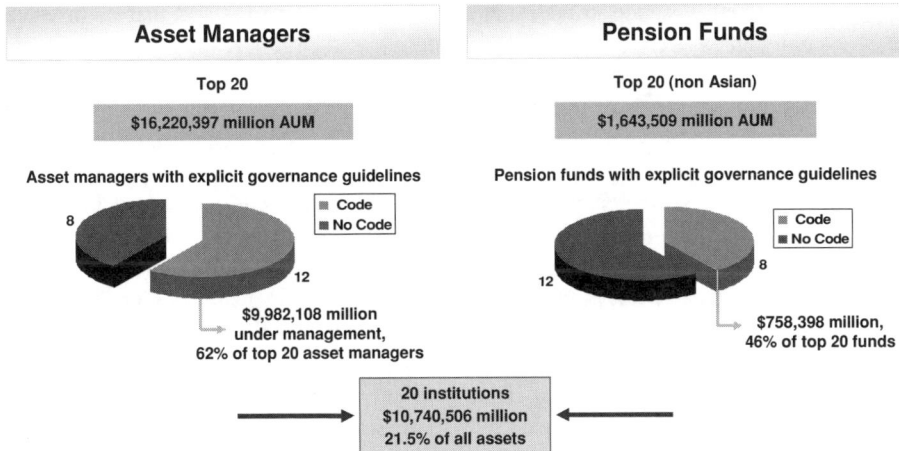

Asset Managers	Pension Funds
Top 20	**Top 20 (non Asian)**
$16,220,397 million AUM	$1,643,509 million AUM
Asset managers with explicit governance guidelines	Pension funds with explicit governance guidelines

8
12
$9,982,108 million under management, 62% of top 20 asset managers

12
8
$758,398 million, 46% of top 20 funds

Code
No Code

20 institutions
$10,740,506 million
21.5% of all assets

Source: Nestor Advisors Ltd, based on Pensions and Investments data

Figure 9.1 Corporate governance requirements of large institutional investors

holdings is indexed, meaning that they *have* to own certain stocks in order to maintain a risk profile that mirrors that of the market; or their positions on specific stocks are so large that they cannot significantly modify them without incurring substantial losses. A rebalancing between the availability of exit and accountability to shareholders might be the order of the day.

In addition to becoming an increasingly dominant force in their domestic equity markets, institutional investors are also becoming more international. Until recently, institutional portfolios were surprisingly local. The percentage of foreign equities in the portfolios of institutional investors is now considerable, having more than doubled over the last decade to more than 25 per cent in the UK and more than 15 per cent in the US. At the end of 2005, foreign investors owned 33 per cent of listed shares in European exchanges.[2]

But home bias is still there. In a 2005 report,[3] the IMF calculated that there is still a considerable divergence from optimum allocation between domestic and international holdings. From a continental European (or, for that matter, Asian) issuer perspective, this means that the invasion of foreign institutional barbarians has barely started.

Whether because of regulatory pressures, as in the US, or because of the discovery of value in governance, institutional investors are adopting a much

[2] Figure compiled by Nestor Advisors, based on FESE 2005 and OECD data from twenty-one markets representing 97 per cent of the capitalisation of European exchanges at the end of 2005.
[3] International Monetary Fund, Global Financial Stability Report – Market Developments and Issues, September 2005, Chapter III.

177

more active stance in addressing their own governance and that of investee companies. According to a representative of a large UK institutional investor organisation, institutions 'must be equipped to manage conflicts of interest, set high standards of transparency, command the right levels of expertise and resource and have a balanced organisational structure, which permits them to carry out their obligations'.[4]

As regards the governance of investee companies, Figure 9.1 suggests that more than two-thirds of the world's largest asset managers and 40 per cent of the largest pension funds, all in all institutions representing more than 20 per cent of global institutional assets, have adopted governance guidelines. These guidelines require institutions to vote, whenever that is not impossible or too risky, and, in voting, to follow certain principles on the way investee companies should be governed. To implement these guidelines, some institutions have built teams that are becoming increasingly vocal in challenging corporate management.

And, of course, there are the 'locusts', as private equity and activist hedge funds have been called by German politicians. The shareowning power of these institutions has grown immensely since the mid-1990s, largely due to growing asset allocations by large institutions. Their emergence has exacerbated the 'great reversal' of ownership dispersion in public corporations, which had been the predominant trend for much of the twentieth century. Hedge funds are becoming bolder by the day in pushing their agenda onto listed companies. They sit on boards, form alliances with other shareholders and pressure companies to change their capital structure and strategy. Hedge funds and private equity seem to have an overall beneficial effect on market efficiency and capital allocation. Their interventions often align management incentives with shareholder interests on the governance side and address inefficiencies in the capital structure, such as under-leverage, a legacy of a bygone era of high inflation and interest rates.[5] What is probably the most objectionable issue with these market players is their secretive ways. This is especially so given the main reason for their prosperity is the amount and quality of public information about companies available as a result of regulatory reform. Transparency of ownership and control by such sophisticated buy-side operations is moving high on the regulatory agenda, as we shall discuss in the next part of this chapter.[6]

---

[4] Peter Montagnon, Chairman of the ICGN's Shareholder Responsibility Committee and Investment Affairs Director of the Association of British Insurers, in *ICGN News* Issue 4, June 2006, p. 1.

[5] See *The Role of Private Pools of Capital in Corporate Governance: Summary and Main Findings about the Role of Private Equity and 'Activist' Hedge Funds*, OECD, May 2007, p. 2.

[6] For a detailed discussion of what is an appropriate regulatory response to hedge funds see Henry Hu and Bernard Black, 'Hedge Funds, Insiders, and the Decoupling of Economic and Voting Ownership: Empty Voting and Hidden (Morphable) Ownership'. Available at Social Science Research Network electronic library, 2007 (http://papers.ssrn.com/abstract=874098).

Regulatory trends in the EU

While Member States have regulated governance in the form of company laws since the nineteenth century, Brussels' entry into the corporate governance arena – long before it was called that – dates back to the adoption of the first company law directive in the late 1960s. However, the first attempt to tackle governance in a comprehensive way came as a response to the recommendations of the Winter Report from a high-level experts group that advised on the future of company law initiatives at EU level. The EU Commission's 'Action Plan on Modernising Company Law and Enhancing Corporate Governance' (ECAP) was adopted in May 2003.[7] ECAP is a crucial element of the European Council's Lisbon Agenda which aims to make Europe the most competitive market in the world by 2010. In addition to measures included in ECAP, some legislative initiatives relevant to corporate governance have been adopted under the Financial Services Action Plan, another important component of the Lisbon Agenda.

Most commentators have judged ECAP to be a success so far, primarily due to its market-driven approach. The EU Commission chose not to prescribe Europe-wide norms aimed at a top-down harmonisation of corporate governance arrangements in markets with distinct, and often long-held, governance traditions and cultures. Correctly diagnosing the changing corporate ownership and control environment discussed in the first part of this chapter, and recognising the difficulty of making top-down changes to Member States' legislative arrangements, the Commission did not attempt to regulate core corporate governance considerations such as the composition, structure, functioning and authority of corporate boards, or the oversight, evaluation and remuneration of executives. Not only did the Commission abstain from attempting harmonisation of core corporate governance issues, it also urged Member States to adopt flexible approaches that allow companies and their shareholders choice in selecting the type of governance that is most appropriate to their individual circumstances.

The Commission has chosen legislative action whenever it was felt that it was needed to facilitate the emergence of market solutions. EC Commissioner McCreevy summed up the Commission's direct regulatory scope: 'our action has been based on two key objectives: (1) bringing more transparency in the way companies operate; and (2) empowering shareholders'.[8] In a further step that favours bottom-up convergence, most legislative action undertaken by the Commission in the context of ECAP constitutes minimum harmonisation

[7] Commission Communication COM(2003)284 final.

[8] Charlie McCreevy, European Commissioner for Internal Market and Services, Speech on 'The European CG Action Plan: Setting Priorities', June 2005 http://europa.eu/rapid/pressReleasesAction.do? reference =SPEECH/05/392&format= HTML&aged=0&language= EN&guiLanguage=en.

through directives that set a minimum standard for all Member States, while allowing for customisation to address local idiosyncrasies.

Nevertheless, the amount of EU legislation related to company law, governance and equity market transparency has been quite impressive: more than twelve directives and implementing directives, two recommendations and one regulation have entered the books between 2003 and 2007. As noted in the Commission's report on the results of the 2006 consultation on the future of the ECAP, 'a number of respondents stated their regulatory fatigue and called for a stabilisation period'.[9] In many instances, the Commission has made it clear that it will heed these calls, take it easy on primary legislation and allow time for bedding-in the changes.

Transparency

Turning to the first of the EC's regulatory objectives in the corporate governance area, the most important development is the emergence of harmonised standards of transparency and disclosure of governance, ownership and control arrangements. This is in addition to earlier harmonisation measures in financial reporting, where IFRS compliance has been implemented since 2005. At the end of the implementation period, investors should benefit from a uniform template for the supply of non-financial information across the EU. This may facilitate the growth of institutional portfolio internationalisation discussed in the first part of this chapter, putting issuers on a competitive footing as they seek capital across borders.

Comply-or-explain

The first, and most important, element of governance transparency has been the positioning of national, comply-or-explain voluntary codes at the heart of European corporate governance policy. The Commission accepted that 'the adoption of detailed binding rules is not necessarily the most desirable and efficient way of achieving the objectives pursued'.[10] It has adopted the UK approach of letting markets regulate governance of listed companies. Investors and other stakeholders benchmark governance arrangements in individual companies against a national codified body of best-practice principles and provisions. These Codes are typically the result of negotiation between market participants, blessed by the regulator. Thus, a key recent regulatory trend has been the proliferation of national corporate governance codes in Member States that are implemented on a comply-or-explain basis. As of July 2007, there is only one Member State,

---

[9] European Commission, Report on consultations for future priorities for Action Plan, July 2006, p. 7. http://ec.europa.eu/internal_market/company/docs/consultation/final_report_en.pdf.

[10] Commission Recommendation 2005/162/EC on the role of non-executive directors or supervisory directors of listed companies and of the committees of the (supervisory) board.

Greece, that does not have a comply-or-explain Code. A recent review[11] of these Codes found that their substantive, normative content is broadly similar across EU borders and follows the lines enshrined in the OECD Principles,[12] which is considered the global benchmark for the development of national policies. This confirms the Commission's initial view that national Codes should act as bottom-up drivers of convergence.

While the Commission decided not to regulate core governance issues that go beyond transparency and shareholder empowerment, it did issue two non-binding Recommendations whose primary purpose is to provide guidance to drafters of national codes. The first EC Recommendation addresses the role of non-executive directors and that of board committees in ways that will seem very familiar to any company that implements the UK Combined Code. Commission officials have made it clear on a number of occasions that, should the Recommendation not produce greater voluntary convergence, they might consider direct regulatory action.

The second Recommendation addresses the issue of director remuneration and lays down basic principles on accountability and transparency in setting pay. In a nutshell, shareholders should be fully informed about the executive remuneration policies of issuers and the remuneration of individual directors, and be given an opportunity to express their views at the annual general meeting; they should also have the right to approve share-based incentive schemes.

Reportedly, the EU remuneration Recommendation strongly influenced the adoption of German legislation in 2005 mandating the detailed disclosure of individual executive pay packages. It was felt that such legislation was needed because of the ineffectiveness of the relevant provisions in the German Code.

Annual disclosures

In order to underpin and consolidate the role of national codes in governance transparency and convergence, the EU has adopted amendments to the fourth and seventh company law directives (the 'amendments'). The amendments provide for a set of annual disclosures pertaining to the governance, ownership and control arrangements of the company.[13] All companies incorporated in EU Member States, and whose securities are traded on a regulated market in the EU, must include a specific corporate governance statement in their annual reports. The statement must be included as a separate part of the annual report (or as a separate report) and must contain at least the following information:

---

[11] Holly J. Gregory, *International Comparison of Selected Corporate Governance Guidelines and Codes of Best Practice*, Weil, Gotshal & Manges, July 2005.

[12] See OECD, Principles of Corporate Governance, available at www.oecd.org.

[13] EU Directive 2006/46/EC.

- a reference to the national corporate governance code applied by the company, and an explanation as to whether and to what extent the company complies with that corporate governance code; if the company does not apply a code, it should explain its corporate governance in the report;
- a description of the company's internal control and risk management systems;
- the information required by Article 10 of the Directive on Takeover Bids (see below);
- the operation of the shareholder meeting and its key powers, and a description of shareholders' rights and how they can be exercised;
- the composition and operation of the board and its committees;
- to the extent a company departs from the national corporate governance code, the company must explain from which parts of the code it departs and its reasons for doing so.

Article 10 of the Takeover Bids Directive, adopted in 2004, requires that the annual reports of companies should include information regarding:

- the structure of their capital and any restrictions on the transfer of securities;
- significant direct and indirect shareholdings;
- the system of control of any employee share scheme where the control rights are not exercised directly by the employees and restrictions on voting rights;
- the rules governing the appointment and replacement of board members and the amendment of the articles of association;
- the powers of board members, and in particular the power to issue or buy back shares;
- any significant agreements to which the company is a party and which take effect, alter or terminate upon a change of control of the company following a takeover bid;
- any agreements between the company and its board members or employees providing for compensation if they resign or are made redundant without valid reason or if their employment ceases because of a takeover bid.

Moreover, according to the amended eight company law directive, adopted in 2006, the audit committee (or, under certain circumstances, other equivalent bodies or the board as a whole) is obliged 'to monitor the effectiveness of the company's internal control, internal audit where applicable, and risk management systems'.[14] The audit committee's monitoring responsibility extends to the whole of the internal control and risk management system, a remit that mirrors the UK Turnbull guidance.

---

[14] EU Directive 2006/43/EC.

In addition to the general requirement to describe internal control and risk management systems, the amendments also require the management and supervisory bodies of listed companies to include a description of the group's internal control and risk management systems in relation to the process for preparing consolidated accounts. This requirement should be read in conjunction with the provision which stipulates the collective responsibility of the board (or supervisory board) for ensuring the integrity of the annual report and accounts.[15] On the one hand, the board's collective responsibility for financial reporting contrasts sharply with the US approach, which places this responsibility squarely on the shoulders of management (the Chief Executive and the Chief Financial Officer). On the other hand, the EU stops short of requiring certification and auditor attestation of the effectiveness of internal control over financial reporting. The high-level responsibility of the board is seen as a guarantee that protects investors while allowing companies to tailor their control system to their special needs and their capacity to absorb control-related costs.

Given the US regulatory paradigm, there is a real risk that Member States, in transposing minimum harmonisation directives, might goldplate them by adding requirements which create onerous and costly obligations for boards and external auditors to certify and provide assurance on the adequacy of financial internal control. With this in mind, the European Corporate Governance Forum, a body set up to advise the Commission on governance issues, issued a statement which underlines that 'the general purpose of risk management and internal control is to manage the risks associated with the successful conduct of business, not to eliminate them'. The Forum 'considers that there is no need to introduce a legal obligation for boards to certify the effectiveness of internal controls at EU level' and 'urges Member States to take account of these points when implementing in national law the associated requirements of the new directives'.[16]

Interim and ad hoc disclosures

In addition to annual reporting on governance issues, EU issuers will have to report, on an interim and ad hoc timely basis, important governance-related information. These new reporting obligations are found in the Transparency Directive which was adopted in December 2004 as part of the Financial Services Action Plan.[17] First and foremost, the Directive requires issuers to file, in addition to their annual report and accounts, non-audited half-yearly results. Along with the financials, the Directive requires half-yearly interim management statements which:

---

[15] COM (2004)725 final, amendments to Directive 83/349/EEC article 36a, Section 3A.

[16] European Corporate Governance Forum, Annual Report 2006, February 2007, p. 10, http://ec.europa.eu/internal_market/company/docs/ecgforum/ecgf-annual-report-2006_en.pdf.

[17] EU Directive 2004/109/EC.

183

- explain material events and transactions that have taken place during the relevant period and their impact on the financial position of the issuer's group;
- generally describe the financial position and performance of the issuer and its group during the relevant period.

As regards control transactions, shareholders should inform issuers within four days at the latest of the acquisition or disposal of voting control above certain thresholds starting at 5 per cent of relevant voting rights. The Directive requires an issuer to disclose publicly the information contained in the notification given by the shareholder, no later than three days after receiving the notification.

Hedge fund and stock lending

As noted above, hedge funds play an increasing role in corporate control challenges. Some companies have voiced fears that these 'short-termist speculators' might hijack corporate strategy and control and that they might be prepared to sacrifice long-term shareholder value for short-term gains by, for example, forcing the company to distribute its cash reserves, or incur excessive leverage, or sell important assets.

The claim that hedge funds are becoming the scourge of issuers is somewhat overstated. A 2007 study by the OECD concluded that activist hedge funds and private equity firms could help strengthen corporate governance practices by increasing the number of investors that have the incentive to make active and informed use of their shareholder rights.[18] Despite the publicity around activist hedge funds, they remain a small part of the capital market: there are only some 120 funds (managing around US$ 50 billion (excluding leverage)) that pursue investment strategies explicitly aimed at influencing publicly held company behaviour and organisation.[19]

Activist hedge funds seek to influence corporate behaviour without acquiring control. They often focus on the company's operational strategies and its use of capital. Their targets are mostly companies that lack a credible long-term strategy or maintain large cash reserves without being able to communicate a credible investment strategy. Hedge funds seem to have a 60–75 per cent success rate in preventing mergers or in supporting takeovers, in changing Chief Executives and board composition, and in altering the capital structure of a company through share buybacks.

Notwithstanding their overall beneficial role, there are two concerns with hedge funds that seem to be justified: the first one regards accountability. Companies need to know who are their important shareholders, and whether they are there for the long term or just a few weeks. Companies should be given the

---

[18] See OECD, The Role of Private Pools of Capital in Corporate Governance: Summary and Main Findings about the Role of Private Equity and 'Activist' Hedge Funds, May 2007, p. 2.

[19] By way of comparison, the global mutual funds industry alone has US$ 18 trillion under management. See OECD, p. 2.

possibility to engage with them. In this respect, the regulatory framework might not be capturing the vesting of significant control rights (de facto or de jure) to stock borrowers in some stock-lending situations. Stock-lending transactions are typically structured in two ways: either as outright sales of stock with a put option on the seller; or as contracts for difference (CFDs), which do not require any transfer but stipulate a certain payment to the borrower. At first glance, the former method would result in the full vesting of control rights to the borrower, who would then presumably be liable to report the crossing of any important regulatory control threshold as set in company law or securities regulation. In the case of CFDs, no transfer of control would normally occur. However, explicit or implicit side arrangements as regards control rights (from an outright proxy to an informal agreement as to how the shares should be voted by the lender) can be made. Any such arrangement that crosses relevant thresholds should, in principle, be captured by disclosure regulation and treated no differently from any other type of change in control. The broad language of the Transparency Directive on this point seems to cover these instances which should thus be subject to timely notification. However, the transposition of these provisions by EU Member States has not yet been tested in the courts. As regards the US,[20] the regulatory framework might be too fragmented to produce comprehensive, timely disclosure of hedge fund positions.

The second concern arises on the investor side, when institutions (usually their back offices) or, even worse, custodians without their client's express authorisation, lend shares with their votes attached to third parties during general meeting periods. A recently issued ICGN code of stock-lending best practice establishes three fundamental principles: transparency of stock-lending practices, especially towards the beneficiaries of the institution's investments; consistency, meaning that 'a clear set of policies which indicates with as little ambiguity as possible when shares shall be lent and when they shall be withheld from lending or recalled is necessary in order to ensure that similar situations are handled in the same way'; and responsibility, meaning that 'responsible shareholders have a duty to see that the votes associated with their shareholdings are not cast in a manner contrary to their stated policies and economic interests'.[21] Many institutions will be looking at the tension between the back office's legitimate objective to earn some extra cash from their stock inventory, and the overall objective to create long-term value and respond to stewardship imperatives. If institutions do not manage to address these issues effectively, it is likely that regulators will take up the baton and impose solutions that limit contractual freedom to a greater extent than the market would like to see.

---

[20] As per Hu and Black, see above note 5.

[21] The International Corporate Governance Network is an investor organisation, grouping some of the world's largest institutional investors, whose members manage collectively more than US$ 10 trillion worth of assets globally. The code can be found at www.icgn.org.

Accountability

The second objective of EU action, according to Commissioner McCreevy, is to empower shareholders. Indeed, a high level of transparency is of little use if shareholders cannot take action to address the incompetence of the directors or straightforward expropriation by unscrupulous managers and/or controlling shareholders.

Here too there are some important emerging regulatory trends. Whereas, in the area of transparency, the European Commission has succeeded in setting the stage for the emergence of a single disclosure system for all European issuers, the jury is still out when it comes to the empowerment of owners to hold companies accountable across EU borders.

Shareholder rights and participation

The key legislative measure in this area is the Commission's directive on shareholder rights.[22] The directive has been hailed by most market participants as a long-needed levelling of the playing field between companies and shareowners. According to the directive's preamble, 'Significant proportions of shares in listed companies are held by shareholders who do not reside in the Member State in which the company is registered. Non-resident shareholders should be able to exercise their rights in relation to the general meeting as easily as shareholders who reside in the Member State in which the company is registered.' The directive facilitates shareholder access and empowerment in the following ways:

- A record date will determine the eligibility of investors to participate in the general meeting, as opposed to current requirements in several EU markets for the blocking of shares, sometimes for several days before the annual general meeting. Blocking has been advanced by many institutional investors as a reason for not voting, as it restricts their ability to move fast when unexpected risks arise.
- Companies will need to publish the AGM agenda well in advance of the meeting, so that it can be transmitted through the custodian chain to the beneficial owners of shares. Most importantly, relevant background information on the decisions shareholders will be asked to make must also be published at the same time as the agenda.
- Member States' laws must not prohibit or create obstacles to the use of electronic shareholder voting. Furthermore, Member States must not overcomplicate the assignment of proxies and thus create obstacles in shareholder participation.

---

[22] See Provisional text of the Directive on the exercise of certain rights of shareholders in listed companies, June 2007, available at http://ec.europa.eu/internal_market/company/docs/shareholders/dir/draft_dir_en.pdf.

- Shareholders will be allowed to ask questions before the AGM.
- Shareholders will have an opportunity to put items on the agenda of the general meeting.

The adoption of the Shareholder Rights Directive should increase the level of participation and engagement of institutional investors in the affairs of European companies. Hitherto, many large institutions have shied away from voting given high share-blocking risks, the disproportionate cost of voting, and the paucity of AGM-related information. These obstacles will be considered later. Facilitation of shareholder engagement should focus boards on addressing investor concerns and raise their shareholder value consciousness. Companies should also start to feel less concerned over the possibility of certain small minorities, hedge funds or other short-termist investors, hijacking shareholder voice to the detriment of long-term shareholder value.

The market for corporate control

From Vodafone's acquisition of Mannesmann in 2000 to the saga of E.ON's bid for Spanish Edensa in 2006, cross-border consolidation has been one of the thorniest areas of EU economic integration. It should come as no surprise that negotiations for the adoption of the EU 2004 Directive on Takeover Bids has been by far the most politically charged of all corporate governance related measures. The Directive was meant to be a legislative lever to limit entrenchment of national elites in inefficiently controlling economic resources by enabling a truly market-driven allocation of these resources through the emergence of an efficient pan-European market for corporate control. The adoption of the Directive came after twenty years of discussions and the last-minute thwarting of a previous draft by a rebellious European Parliament in 2001. The issue over which the earlier draft fell was the protection of large German companies from mostly foreign predators. For over three decades, these large corporates had served masters other than their shareholders. By law employee interests were (and still are) considered equal to those of shareholders, and worker representatives fill half of the seats on supervisory boards of companies. Employee co-determination combined with a vast network of cross-shareholdings had managed effectively to shield managers from serious shareholder scrutiny for the better part of the twentieth century. No surprise then that German companies had become laggards in generating shareholder wealth. This resulted in their undervaluation, which made them attractive to various bidders including private equity and hedge funds. Ironically, one of the reasons that German companies became fair game was an earlier round of domestic company law reform aimed at enhancing shareholder power by outlawing most anti-takeover defences (most importantly board-driven poison pills).

Being the outcome of this twenty-year policy wrangle, the Takeover Bids Directive is unlikely to bring about the changes of momentum sought by the

187

Commission. Moreover, some of the regulatory solutions it has espoused may prove to be counterproductive.

There are, certainly, some positive aspects to the Directive. It sets a minimum level of transparency requirements regarding ownership structure and control arrangements (discussed above). It requires timely and orderly provision of information to the market in the form of an offer document, and it establishes squeeze-out and sell-out rights for small stranded minorities after a takeover battle. The Directive also spells out the principle of a mandatory bid to all holders of securities when control is sought – although it does leave a lot of leeway to Member States in shaping mandatory bid thresholds, thus providing the potential for regulatory arbitrage and divergence rather than convergence of regulatory regimes. For example, an Italian shareholder holding 40 per cent of shares may be able to sell for a substantial control premium without extending benefits to free float shareholders, while bidders of UK companies will need to launch expensive bids for 100 per cent of the equity once they acquire more than 29.9 per cent of voting securities.

The most sensitive issue was the regulation of anti-takeover defences. The approach of the Directive is three-pronged: limiting the power of the board to raise obstacles by calling for shareholder approval of any major defence move; a temporary non-applicability of special voting rights or voting limits when such decisions are taken – so that minority shareholders with multiple voting rights cannot impose their will on the majority holding one vote per share; and the so-called breakthrough clause allowing bidders who have acquired more than 75 per cent of outstanding voting stock to adopt amendments to the articles of association during the first post-bid general meeting that remove multiple voting shares or other control arrangements. This solution was advocated by the Winter Report and effectively addresses two difficult policy tradeoffs:

- a fair and effective balance between the often conflicting objectives of accountability to outside investors and the existence of strong, responsible owners;
- a balance between the need to protect existing, long-standing contractual arrangements (such as multiple voting rights) and the public policy imperative of making the European takeover market more efficient and integrated.

The final compromise made the above approach optional for Member States by giving countries the choice to allow individual companies to opt out of the regime. Moreover, even when companies are subject to the regime, the 'reciprocity exception' allows them to opt out when they are the target of a bidder who is not subject to the same regime. This optional approach is counterproductive first, because of its complicated and unpredictable nature. It is difficult, for example, to predict the defensive options available to a target company, as these depend on whether potential bidders are themselves subject to the Directive's regime. It is also unclear what will happen in a three- or four-way contested bid. Investors will find it hard to price the availability of takeover exits into the share price. In addition to the lack of transparency, the Directive may actually be setting the clock back in terms of company law in some countries. A 2007 European Commission report on the implementation of the Directive confirms our view of the Directive being rather counterproductive. According to the Report, two Member States, Cyprus and Spain, which had board neutrality (i.e. the board was not able to adopt anti-takeover measures without shareholder approval) in place by the time of the publication of the report, have decided to implement the Directive by introducing reciprocity. Italy may also decide to do the same. As regards the breakthrough rule, the vast majority of Member States have not imposed (or are unlikely to impose) this rule, but have made it optional for companies. Just 1 per cent of listed companies in the EU will apply this rule on a mandatory basis since only the Baltic States have imposed the requirement in full. In contrast, Hungary had a partial breakthrough rule before transposition, which has been eliminated.[23]

One-share-one-vote

The unsatisfactory regime of the 2004 Takeover Bids Directive suggests that the EU corporate control market will continue to be marked by regulatory divergence. Nevertheless, consolidation is continuing to occur. The significant increase in the level of transparency, combined with the expected increase in shareholder engagement by Anglo-American institutional shareholders in European cross-border situations, should limit the damage from regulatory back-stepping on poison pills.

But poison pills are only part of the anti-takeover arsenal. In many European large companies there are important asymmetries between pecuniary rights related to shares (cash flow rights) and control, most importantly voting rights attached to shares. A 2007 study on the proportionality principle in the EU ('Proportionality Principle study') commissioned by the European Commission found that Control Enhancing Mechanisms (CEMs), enabling asymmetries between cash flow rights and voting rights, are widely available in Europe: 44 per cent of the 464 European companies considered in the study have CEMs; this includes a majority of large caps (52 per cent of the companies analysed) and one quarter of recently listed companies.[24]

In principle, markets welcome flexibility in shaping rights along the risk–return curve. For example, most company laws uncontroversially allow voting rights to be forfeited in return for privileged status in cash distributions, as

---

[23] European Commission, Report on the Implementation of the Directive on Takeover Bids, February 2007, pp. 6 and 7.

[24] See ISS, Shearman & Sterling & ICGN, 'Report on the Proportionality Principle in the European Union', May 2007, p. 9. The study covers sixteen Member States (Belgium, Denmark, Estonia, France, Finland, Germany, Greece, Hungary, Ireland, Italy, Luxemburg, The Netherlands, Poland, Spain, Sweden and the United Kingdom) and three other jurisdictions (Australia, Japan and the United States).

is the case with most classes of preferred stock. Investors, however, recoil at arrangements that undermine one-share-one-vote where the only purpose is to protect and entrench management, even if such arrangements are described as protecting the long-term stability of the company. Voting rights ceilings are a good example of such an arrangement. The EU study found that voting rights ceilings, along with priority shares, golden shares and multiple voting rights, are among the CEMs that are most negatively perceived by investors. According to the study, voting rights ceilings 'hinder the emergence of large shareholders, thereby making takeovers virtually impossible. At the same time, they fragment power and impede effective monitoring. That is, they simultaneously undermine the two primary mechanisms for disciplining managers: outside monitoring and control contestability.'[25]

What should EU public policy have to say about the most prevalent of asymmetries, that of multiple voting rights? In Sweden, where these rights are most popular among large listed issuers, block holders typically hold more than 50 per cent of control rights while being exposed to between 12 and 20 per cent of the equity risk. That is because the risk–return characteristics of the multiple voting class of securities are identical to those of the single vote class. According to their proponents, multiple voting rights allow companies to have their cake and eat it: strong, engaged owners with the power to act as true principals in overseeing and remunerating management, on the one hand; and a wide equity base and capital market access providing companies with growth funding, on the other hand. Conceptually, however, this arrangement is suspect because it makes little economic sense for the controlling owners. Like private equity investors, they put in the effort and underwrite the cost of long-term active engagement in the governance of the company. But unlike them, they agree to share disproportionately the resulting benefit with other shareholders. As the theory goes, rational economic actors would have to compensate for this free rider loss by appropriating private benefits of control. These may range from company perks to much more serious appropriation of corporate opportunities and, *in extremis*, to the 'tunnelling' of assets and cash flows. The latter is often the case in emerging market companies where large cash flow to control rights asymmetries exist in the context of a weak legal and institutional environment. Ultimately, the question is whether, and to what extent, in an environment where the rule of law is highly developed, the risk of private benefits outweighs the public benefits of better managerial monitoring combined with broader capital market access.

In an *FT* op-ed, two prominent investor representatives support the idea that the EU should adopt rules imposing one-share-one-vote on listed companies, albeit recognising that this might, in the short term, be politically unfeasible. In their words, 'distortions of the proportionality between voting rights and share

---

[25] See 'Report on the Proportionality Principle in the European Union', May 2007, p. 16.

capital should not be part of the solution'.[26] And yet, the world's deepest and most liquid capital markets have no rules outlawing such distortions, as testified by the 2005 listing of Google with its two classes of voting shares, allowing the two founders a free hand in most strategic decisions. It is also interesting to note that the UK has never used regulation against multiple voting shares as a tool of shareholder empowerment. One-share-one-vote became the overriding (but not universal) standard in the London market as a result of investor pressure. Because of the higher cost of capital for companies that do not espouse the principle, an issuer now needs a very good reason to maintain control structures that do not conform to the standard.

The EU Commission's 2007 study on one-share-one-vote confirmed the poor case for any legislative action in this area. Commissioner McCreevy has backtracked from his earlier position in favour of a recommendation promoting one-share-one-vote, as even a set of soft law principles might prove to be hard to agree on. What might prove more effective, and less costly in political capital, is to wait for the new transparency and shareholder rights regime for EU issuers to be fully implemented, and give the market another chance to develop its own ways to value asymmetric control arrangements.

Shareholder communications

One area which straddles both objectives of the Commission's agenda for transparency and empowerment is that of communications between shareholders and the company, and communications among shareholders themselves with respect to a particular company. Both are essential for active shareholder engagement and for a board to understand the views and wishes of its shareholders before crises break out.

Communications between shareholders and the board became a central issue in the highly contested, albeit unsuccessful, cross-border bid by Deutsche Börse (DB) to acquire the London Stock Exchange (LSE).[27] When such a strategic move is anticipated, the clear agreement of the non-executive directors is important in winning the support of investors. Indeed, the UK Combined Code explicitly stipulates that, while the Chief Executive and Chief Financial Officer should be the main parties regularly talking to shareholders, the board as a whole bears responsibility for maintaining a good dialogue. The Combined Code also recommends that the Chairman and senior independent director should regularly meet with large shareholders, update them on the situation and gauge their feelings. In contrast, the DB supervisory board never took a proactive stance with investors. Rolf Breuer, its Chairman, started taking an active part in discussions with investors only a few days before the deal died. His intervention

---

[26] Peter Montagnon and Roderick Munsters, 'One share, one vote is the way to a fairer market', *Financial Times*, August 2006.

[27] A more extensive discussion of these issues can be found in the article by Stilpon Nestor, 'How board governance cost Deutsche Börse its deal', *International Financial Law Review*, 13, 2 (March 2005), pp. 137–55.

came too late to reverse the ill-feeling created between DB and its investors. It is worth noting that Rolf Breuer's absence from the dialogue was not an exception to the German practice, nor was it contrary to the German code of corporate governance (Cromme Code), which does not have provisions equivalent to those of the UK Combined Code. In Germany it is the Chief Executive (the 'spokesman of the Vorstandt') not the Chairman of the Supervisory Board who talks to investors. This seems an aberration, given the fact that it is the supervisory board alone that is directly accountable to shareholders, according to German corporate law.

A key task of the non-executive Chairman should be to build and maintain strong relationships with the company's key investors. Part of his role is to present to the board investor concerns independently of management. In the case of Deutsche Börse, it was the Chief Executive who reported to the Supervisory Board on these matters. Yet, the Chief Executive was the person most committed to pursuing the LSE's takeover. Continental European boards are at the very beginning of a steep learning curve in their communications policy towards investors. While there is no regulatory solution to this problem, many continental European boards will need to review and redefine their role, duties and limits in communicating with investors, especially as the latter step up their engagement activities, whether friendly or hostile.

As regards communications among shareholders, it is becoming apparent from recent shareholder engagement actions (such as the DB/LSE bid) that there is a risk of consultations between investors regarding the corporate governance of a specific company being viewed as a concert party practice by securities regulators. If found to be in concert, investors might be asked to place a bid for the company. Such a prospect would obviously deter them from engaging in any such dialogue, even in the face of the most flagrant managerial incompetence or expropriation of shareholder wealth. Clarity and predictability on this issue are essential if investors are to meet their stewardship obligations. As long as the objective is not to take control of the company, communications among shareholders should be allowed, and not just on the issue of director elections. Dialogue between shareholders enhances the capacity of markets to arrive at efficient solutions that are good for companies. It also helps to avoid public confrontation between companies and major shareholders. In the context of the 2006 consultation on ECAP, the ICGN proposed that the Commission take action to clarify and, if needed, limit concert party action rules in Member States, in a way that promotes shareowner empowerment and legal certainty.[28]

Trends in the US

While the EU regulatory environment is entering a stabilisation phase, the US is still reeling from the realisation of the inadequacies in its corporate

---

[28] See ICGN submission on the Consultation on the EU Action Plan at www.icgn.org.

governance. The Sarbanes-Oxley Act (SOX) has contributed to retrieving some of the trust that was lost in the wake of the turn-of-the-century corporate scandals. It has created other problems of its own that threaten to undermine the global supremacy of US capital markets. The exclusive competence of the States to adopt company law rules, combined with the ageing philosophy and framework of federal securities regulation as discussed in the first part of this chapter, has resulted in a system that relies more on regulatory and judicial enforcement and less on the accountability of companies to their shareholders.

In the US, responsibility for corporate governance-related regulation is divided between States and Federal jurisdictions. Federal regulation has been limited to issues of transparency and the functioning of the capital market. In contrast to the EU's principles-based, minimum-harmonisation approach, Federal regulation is based on detailed rules that apply uniformly to all issuers. Core corporate governance rules are found in corporate law shaped by statutes and case law of individual States. Delaware is by far the most influential among the States, being the host of most US listed corporations. In addition, US listed companies face a rules-based corporate governance framework set out in the listing requirements of the major stock exchanges, implemented by the exchanges themselves. These requirements are mandatory for domestic US issuers. Foreign issuers in US markets have to disclose the main differences between their corporate governance and the requirements of the US exchange on which their shares are listed.

Transparency

Internal control over financial reporting and the vanishing international issuer

Given the limits of Federal regulatory jurisdiction, SOX should be read and interpreted in the context of regulating market transparency, not core corporate governance subject matter. Many commentators have pointed out that certain SOX provisions, such as the prohibition of lending to corporate officers, do not fit the context and might be going beyond the constitutionally prescribed jurisdiction of the Federal government. These jurisdictional limits help explain why, in contrast to the UK and the EU, US Federal regulation focused exclusively on internal control over financial reporting,[29] when it came to regulating responsibility for internal control.

Section 404 mandates the annual filing of an internal control report that states management responsibility for establishing and maintaining an adequate internal control structure for financial reporting, and contains an assessment of

---

[29] According to Exchange Act Rules 13a–15(f) and 15d–15(f), internal control over financial reporting is 'a process designed by, or under the supervision of, the issuer's principal executive and principal financial officers, or persons performing similar functions, and effected by the registrant's board of directors, management and other personnel, to provide reasonable assurance regarding the reliability of financial reporting and the preparation of financial statements for external purposes in accordance with generally accepted accounting principles'.

the effectiveness of internal control over financial reporting. This assessment is further attested by the external auditor. In the three years since implementation started, howls of protest have been raised over the enormous cost of this provision to issuers, with few benefits to show. On the cost side, one study suggests an average annual cost per company of US$ 8.5 million[30] for the implementation of SOX 404. According to the Chief Financial Officer of Deutsche Telecom, the company spent over 20 million euros to prepare for SOX 404 implementation. This does not include 'indirect costs of full international compliance with all kinds of stock requirements' which are likely to double the figure.[31] While it is true that some of these costs are once off, the breadth of the obligation is such that companies need to incur considerable ongoing costs to maintain and adapt the system, not to speak of the audit costs which have more than doubled as a result.

American commentators maintain that the SOX 404 approach of annual assessment, attested to by the auditors, is beneficial in raising trust in the post-Enron US capital markets. This is not clear from a European perspective: while the board and management should have overall responsibility for maintaining effective internal control, an annual assessment and audit against a detailed 'internationally recognised' benchmark increases legal risk to an extent that goes far beyond what is reasonable and proportionate to the relatively limited incidence of expropriation and fraud. On the other hand, the increased legal significance attributed to internal control might severely inhibit the capacity of a private firm to make timely entrepreneurial decisions.

The US Securities and Exchanges Commission (SEC) and the Public Company Accountancy Oversight Board (PCAOB), the audit oversight body, have both been looking for ways to attenuate the cost impact of SOX. In December 2006, the SEC released new rules exempting smaller US companies from the requirement to produce a management report until December 2007, as well as the requirement to file the auditor's attestation report until December 2008. The SEC also postponed section 404 implementation for foreign private issuers, who are not required to provide the auditor's attestation report until July 2007,[32] while making it easier for foreign private issuers to deregister with the SEC and terminate the corresponding duty to file reports.[33]

The SEC released in June 2007 new guidance regarding management reporting on internal control over financial reporting.[34] The guidance promotes a risk-based approach allowing management to use their judgement and focus on the financial controls that might carry the risk of having a material impact on

---

[30] Figures cited in *The Economist* online edition, 'The trial of Sarbanes Oxley' (April 2006).

[31] Remarks by Dr Eick, CFO of DT in 'Shareholder rights and responsibilities: the dialogue between companies and investors', discussion paper issued by the Deutches Actieninstitut (2006), p. 23.

[32] See Securities and Exchange Commission, Final Rule 33–8760, December 2006.

[33] See Securities and Exchange Commission, Final Rule 34–55540, March 2007.

[34] See Securities and Exchange Commission, Final Rule 33–8810, June 2007.

financial statements, without the need to look to auditing standards. By limiting the scope of certification and assurance, the aim is to lower implementation costs. In line with the SEC, the PCAOB also modified its auditing standards to reflect a more principles-based approach to assurance. The area is financial controls that are more based on materiality.[35]

Looking to the future, US policy makers face a stark choice: further redraw the regulatory map – and it is unlikely that the SEC can do this without Congressional support – or see the competitiveness of the US capital markets continue to diminish. According to a 2007 report by McKinsey the threat to US and New York global financial services leadership is real. The report found that the decline in the pre-eminence of the US equity markets is already under way and is cause for concern 'not only because of the significant linkages that exist between IPOs and other parts of the financial services economy, but also because of the importance of financial services jobs to the US, New York, and other leading US financial centers in terms of both direct and indirect employment, as well as income and consumption tax revenues'.[36] Another 2006 study, commissioned by the City of London Corporation and the London Stock Exchange, concluded that 'the rise in US compliance costs has increased the competitive position of the London markets'.[37] Indeed, recent acquisitive behaviour by US stock exchanges in Europe can be explained in two ways: their desire to recapture a slice of global issuance that has permanently migrated as a result of US overregulation; and the building of a platform for US companies to avoid home country regulatory costs in raising capital.

Executive remuneration

While the SEC is limited in what it can do to address the shortcomings of the costly rules-driven US regime on financial internal control post-SOX, it has moved decisively to address growing concerns over transparency of executive remuneration arrangements.

Executive compensation has long been a battleground between investors and companies in the US. In contrast to the UK, over 90 per cent of S&P 500 executive teams are not remunerated for business performance beyond a two-year period.[38] Long-term incentive stock-based plans focus on share price appreciation and do not include any performance or other option vesting or exercise hurdles.

---

[35] See PCAOB, Auditing Standard No. 5, June 2007.

[36] See McKinsey, *Sustaining New York's and the US' Global Financial Services Leadership*, January 2007, pp. 11 and 12. See also the Interim Report of the Committee on Capital Markets Regulation, November 2006.

[37] Leonie Bell, Luis Correia da Silva and Agris Preimanis, *The Cost of Capital: An International Comparison*, Oxera Consulting, June 2006, p. 5.

[38] B. Atkins, 'Pay for the long term', *Directors Monthly*, NACD, April 2006.

As Bebchuk and Fried[39] have documented, US firms have been considerably opaque in their remuneration reporting, and often use pay practices that purposefully obscure the total amount of executive compensation and the extent to which managers' compensation is decoupled from their own performance. To this end, they have been assisted by a remuneration disclosure regime that has been built piecemeal and contains many inconsistencies.

The US exchanges, with the approval of the SEC, have been tasked with developing process rules for the way remuneration is set. These include a compensation committee of the board, consisting of independent non-executive directors, that should function transparently in setting executive remuneration. A considerable body of US board practice has evolved around these rules, but many critics doubt the degree to which it is truly effective. In its August 2006 initiative,[40] the SEC sought to address the transparency of pay policies and practices and their outcomes – the levels and structure of executive remuneration – so investors can make their own considered judgements. The aim has been to consolidate and, in some respects, overhaul the disclosure regime. Many buy side organisations and investor groups (including the Council of Institutional Investors, the ICGN and the ISS) have hailed this effort as a milestone in promoting transparency in US capital markets.

At the heart of the SEC's approach is a requirement for Compensation Discussion and Analysis, a plain English narrative of the company's approach to compensation, much like the remuneration report required of UK listed companies. The rules focus on eliminating double-counting while providing more comprehensive disclosure of all elements of executive compensation. The 2006 rules require the disclosure of 'total compensation' in the Summary Compensation Table and enumerate the elements that comprise total compensation, including fair value basis for reporting option grants. Also, post-employment compensation disclosures are now required, including the potential payments from retirement plans, non-qualified deferred compensation and other potential post-employment payments.

According to ISS,

> shareholders and board members should receive immediate benefits from the new tally sheets providing information on the total annual compensation packages paid to senior executives at U.S. companies. Additionally, we would expect abuses in the pensions, deferred compensation, severance and perquisites areas to dry up now that light will finally reach those previously dark recesses of the compensation landscape.[41]

---

[39] Lucian Bebchuk and Jesse Fried, 'Executive Compensation as an Agency Problem', Discussion Paper 421, Harvard Law School Olin Center for Law, Economics and Business, July 2003. Available at www.ssrn.com.

[40] Securities and Exchange Commission, Release No. 33–8732; 34–54302, August 2006.

[41] ISS statement at www.isssproxy.com.

In addition to the new disclosure regime on executive compensation, the SEC has adopted a requirement that calls for a narrative explanation of the independence status of directors, and consolidated other disclosure requirements regarding director independence and board committees, including new disclosure requirements about the compensation committee.

The new rigour of compensation disclosures will not be applied to foreign private issuers. They can continue following their home country rules and practices. The SEC's reluctance to level the playing field is understandable. The London market has no requirements that apply to foreign issuers on compensation disclosures, not even on a comply-or-explain basis. Transparency of remuneration arrangements in continental Europe is still at a very early stage and, as discussed earlier, EU action is limited to a recommendation. One still hears the argument that it is full disclosure of remuneration that has driven pay levels in the US and the UK to their current, some would say dizzying, heights.

Accountability

Under US law, 'the board is king'. In contrast to the UK and most other European jurisdictions, shareholders in US companies do not have the power to initiate any corporate action nor do they have to be consulted on any action unless the articles of association so provide.[42] In contrast, UK shareholders are called on to approve major transactions, while in some other EU countries shareholders have to approve certain related party transactions contrary to the EU mandatory regime established in the second company law directive. Increases in capital in the US are approved by the board, which can easily waive any pre-emption rights of existing shareholders. In all EU companies, shareholders representing anywhere from 5 to 20 per cent of the outstanding voting equity may call an extraordinary general meeting and pass resolutions, including the ousting of the board. In the US, most State company laws (including Delaware) do not grant such rights to shareholders and, at least until recently, companies could not provide for such rights in their articles of association. Many companies require a so-called supermajority vote making it very difficult for even a majority shareholder to influence the course of the company against the will of the incumbent board.[43]

The only way that shareholders can really influence board decision-making in the US is by electing suitable board members. Here too, the US law and practice differ from European countries. In Europe, shareholders, either individually or representing a minimum percentage, can propose candidates to the board at the general meeting. In the US, the only way shareholders have to propose candidates independently of the board slate is to request the approval of the SEC for the distribution of a separate proxy. Such a proxy fight with the incumbent

---

[42] See Robert Clark, *Corporate Law*, New York: Macmillan, 1986, pp. 21–4.

[43] In contrast, in Europe supermajority provisions are perceived by shareholders as a protection against abusive change of the 'rules of the game' by major shareholders.

board and management entails enormous costs for the challenger. Importantly, in most US corporations shareholders are not allowed to vote against board-nominated candidates. Under the so-called plurality system, shareholders are given the possibility either to vote for a candidate or to withhold their vote. They cannot vote against a director since, in the absence of an alternative slate, there would be an empty seat if a candidate were voted down. Thus, a director can be elected even if only one vote is cast in his favour.

It follows that the power vested in the incumbents is enormous. Even though changing the board is the only way shareholders have to express their dissatisfaction with the management of the company, this option is not available unless a full change in control occurs. Incumbent boards are left with extensive powers to frustrate any such change. In addition to various forms of poison pills, many US companies have adopted staggered board provisions whereby only a certain percentage of directors can be replaced in any given year, thus making it extremely time consuming and costly to change the board, even as a result of a successful takeover bid or proxy fight.

Entrenchment is not only harmful in theory, but is also an empirically proven destroyer of value. According to Professor Clark,

> studies about the impacts of the most costly reforms, those concerning audit practices and board independence, are fairly inconclusive or negative, while studies about proposals for shareholder empowerment and reduction of managerial entrenchment indicate that changes in these areas – which in general are only atmospherically supported by the SOX-related changes – could have significant positive impacts.[44]

The SEC put forward a modest proposal to give shareholders access to the corporate ballot and propose their own nominees without launching a full-scale proxy fight. In spite of the conditions for access being extremely stringent, US corporations fought bitterly against the proposal and it was withdrawn in 2005.

However, the objections to managerial entrenchment have started to get through and several large caps have retracted supermajority provisions and retreated from staggered boards, opting instead for UK-style annual elections of directors. More recently, in the face of growing investor opposition to the plurality system, some respected US companies have moved to address shareholder disenfranchisement in director nomination. For example, Pfizer, the pharmaceuticals giant, has amended its bylaws, making it mandatory for a director to resign if more than 50 per cent of the votes are withheld.

This emerging corporate change of heart can be largely explained by some of the market trends discussed in the first part of this chapter: the institutionalisation of the US equity market has made accountability to shareholders a

---

[44] Robert Clark, 'Corporate Governance Change in the Wake of Sarbanes Oxley Act', Discussion Paper 525, Harvard Law School Olin Center for Law, Economics and Business, September 2005, p. 2. Available at www.ssrn.com.

realistic alternative to intensive regulation and litigation, and the globalisation of US institutional portfolios has meant that large US issuers are competing for institutional capital with European (and other international) issuers.

There is also another factor that might limit widespread board entrenchment in the US: the possibility to use the internet more extensively in the proxy process. In January 2007, the SEC released new rules allowing issuers and other persons to furnish proxy materials to shareholders by posting them on an internet website and providing shareholders with notice of the availability of the proxy materials.[45] This rule may drastically cut the costs of proxy challenges and render the plurality system more palatable to investors.

Concluding remarks

The preceding pages of this chapter have told a story of a remarkable change that has been taking place in the corporate governance regulatory arena during the first few years of the twenty-first century: the EU regulatory environment for the capital markets is outperforming that of the US. In this, it is largely inspired by the UK's philosophy of principles-based regulation and transparent choice – as opposed to detailed, prescribed behaviour for market participants. In contrast, US regulation, which has been perceived as the gold standard since the 1930s, has fallen victim to a knee-jerk legislative reaction to the well-known corporate scandals in the wake of the tech bubble. Most importantly, US regulators seem to be still in thrall to the twentieth-century paradigms of widely dispersed ownership and the 'Wall Street walk'; the latter being essentially the only way shareholders may hold companies accountable. Policy seems to be in denial of the growing preponderance of large institutional owners and the omnipresence of active investors with a very loud voice to match their walking prowess.

The significance of this change has been reflected in the vast relative increase of international capital market activity in Europe as compared to the US; in the growing internationalisation of US institutional portfolios; and, arguably, in the recent drive by US exchanges to expose themselves to non-US capital market issuance and trading.

European regulatory upgrading also translates into increased transparency and accountability for corporate Europe. With this comes a newfound vulnerability to outside forces, activist investors of every sort and private equity 'locusts'. As outsiders arm themselves with vast amounts of newly available information, the long-standing friendliness of European company law towards shareholders is coming into play. Corporate elites and national champions are seeing the ground shift under their feet. Policy makers should rejoice in this challenge: European economies and consumers may only gain from increases

---

[45] Securities and Exchange Commission, Rule 34–55146, January 2007.

in productivity and allocative efficiency, as corporate giants come under the acid test of shareholder value.

But it is too early for self-congratulation. The risk of political backlash driven by economic nationalism and the fear of loss of power from well-entrenched elites is very real. The EU reformers may face a big challenge in the next phase of company law and governance reform: allowing European companies to transfer their corporate seat by choosing the jurisdiction that provides them with the most efficient, adequately implemented set of rules, as constitutional arrangements have allowed Delaware to become the corporate capital of the US. Local stakeholders (for example, German trade unions that appoint half of large company boards) will fight tooth and nail to maintain the status quo. Another risk is that the openness of the European approach, based on transparency and comply-or-explain corporate governance, might be undermined by an ill-considered flexibility towards emerging market foreign issuers with much lower governance standards. In the UK, the FSA is debating the adequate minimum level of corporate governance that such issuers should commit to when coming to the London market.

If the US model drove international regulatory trends and convergence up until the 1990s, it is the UK/EU model that is gaining the intellectual upper hand in the early twenty-first century: the long-term development and prosperity of companies should rely less on overpowerful Chief Executives, omnipresent regulators and trigger-happy plaintiffs; and more on accountable boards and informed shareholders for their long-term direction and prosperity. That is, after all, the message not only of Europe but of some of the most admired contemporary US business icons, like Stephen Schwartzman of Blackstone and Warren Buffet of Berkshire Hathaway.

10

Corporate governance and performance: the missing links

COLIN MELVIN AND HANS-CHRISTOPH HIRT

Introduction

The question of whether there is a link between corporate governance and performance is significant for a fund manager such as Hermes which undertakes corporate governance activities on behalf of three of the UK's five largest pension funds. Such funds are the classic long-term investors who will be shareholders for decades and, as they represent thousands of individuals who depend on them for their long-term financial well-being, have a strong interest in the sustainable, wealth-creating capacity of the companies in which they invest.

The corporate governance activities carried out by Hermes, on behalf of its clients, are based on the fundamental belief that companies with governance structures that allow shareholders to hold their management to account, and those that have active, interested and involved shareholders, will ultimately perform better and be worth more than those where either of these factors is missing. At the very least, we are convinced that sensible corporate governance activities may prevent the destruction of value. In our view, the key to the long-term success of a business is a constructive dialogue between companies and investors, commonly described as active ownership. Management and boards which have a dialogue with and are accountable to their owners will tend to operate more effectively in the long-term interests of the business and its investors.

Given this fundamental belief, the evidence for a link between corporate governance and performance is of great importance to Hermes and its clients. There has been much research in this area in recent years, which has often come to inconclusive results. We will review some of the findings in this chapter. We will then discuss the difficulties with research into, and other evidence on, the relationship between corporate governance and performance and explain possible reasons for inconclusive results of some of the studies. We will also highlight some of the evidence supporting our view that it is a combination of a company's governance structure and active ownership that matters in terms of performance.

Before reviewing the existing research and evidence, it is necessary briefly to consider the methodological and evidentiary difficulties that studies in this area face. To begin with, there are many different interpretations of both 'corporate governance' and 'performance'. The term corporate governance has come to mean many things. Traditionally and at a fundamental level, the concept refers to corporate decision-making, control and accountability, particularly the structure of the board and its working procedures. However, the term corporate governance is sometimes used very widely, embracing a company's relations with several different stakeholders or very narrowly referring to a company's compliance with the provisions of best-practice codes. The problem that researchers face is not only to define what is meant by corporate governance but also what amounts to 'good' or 'bad' corporate governance. Similarly, the term 'performance' may refer to rather different concepts, such as the development of the share price, profitability or the present valuation of a company. As such, the body of research into the link between corporate governance and performance contains studies that seek to correlate rather different concepts of corporate governance and measures of performance. We would define good corporate governance simply as good management, involving accountability to and a constructive dialogue with investors, as well as consideration of the interests of other stakeholders where appropriate. However, many of the studies that we have reviewed use their own definition of corporate governance and it is necessary to keep that in mind when assessing the research and drawing conclusions.

Evidentiary difficulties of research into and evidence on the relationship between corporate governance and performance include the issue of causation, which is notoriously hard to prove, and the limited availability of reliable historic data. We note that improved corporate governance may only have an effect on the performance of a company in three, five or even ten years, and that studies that cover only a few years of data may thus come to wrong conclusions.

If corporate governance is simply regarded as a risk factor, its significance for the performance and ultimately the valuation of a company, which follows from the relationship between a company's Equity Risk Premium and its market value, is immediately apparent. There is a direct inverse relationship between the Equity Risk Premium and the market valuation of a company. As such, it follows that by decreasing a company's Equity Risk Premium, for example by improving its corporate governance structure, its market value can be improved. The relationship between a company's Equity Risk Premium and its valuation also seems to be the basis for the findings of McKinsey's *Global Investor Opinion Survey* (2000 (updated in 2002)), which is the most widely quoted opinion-based research into the link between corporate governance and performance as measured by the valuation of the company. McKinsey surveyed over 200 institutional investors and found that 80 per cent of the respondents would pay a premium for well-governed companies. The size of the premium varied by market, from 11 per cent for Canadian companies to around 40 per cent for companies operating in countries where the regulatory backdrop was less certain, such as Egypt, Morocco and Russia. The UK and the US scored 12 per cent and 14 per cent respectively. Although the study is opinion-based and therefore of limited evidentiary value, the finding reflects a growing perception amongst market participants that well-governed companies, which are perceived to be run in the interests of investors, may benefit from a lower cost of capital.

However, knowledge of the relationship between the Equity Risk Premium and market valuation in itself is not sufficient for investors to embrace a corporate governance-based investment strategy that seeks to improve the performance and ultimately the value of investee companies. To begin with, while governance risk may be measured in different ways, both quantitatively and qualitatively, its interrelation with and precise effect on the Equity Risk Premium is difficult to assess. Moreover, there are difficulties with identifying corporate governance changes that reduce the governance risk and then the practical problem of bringing about the necessary improvements. As such, in terms of the relationship between corporate governance and performance, the knowledge that corporate governance affects the Equity Risk Premium is only a starting point.

More recent research assessing the link between corporate governance and performance in Asian markets (Gill and Allen 2005) points to another difficulty with looking at governance simply as a risk factor. It found that companies and markets with high levels of corporate governance do not necessarily outperform those with low levels when markets are rising, especially when there are strong liquidity inflows into markets. The researchers explain this finding with a negative correlation between the performance of companies with high levels of corporate governance and the appetite of investors for risk. They point out that one reason for this is that well-governed companies tend to have already strong valuations when markets start rising. Moreover, the study suggests that when liquidity enters markets, it raises risk appetite and effectively reduces the risk premium, thus making investment in less well governed companies more attractive. According to the research, it is only when markets are falling that companies and markets with high levels of corporate governance outperform those with low levels, as investors abandon risky companies.

From this brief discussion, it follows that there are two important questions that an investor must be able to address before trying to use corporate governance as part of an investment approach that seeks to improve the performance and ultimately the value of investee companies: what exactly are the corporate governance issues that matter for a particular company at a certain time, and how can positive change be achieved? It seems that research into the relationship of corporate governance and performance has failed until today to recognise appropriately both issues and to incorporate them effectively into methodology. Given these missing links, it is perhaps not surprising that the results of some of the research are inconclusive. In the following two sections, we review and assess evidence based on governance-ranking research and consider the performance of companies included in focus lists and shareholder engagement funds. We also provide a case study of how shareholder engagement works in practice. On the basis of our review and our assessment of existing research and evidence, we then provide our views on the two questions and identify what we consider to be the two missing links in the research into the relationship between corporate governance and performance.

Governance-ranking-based research into the link between corporate governance and performance

Overview of governance-ranking research

Governance-ranking research seeks to establish a link between one or more governance factors or standards and performance. In the following discussion, we will use the term standards to refer to a broad range of criteria on the basis of which the quality of governance may be assessed. The rankings are generally based on an assessment of the presence of certain factors (for example, a poison pill provision) or compliance with certain requirements (for example, that half of the board members are independent non-executive directors). Standards are used as a proxy objectively to measure a company's governance quality. The focus on certain standards by reference to which the quality of corporate governance can be objectively measured has superficial attractions. However, it also causes problems and distortions in the findings of the research trying to link corporate governance and performance. To begin with, any single governance standard may, for a number of reasons, be unrelated to the performance of companies in a particular market during a given period of time. Research that focuses on a single standard, such as the composition of boards, in isolation, may thus lead to incorrect conclusions. Moreover, such research does not effectively capture the general benefits that may result from active ownership involving engagement regarding a larger set of standards. More complex research considers a range of governance standards against which the corporate governance qualities of the companies investigated are assessed. The selection of a set of governance standards introduces a subjective element into governance-ranking research. In addition, researchers may attach different weight to the standards investigated for the purposes of the ranking that underlies the studies, introducing further subjectivity.

Many of the studies that suggest that there is no link between corporate governance and performance focus on a single governance standard (for example, Bhagat and Black 1999, 2002; Dalton et al. 1998; Dulewicz and Herbert 2003). For the reasons explained above, such a result is perhaps unsurprising. Similarly, research involving a ranking based on compliance with too many potentially insignificant governance standards may distort the finding of a link between certain core standards and performance. We therefore believe that the most valuable research focuses on a relatively small set of governance standards and seeks to identify which standards are directly related to performance.

The most celebrated governance-ranking study, which supports the proposition that there is a link between the quality of corporate governance, measured in terms of shareholder rights, and performance was carried out by Gompers et al. (2003). The research is based on an assessment of the governance of 1500 US companies using twenty-four governance provisions analysed by the Institutional Investors Research Center (IRRC) during the 1990s. The IRRC tracks both company-level rules and coverage under six state takeover laws. The twenty-four provisions fall into five broad groups: measures for delaying hostile bidders, voting rights, director protection, other takeover defences and state laws. The study found that if a fund had taken long positions in companies scoring in the top decile of their governance ranking and short positions in companies in the bottom decile, it would have outperformed the market by 8.5 per cent per year throughout the 1990s. The research also supported the proposition that companies with a good governance ranking were higher valued and had higher profits than those with a bad ranking. Prior to Gompers et al., Millstein and MacAvoy (1998) had found that, over five years, well-governed companies (identified on the basis of CalPERS ratings) outperformed by 7 per cent. Support for a link between good governance practice and shareholder returns was also found in research conducted by Governance Metrics International in 2003 and 2004. Drobetz et al. (2004) replicated the finding of Gompers et al. in respect of the German market. The research by Bauer et al. (2004), based on an analysis of corporate governance data on a sample of European companies included in the FTSE Eurotop 300, provided somewhat mixed support. They found a positive relationship between the corporate governance standards investigated and share price and company value but not operating performance.

Following on from the research by Gompers et al., Bebchuk et al. (2004) investigated which of the twenty-four governance provisions tracked by the IRRC are correlated with company value and shareholder returns. They identified six such provisions: four concerning the extent to which a majority of shareholders can impose its will on the management and two relating to mechanisms that facilitate the defence of a hostile takeover. Based on their assessment of the six provisions, they then constructed an 'entrenchment index' and investigated the empirical relationship between this index and performance. They found that increases in the level of this index are consistently associated with economically significant reductions in the valuation of companies measured by Tobin's Q and that companies with higher index levels were associated with significant negative abnormal returns during the 1990–2003 period. Most significantly, Bebchuk et al. found that the six provisions on which their entrenchment index was based fully explained the correlation identified by Gompers et al. between the twenty-four IRRC provisions and reduced company value and lower share returns during the 1990s.

205

In contrast to the research by Gompers et al. and Bebchuk et al., the research into the link between corporate governance and performance carried out in recent years by Deutsche Bank (Deutsche Bank 2003, 2004a, 2004b, 2005a, 2005b, 2006) covers several of the main markets including Asia, Continental Europe, the UK and the US. Deutsche Bank's updated UK research (Deutsche Bank 2004a, 2005b) is based on an assessment of the governance of the FTSE 350 companies at the end of 2000, 2003 and June 2005 using fifty differently weighted corporate governance standards. It found a clear link between the quality of corporate governance and share price performance of the companies considered. During the four and a half year period investigated, the top 20 per cent of the companies in terms of governance structure and behaviour outper-formed those in the bottom 20 per cent by 32 per cent. Deutsche Bank also carried out a momentum analysis in which companies were ranked on the basis of how their governance practices evolved over the period investigated. Here the outperformance of the companies which were consistently in the top 20 per cent, as compared to the companies consistently in the bottom 20 per cent, was 59 per cent.

Furthermore, the study found that companies which improved from the low-est quintile outperformed those companies that remained in the lowest quintile by 7 per cent. Deutsche Bank's research also showed that there was a positive relationship between the historic governance assessment of the companies and their profitability (ROE). For example, the top 20 per cent companies (average 2005 ROE estimate of 20.9 per cent) were significantly more profitable than the bottom 20 per cent (average 2005 ROE estimate of 10.9 per cent). Similarly, the research found that the profitability of the top companies was significantly better than that of the bottom companies using ROA and EBITDA margin. However, the research did not find a clear relationship between the quality of governance and investors' current valuations, measured by P/E, P/CF and P/BV, as opposed to the historic share price performance. This would seem to support the view that the knowledge that corporate governance affects the Equity Risk Premium in itself is only a starting point in respect of the link between corporate governance and performance.

In an academic study, Bauer et al. (2005) investigated the importance of cor-porate governance for Japanese companies. Using a unique data set provided by Governance Metrics International, which rates firms on six different corporate governance categories, the researchers analysed whether companies with a high governance ranking perform better than companies with a low governance rank-ing. They measured corporate performance by share price, company value and operating performance. Using an overall index, the authors found that corpo-rate governance positively affects share price and company value but negatively affects operating performance. They suggest a number of explanations for the finding regarding operating performance, for example the possibility that com-panies with good governance tend to apply more prudent accounting policies leading to more conservative financial reporting. Moreover, using the individual corporate governance categories, the study found that they differently affect the variables investigated. For example, whereas provisions towards financial disclosure, shareholder rights and remuneration matter in terms of share price and company value, provisions falling into the market for control category reduce company value. The authors explained this by the fact that takeovers in Japan are rare and hence any provisions in this area are futile.

Most recently, clear support for the proposition that corporate governance matters in terms of performance was found by a Goldman Sachs study on Australian companies (Goldman Sachs 2006). The research, which used corporate governance rating data from Corporate Governance International, tested the investment returns from buying companies that are top rated and selling those that are bottom rated. The study found that such an investment strategy would have generated a 10.9 per cent return above the passive market return for the period from September 2005 to May 2006. The research, which was back tested over a period from August 2001, also sought to identify which of the five proxies of good corporate governance used by Corporate Governance International matter in terms of returns. According to the study, the overall structure of the board and the skills of its members are the most relevant governance factors in terms of excess returns. The study also examined the relevance of corporate governance ratings as a forward indicator for the likelihood of earnings surprises. The research found that in the June 2005 reporting season, top-rated companies reported average positive earnings surprises of 2.6 per cent versus an average negative earnings surprise of –0.4 per cent for low-rated companies. Thus, a further finding of the study was that corporate governance ratings can help investors to assess the potential for companies to surprise on their earnings.

Assessment of governance-ranking research

Most of the governance-ranking research provides support for the proposition that good corporate governance improves performance and ultimately the value of companies. We acknowledge that there is some research falling into this category that raises doubts on the existence of a link between corporate governance and performance. We also note that the governance-ranking studies are based on the assessment of certain governance standards in the past and thus on historic data. The standards investigated and often the weights attached to them vary between the studies. Moreover, as the standards assessed depend on the regulation applicable in a particular market and may vary over time, it is difficult to draw general conclusions.

Some of the more sophisticated research partly addresses these issues by considering international standards and using momentum analysis. However, particularly the finding by Bebchuk et al. (2004), which suggests that corporate governance activities may need to be focused on certain core standards effectively to improve performance, needs to be treated with care. The governance provisions investigated by the IRRC are principally concerned with mechanisms enabling management to prevent or to delay takeovers. As the regulation of takeovers differs significantly between the main world markets, the six provisions identified by Bebchuk et al. in respect of the US may not be of similar relevance elsewhere. Before any general conclusions are drawn, research replicating the finding by Bebchuk et al. in respect of markets other than the US is required to identify those specific governance standards that are directly linked to performance. In spite of these qualifications, the governance-ranking research on the whole supports the proposition that good corporate governance enhances performance, and ultimately the value of companies.

Having said this, there remains a fundamental question regarding research that seeks to establish a link between corporate governance and performance, which is based on corporate governance ratings and rankings, namely, whether standards that are meant objectively to measure the corporate governance quality of a specific company matter in respect of the performance of that particular company. Before considering the issue at the company level, there is of course the question whether it is sensible to use the same set of standards to assess governance quality in different markets with their respective legal frameworks and best-practice recommendations. For example, how much do we learn about the corporate governance quality of a German company by the fact that the majority of the members of its supervisory board are not independent as internationally defined, because of a law which requires that half of the board members must be employee representatives? Not a lot, it would seem. Nevertheless, the standard 'majority independence' continues to be widely used to assess the quality of corporate governance across the world.

Moreover, the typical ownership structure of companies varies significantly between markets. There are different problems, or agency conflicts, in companies that are closely held and controlled by one shareholder (majority shareholder versus minority shareholders) than in those that have a dispersed shareholder structure (management versus shareholders). This makes comparisons of the quality of corporate governance across markets with different ownership structures based on the same set of standards even more questionable. Research into the link between corporate governance and performance which takes this important consideration into account is rather limited to date (for an example, see Beiner et al. 2004, a study that finds a positive relationship between corporate governance and Tobin's Q).

Even in respect of companies in the same market – and thus subject to the same regulation – with similar ownership structures, different governance standards may matter in terms of performance, for example because they operate in different sectors with particular opportunities or threats. Clearly, the governance structure of a steel manufacturer may need to be different from that of a management consultancy. Finally, it seems intuitive that certain governance arrangements, such as combining or separating the roles of Chairman and Chief

Executive, may be more or less appropriate for companies at different stages of their life cycle and in particular in crisis situations. What seems clear from this discussion is that in terms of the most appropriate governance structure, one size does not fit all companies

What is the conclusion of the view that the most appropriate and effective corporate governance structure for a company is contingent on a number of factors that differ not only between markets and sectors, may change over the life cycle of a company but generally seems to be highly company specific? If one subscribes to this view then it becomes clear that producing reliable corporate governance ratings and rankings, which are useful across different markets and sectors, is very challenging. As a consequence, the task to produce robust evidence that adherence to certain corporate governance standards may enhance the performance of companies and ultimately create value for shareholders is even more difficult than previously assumed, and perhaps impossible. The findings of the research carried out by a group of independent academics on behalf of the Dutch Corporate Governance Research Foundation for Pension Funds (SCGOP) in 2004 makes this very clear (de Jong et al. 2004).

If one believes that corporate governance can be used as part of an investment technique to improve performance and ultimately to increase the value of investee companies, there must be something in addition to the skill of identifying companies with objectively measured high or low governance quality. On the basis of the evidence we review in the next section, we would argue that, other things being equal, the difference can be made by active, interested and involved shareholders.

Further evidence for a link between corporate governance and performance: effectiveness of shareholder engagement

Performance of companies in focus lists

Focus lists are issued by a number of investors and investor groups. In essence, they attempt to induce the management of the companies listed to address performance- or governance-related problems by publicising them. The inclusion of a company in a focus list generally also represents a statement of intent of the issuer of the list to engage with the companies listed to encourage improvements. The rationale for focus lists is that by publicising the problems of companies and announcing an intention to engage with them to address the failings, their performance may improve at some point after they are included in a list. In addition, the expectation that a company's problems will be addressed following its inclusion in a list can lead to an immediate positive market reaction.

The best-known focus list is issued by CalPERS. The so-called 'CalPERS effect', that is, the improvement of a company's performance following its inclusion in the CalPERS focus list, was first described in 1994 (Nesbitt 1994). This research, which was updated in 1995, 1997, 2001 (Nesbitt 2001) and 2004 2004 (Hewsenian and Noh 2004), is generally regarded as the most compelling in this area. Until the most recent update of the research, it showed that companies included in the CalPERS focus list substantially outperformed in the five years after their inclusion in the focus list (by 41 per cent in the original 1994 study and by 14 per cent in the 2001 update). Results from the 2004 update provide more limited support for the long-term positive effect, showing excess returns of just 8 per cent over the five-year period after listing.

Studies of the CalPERS effect were also undertaken by Anson, White and Ho of CalPERS (2003, 2004). In their 2003 study they found that there was a significant short-term price impact after companies were included in the CalPERS focus list. The study documented that the average excess return, defined as the return earned over and above the risk-adjusted return required for the focus list companies, earned by each company in the focus list for the ninety-five days period after inclusion in the list was 12 per cent. As such, the authors concluded that the focus list had a significant short-term wealth enhancing effect. In their 2004 paper, Anson et al. revised their original paper, focusing on the longer-term wealth effect of including companies in the CalPERS focus list. They found that on average a company that is included in the focus list earns a return over and above its risk-adjusted rate of return for the one-year period after publication of the list that is 59 per cent greater than the risk-adjusted rate of return that shareholders would normally expect to receive for their investment. The authors thus concluded that the focus list approach of CalPERS adds significant value to the investee companies targeted.

The methodology used by Anson et al. has been questioned in the literature (Nelson 2005). However, there is very recent independent academic evidence to back up their findings. Barber analysed the gains from CalPERS corporate governance activities relating to the companies in the focus list from 1992 to 2005. He concluded that through these activities CalPERS had added an estimated $3.1 billion of value to its investments over that period (Barber 2006). Research into the effects of other focus lists also showed that after a company's inclusion in such a list its performance improved (Opler and Sokobin 1998).

The research on the performance effect of focus lists supports the view that the process of publicising problems of companies and, when appropriate, active engagement by investors with such companies to address the failings identified can improve their performance. We consider that this finding in itself provides a sound justification for investors to act as active owners. We note that there is some research that does not fully support the proposition that inclusion of a company in a focus list is likely to improve its subsequent performance. Such inconclusive results may be explained by the fact that companies included in a focus list may not have the potential to respond to investor oversight and pressure (Caton et al. 2001). More limited support provided by some research may also be explained by other factors determining the success of investors' engagement with companies, such as the shareholding structure. Certain companies, for example those with a family block holding, are less susceptible to change through engagements. The performance of shareholder engagement funds, which can take a company's potential to respond to constructive proposals and other factors, such as the shareholding structure, into account when selecting companies for investment and engagement, provides the most valuable evidence that corporate governance matters in terms of performance.

Performance of shareholder engagement funds

The success of shareholder engagement funds is the most compelling evidence supporting the proposition that active ownership with the objective of improving corporate governance can lead to better performance and ultimately a higher value of investee companies. Shareholder engagement funds invest in underperforming companies with governance problems which have the potential for improvement. As such, their performance provides a real-life test involving a significant financial commitment to the proposition. By engaging with such companies and, if necessary, by using their ownership rights, active investors seek to encourage corporate governance improvements that they consider will ultimately lead to an increase in the value of their investment. Hermes' Focus Funds take this approach. They invest in companies that are fundamentally sound but underperforming as a result of weaknesses in their strategy, governance or financial structure. The Focus Fund team then engages with the companies' executive and non-executive directors and liaises with other shareholders and stakeholders as appropriate. Significantly, the Focus Funds team works constructively and cooperatively with the boards of investee companies and does not seek to micro-manage them. Indeed, the shareholder engagement programmes are intended to assist boards in taking tough decisions rather than to take such decisions for the boards and to support them in implementing decisions once taken. Thus, over a period of time and through a constructive dialogue, the Focus Fund team uses its influence as owner to help resolve the problems causing underperformance.

Hermes' original UK Focus Fund has outperformed the FTSE All Share Total Return Index by 3.1 per cent on an annualised basis (net of fees) since its inception in 1998 (to 30 June 2006). Similarly, since its inception in 2002, the European Focus Fund has outperformed its benchmark by 3.9 per cent on an annualised basis (net of fees) (to 30 June 2006). In the US, Relational Investors LLC outperformed its benchmark by 6.3 per cent on an annualised basis (net of fees) since inception (to 30 June 2006). We believe that the outperformance of shareholder engagement funds in difficult market conditions – effectively using active ownership to improve corporate governance as an investment technique – provides the strongest evidence in support of the view that there is a link between corporate governance and performance.

The effectiveness of the investment approach taken by Hermes' Focus Funds in terms of returns for shareholders was recently investigated by four independent academics (Becht et al. 2006). The researchers were given unlimited access to Hermes' resources, including letters, memos, minutes, presentations, transcripts/recordings of telephone conversations and client reports, documenting its work with the companies in which Hermes' UK Focus Fund invested in a period over five years (1998–2004). They reviewed all forms of public and private engagement with forty-one companies. One of the main objectives of their research was to determine if the achievement of the Focus Fund's engagement objectives, generally substantial changes in the governance structure of target companies, such as significant asset sales, divestments, or replacement of the CEO or Chairman, is ultimately value increasing. The researchers found that when the engagement objectives led to actual outcomes, there were economically large and statistically significant positive abnormal returns around the announcement date. Excluding events with confounding information, such as earnings announcements or profit warnings, the mean abnormal returns were 5.3 per cent in the seven-day window around the announcement date. There were thus large positive market reactions to events initiated through the intervention of the Focus Fund. Importantly, the researchers also established that the Focus Fund succeeded in accomplishing its desired outcomes in the large majority of cases. On the basis of their findings, the researchers concluded that shareholder activism can produce corporate governance changes that generate significant returns for shareholders. Using a novel research methodology, the researchers were also able to show that a high proportion of the Focus Fund's strong outperformance was attributable to activism and not stock picking. The independent academics thus found a clear link between shareholder activism and fund performance.

The strong performance of Hermes' Focus Funds and the results of the recent independent study of the investment approach they take support our fundamental belief that companies with active, interested and responsible shareholders are more likely to achieve superior long-term returns than those without. Hermes has extended its successful Focus Fund approach and also carries out engagements with selected companies held as part of its clients' indexed core holdings, thus leveraging the unique resource it has built up since the early 1990s. In the following section, we describe one of these engagements, which we carried out between 2000 and 2003.

Shareholder engagement in practice: Premier Oil plc

By 2000, Premier Oil plc ('Premier') had become a *cause célèbre* amongst those concerned with governance, and more particularly with the social, ethical and environmental responsibilities of business. Most concerning, Premier's share price had dramatically underperformed the market for several years and it appeared unable to deliver on its stated strategy. Working with the company, with other shareholders and with NGOs, Hermes helped the company to resolve these issues.

Hermes accelerated its engagement with Premier in mid-2000. For several years previously, Hermes had communicated its concerns over the company's board structure and had voted against the re-election of several of the non-executive directors whom it did not regard as being independent. On the governance side, the fundamental issue was that the company was dominated by two major shareholders: Amerada Hess, a US company, and Petronas, the Malaysian National Oil Company, each of which held 25 per cent of the shares. Not content with the control and influence they wielded as major shareholders, each of them also had two non-executive directors on the board. Two further non-executive directors were also deemed non-independent.

These board problems were reflected in a failure by the company to address some of the severe problems that Premier was facing. The strategy was not clear to shareholders. It appeared that the strategy proposed in November 1999 when Petronas invested in the company (and on the basis of which independent shareholders had approved that investment) was not being followed, and it was not apparent to investors that an alternative had been developed. The company was in a strategic hole: it was not large enough to compete in production and downstream work with the emerging super-major oil companies, but it was also not as lightweight and fleet-of-foot as it needed to be in order fully to exploit the exploration opportunities opened up by the super-majors' focus on larger-scale fields. Its freedom of action was also limited by the company's high level of gearing.

In addition, the company had allowed itself to become exposed to major ethical and reputational risks as a result of being the lead investor in the Yetagun gas field in Myanmar. Myanmar, formerly known as Burma, was a country ruled by a military dictatorship which had refused to accept the results of democratic elections in 1990, where summary arrest, forced labour and torture were widely reported, and which had therefore become a pariah state. Premier's involvement in the country had brought public criticism of the company from a range of sources including Burmese campaigners, Amnesty International, trade union groups and, not least, the UK Government. It was not clear to shareholders that the company was effectively managing the reputational and ethical risks it faced as a result of its involvement in Myanmar.

To begin exploring these concerns, Hermes held a meeting in mid-2000 with Premier's Corporate Responsibility and Finance Directors. This provided an opportunity to understand Premier's considerable positive work on the ground in Myanmar, which included building schools, funding teachers, AIDS education and environmental remediation. While Hermes recognised that positive work, there were continuing concerns. The board had not publicly stated that it believed it was effectively managing all the risks that were associated with

213

its presence in Myanmar; nor did Hermes have the confidence that the board, as then constituted, could give shareholders the reassurance that they needed in that regard.

When Hermes had analysed all these issues, it came as no surprise that, in the absence of a clear strategy, with a restrictive capital structure, with its involvement in Myanmar not clearly being managed and a board which did not seem designed to address these issues in the interests of all shareholders, Premier's share price had dramatically underperformed the market for several years. The next step in Hermes' engagement was a letter to the Chairman of Premier, Sir David John, requesting a meeting to discuss the full range of concerns.

While Hermes was awaiting that meeting, it was approached by two separate groups asking it to engage on the social, ethical and environmental issues raised by Premier. The first group consisted of its clients, principally led by trade union pension fund trustees. The second was from NGOs who were focusing on disinvestment from Myanmar/Burma. Subsequently Hermes had discussions with representatives of both groups. Though Hermes did not share the rather limited engagement agenda of the NGOs, the meetings provided it with useful information and contacts.

The meeting with Sir David John took place in January 2001 and was a frank and honest one. It was rapidly apparent to Hermes that Sir David understood its concerns. In December 2000, the company had already added a new, fully independent non-executive director. Sir David assured Hermes that further developments on the governance side were in train. Hermes approved of these developments, but queried whether they would ultimately be adequate to address all the issues identified. Sir David was also willing to discuss strategic and ethical concerns. Importantly, he agreed to the request of Hermes for him to meet representatives of the NGO Burma Campaign (until that point their contact with the company had only been through the Corporate Responsibility Director).

Hermes followed up this meeting with a detailed letter outlining its concerns and asking Sir David to begin addressing them in the interests of all shareholders. Sir David's prompt response assured Hermes that the board would continue to work for a solution to 'enable the true value of the company to be reflected in the share price'. In March 2001, Premier added another fully independent non-executive director, a banking executive with extensive experience in Asia, and Malaysia in particular.

At the AGM in May 2001, Sir David made a very important public statement with regard to the shareholding structure of the company. It was an acknowledgement that the presence of two 25 per cent shareholders was a burden on the company's share price – a point Hermes had clearly made in a meeting with him – and a statement of intent about seeking a resolution to this problem. He said: 'We believe that the current share price remains low relative to the underlying value of the business partly as a result of the concentration of share ownership. The board is continuing to seek ways to reduce the discount on assets for the benefit of all shareholders.'

The first year of Hermes' engagement had brought some progress but had failed fully to address Premier's fundamental problems. Hermes met Sir David and the Chief Executive in early 2002. This was an impressively frank meeting, where they were willing to be more open with Hermes about the work they had been undertaking to resolve Premier's problems. Over the years since 1999, they had proposed a number of solutions to the company's strategic impasse, but each had been in some way barred by one or other of the two major shareholders. They were, however, confident that both shareholders now had a different attitude and that a resolution in the interests of all investors could now be achieved, though it might take a number of months.

Following this meeting, Hermes sent Sir David a further letter expressing its concerns at the actions of the major shareholders and putting in writing its offer to lend him support in the negotiations, should that prove valuable. Hermes offered to call on its contacts at global institutions and share with them its concerns that certain directors of Premier had not proved themselves to be the friends of minority investors. Hermes hoped that the implication of potential difficulties this might cause for fundraising by companies with which those directors were involved could bolster Sir David's hand in negotiations. Hermes also raised its concerns that public statements by Amerada that its investment in Premier was somehow ring-fenced from Myanmar, and that its directors did not participate in any discussions on the company's involvement in that country, seemed to be out of line with UK company law and the fiduciary duties of directors to all their shareholders.

The company's preliminary results announcement in March 2002 high-lighted the positive progress the business was making operationally, but more importantly it detailed the progress being made in relation to the company's fundamental problems. It made clear the roadmap the company was using to solve its problems, talking about shedding mature assets in return for the exit of the major shareholders, and turning itself into a focused, fleet-of-foot exploration company once again. The statement read: 'We are in specific discussions with our alliance partners on creating a new Premier, better balanced to achieve our objectives. While the restructuring process is complex and involves careful balancing of the interests of all shareholders, we are committed to finding a solution before the end of this year and I am hopeful this will be achieved.'

As part of Hermes' usual series of financial analysts meetings following preliminary or final results announcements, it met representatives of Premier – this time the Chief Executive and the Finance Director. This meeting gave Hermes further encouragement that genuine progress was being made, as they suggested that the major shareholders both now clearly understood that any deal that they agreed would have to be approved by independent shareholders without them having the right to vote. Therefore, any deal would have to offer minorities full value to be allowed to proceed. The implication that Hermes took away from this meeting was that negotiations were now on track to reach a resolution.

That resolution was announced in September 2002. Premier said that it was to 'swap assets for shares', with Petronas taking the Myanmar operation and a share of Premier's Indonesian activities, and Amerada a further segment of the Indonesian interest (in which Premier retained a stake). This was in return for cancelling their 25 per cent shareholdings, and losing their rights to appoint non-executive directors – as well as a substantial cash payment from Petronas. Thus the shareholding and governance issues were resolved in one step, and the cash was to be used dramatically to cut Premier's debt burden. By the same action, Premier reduced its oil and gas production activities and focused on fleet-of-foot exploration. And finally it had withdrawn from Myanmar in a way which was fully acceptable to the Burma Campaign, to other NGOs and to the UK Government.

However, most critically for minority shareholders, the share price of Premier rose 10 per cent on the announcement. Indeed, news of Premier's change in direction had been anticipated by the market for many months. As a result, Premier's share price doubled (relative to the oil and gas sector) during the period of Hermes' engagement, netting an excess return to the clients of over £1 million, and more than fifty times that sum to other minority shareholders. The price continued to rise thereafter until 12 September 2003 when the reconstruction was completed with the exit of the major shareholders and a 10:1 share consolidation. Premier is now established as a strong independent company and continues to create value for its shareholders.

Assessment of the research and evidence for a link between corporate governance and performance

Focus list research and the effectiveness of shareholder engagement in general and the performance of shareholder engagement funds in particular provide convincing evidence for a link between active ownership that seeks to improve corporate governance and better performance of companies thus targeted. Unlike the evidence for a link between corporate governance and performance established by governance-ranking research, this evidence would seem to be relevant regarding markets with different regulation and for companies operating in different sectors. Indeed, the results of focus list research and the success of shareholder engagement suggest that compliance with certain standards is less important than the extent to which ownership oversight and, if necessary, pressure is exercised. The evidence in this category thus supports the proposition that it is not simply the absolute quality of governance but also the process of active ownership and oversight of management that is important in terms of performance and value creation. This process is important not only in respect of companies where performance- or governance-related problems have been identified and possibly addressed but as an ongoing and general approach to the management of investments with the objective of preventing the occurrence of such problems.

Governance-ranking research, which focuses at least in principle on objectively measurable corporate governance standards, provides clearer evidence than focus list research and the performance of shareholder engagement funds in respect of a link between corporate governance strictly defined and performance. However, in our experience, weaknesses in strategy and financial structure and governance-related problems strictly defined often go together. Moreover, there may be a relationship between a company's adherence to standards and active ownership. This leads us to the main qualification of the existing body of research, namely, the question of causation. It is notoriously difficult to prove causation, even where research establishes a correlation between corporate governance and performance. The issue of causation arises not only with regard to the significance of certain standards, but also in the extent to which active ownership influences the governance structure and possibly the running of investee companies. We note that the authors of many of the studies we have reviewed acknowledged that there was a need for further empirical work addressing the issue of causation. We recognise the problems with the available body of research and studies. Nevertheless, we consider there to be sufficient evidence in support of our view that good corporate governance improves the long-term performance and ultimately the value of companies.

Conclusion

The corporate governance activities that Hermes undertakes on behalf of its clients are based on the belief that both companies' adherence to certain governance standards and particularly active ownership to improve corporate governance will lead to better performance of investee companies and ultimately increase their value. The belief that good corporate governance may help to prevent major corporate disasters is less controversial than the proposition that it can actually create additional value for an investor. However, in spite of some evidence to the contrary, we are convinced that active ownership based on corporate governance is an investment technique that can effectively improve performance and ultimately increase the value of a portfolio of investee companies. Indeed, this belief underlies Hermes' engagement programmes in relation both to its Focus Funds and to its clients' passive and actively managed core investments. What is the foundation for this belief?

At the beginning of this chapter we set out two fundamental questions that an investor needs to be able to address before trying to use corporate governance as part of an investment approach which seeks to improve the performance of investee companies: what exactly are the corporate governance issues that matter for a particular company at a certain time and how can positive change be achieved? Having reviewed the relevant research and other evidence available, we are now in a position to describe how these issues can be addressed and what resources are required. In fact, we can identify the missing links in the research into the relationship between corporate governance and performance.

One size does not fit all: towards a contingent model of corporate governance

Even the best corporate governance ratings and rankings are just a starting point for further company-specific analysis by specialised personnel taking the particular circumstances of a company into account before passing judgement regarding the quality of its governance. The main problem with ratings, particularly if used for different markets and across sectors, is that they seek to be objective. It is highly questionable whether standards that are meant objectively to measure the corporate governance quality of a certain universe of companies matter in respect of the performance of a particular company. We believe that the most appropriate and effective corporate governance structure for a company is contingent on a number of factors that differ between markets and sectors, may change over the life cycle of a company and generally seem to be highly company specific. As such, an assessment of the governance quality of a company based on objective criteria will – depending on the relevance of the standards used – be unreliable at best.

To assess effectively the corporate governance quality of a specific company and identify areas where changes could improve performance and thus add value, an investor needs a significant number of personnel with a wide range of qualifications, skills and experience, including direct experience of corporate management. We would note that this is not normally available to fund management companies or rating agencies. In this regard the finding of the momentum analysis of Deutsche Bank, which suggests that companies that improve their corporate governance arrangements over the period under investigation very significantly outperform those that do not, is of great interest. It provides support for the view that relevant areas for governance improvement need to be determined on a case by case basis, and that it may be informed investors that are best placed to identify the relevant performance-enhancing factors. However, identifying areas where changes could lead to improved performance is only part of the role of active, interested and involved shareholders.

Investors play an important role in using corporate governance as an investment technique

A detailed, company-specific corporate governance analysis to identify changes that could unlock value should only be part of an effective corporate governance based investment strategy. In terms of creating (or at least preserving) value, the most important part of the investors' role seems to be engaging in a constructive dialogue with companies to encourage governance changes where necessary, or at the very least taking an active interest in and overseeing their affairs. In our view it is not simply the quality of the governance arrangements that is important in terms of performance but to a significant extent the appropriate engagement of investors with companies on a wide range of issues as part of an active ownership approach involving continuous oversight of the management. The performance of companies included in CalPERS focus list and the success of Hermes' Focus Funds provide firm support for this view. In order to make their corporate governance based investment strategies work, both CalPERS and Hermes devote significant resources to that end. At Hermes more than fifty people with a wide range of qualifications, experiences and skills are involved in corporate governance analysis and engagement work. This suggests that, going forward, there will be a need for institutional investors to cooperate more closely in respect of corporate governance and engagement and to pool their capabilities. Only by doing so will the potential of a corporate governance-based investment strategy be fully realised.

References

Anson, M., T. White and H. Ho (2003), 'The Shareholder Wealth Effects of CalPERs' Focus List', *Journal of Applied Corporate Finance* 15, 3: 8–17.

(2004), 'Good Corporate Governance Works: More Evidence from CalPERS', *Journal of Asset Management* 5: 149–56.

Barber, B., 'Monitoring the Monitor: Evaluating CalPERS' Shareholder Activism', Working Paper, March 2006.

Bauer, R., B. Frijns, R. Otten and A. Tourani-Rad (2005), 'The Impact of Corporate Governance on Corporate Performance: Evidence from Japan', Maastricht University/Auckland University of Technology, May 2005.

Bauer, R. and H. Guenster (2003), 'Good Corporate Governance Pays Off! Well-Governed Companies Perform Better on the Stock Market', Working Paper, April 2003.

Bauer, R., H. Guenster and R. Otten (2004), 'Empirical Evidence on Corporate Governance in Europe: The Effect on Stock Returns, Firm Value and Performance', *Journal of Asset Management* 5, 2: 91–104.

Bebchuk, L., A. Cohen and A. Ferrell (2004), 'What Matters in Corporate Governance?', Olin Paper No. 491, Harvard Law School, September 2004.

Becht, M., J. Franks, C. Mayer and S. Rossi (2006), 'Study on Shareholder Activism in the U.K.', *Journal of Applied Corporate Finance* 18: 8–27.

Beiner, S., W. Drobetz, M. Schmid and H. Zimmermann (2004), 'An Integrated Framework of Corporate Governance and Firm Valuation – Evidence from Switzerland', ECGI, Finance Working Paper No. 34/2004.

Bhagat, S. and B. Black (1999), 'The Uncertain Relationship between Board Composition and Firm Performance', *Business Lawyer* 54: 921–63.

Caton, G., J. Goh and J. Donaldson (2001), 'The Effectiveness of Institutional Activism', *Financial Analysts Journal* 57, 3: 21–6.

Coombes, P. and M. Watson (McKinsey) (2000, 2002), 'Global Investor Opinion Survey'. See www.mckinsey.com/governance.

Dalton, Daily, Ellstrand and Johnson (1998), 'Meta-Analytic Reviews of Board Composition, Leadership Structure, and Financial Performance', *Strategic Management Journal* 19, 3: 269–90.

De Jong, A., D. Dejong, G. Mertens and C. Wasley (2004), 'International Corporate Governance and Performance: A Comparative Analysis of Corporate Governance and Performance in France, Germany and the U.K.', published by Corporate Governance Research Foundation, the Netherlands, November 2004.

Deutsche Bank (2003), Global Corporate Governance Research, 'Beyond the Numbers – Corporate Governance: Unveiling the S&P 500', August 2003.

(2004a), Global Corporate Governance Research, 'Beyond the Numbers – Corporate Governance in the UK', February 2004.

(2004b), Global Corporate Governance Research, 'Beyond the Numbers – Corporate Governance in South Africa', October 2004.

(2005a), Global Corporate Governance Research, 'Beyond the Numbers – Corporate Governance in Europe', March 2005.

(2005b), Global Corporate Governance Research, 'Beyond the Numbers – UK Corporate Governance Revisited', July 2005.

(2006), Global Corporate Governance Research, 'Beyond the Numbers – Corporate Governance in Asia and Australia', March 2006.

Drobetz, W., A. Schillhofer and H. Zimmermann (2004), 'Corporate Governance and Expected Stock Returns: Evidence from Germany', *European Financial Management* 10, 2: 267–93.

Dulewicz, V. and P. Herbert (2003), 'Does the Composition and Practice of UK Boards Bear Any Relationship to the Performance of Listed Companies', Henley Management College, Working Paper, March 2003.

Gill, A. and J. Allen (2005), 'CG Watch 2005 – Corporate Governance in Asia: The Holy Grail – Quality at a Reasonable Price', CLSA Asia-Pacific Markets, October 2005.

Gompers, P., J. Ishii and A. Metrick (2003), 'Corporate Governance and Equity Prices', *Quarterly Journal of Economics* 118, February: 107–55.

Gray, A., Goldman Sachs, Environmental, Social & Governance Research, 'Good Corporate Governance = Good Investment Returns', June 2006.

Hewsenian, R. and J. Noh (2004), 'The "CalPERS Effect" on Targeted Company Share Prices', Wilshire Associates, July 2004.

Millstein, I. and P. MacAvoy (1998), 'The Active Board of Directors and Performance of the Large Publicly Traded Corporation', *Columbia Law Review* 98: 1283–1321.

Nelson, J. (2005), 'Does Good Corporate Governance Really Work? More Evidence from CalPERS', *Journal of Asset Management* 6: 274–87.

Nesbitt, S. (1994), 'Long-term Rewards from Shareholder Activism: A Study of the "CalPERS Effect"', *Journal of Applied Corporate Finance* Winter: 75–80.

—— (2001), 'The "CalPERS Effect" on Targeted Company Share Prices', Wilshire Associates, January 2001.

Opler, T. and J. Sokobin (1998), 'Does Co-ordinated Institutional Activism Work? An Analysis of the Activities of the Council of Institutional Investors', Working Paper, October 1995, updated in 1998.

11

Is the UK model working?

SIMON LOWE

The evolution of UK corporate governance

To find evidence of the first statutory recognition of the importance of internal controls we must look at US law. During the 1970s, the Foreign Corrupt Practices Act 1977 (FCPA) was enacted as a result of investigations by the Securities and Exchange Commission (SEC), which found that over 400 US companies admitted to making questionable or illegal payments in excess of $300 million to foreign government officials, politicians and political parties.

The FCPA set out anti-bribery laws, but also considered the requirement for maintaining books and records, and a sufficient system of internal controls.[1] In 1988, US Congress believed that US companies were at a disadvantage in international markets as elements of bribery appeared to be routine practice in other countries. US Congress contacted the Organisation for Economic Cooperation and Development (OECD), highlighting these concerns. However, it took almost ten years for member states to sign the OECD convention on Combating Bribery of Foreign Public Officials in International Business Transactions 1997. The convention drew on recommendations taken directly from the FCPA for accounting requirements, independent external audit and internal company controls.

In the UK, statute and case law in relation to company and director responsibilities and internal controls were also being established. The requirements for the management and structure of companies in the UK were being strengthened through Acts of Parliament (primarily in the Companies Act 1985), case law (such as directors exercising care and skill in carrying out duties[2]) and regulations. However, at the time there was little guidance specifically on corporate governance. As a consequence, in May 1991 the Financial Reporting

---

[1] The FCPA prohibits both United States and foreign corporations and nationals from offering or paying, or authorising the offer or payment, of anything of value to a foreign government official, foreign political party, party official, or candidate for foreign public office, or to an official of a public international organisation in order to obtain or retain business. In addition, the FCPA requires publicly held United States companies to make and keep books and records which, in reasonable detail, accurately reflect the disposition of company assets and to devise and maintain a system of internal accounting controls sufficient to reasonably assure that transactions are authorised, recorded accurately, and periodically reviewed. From www.usdoj.gov/criminal/fraud/fcpa/fcpastat.htm.

[2] *Dorchester Finance Co. v. Stebbing* (1977).

Council (FRC), the London Stock Exchange (LSE) and the UK accountancy profession set up a committee to consider the Financial Aspects of Corporate Governance. The result of this review was the Cadbury Report (1992), which started to establish best practice on financial reporting and accountability for public companies.

Later that year, the final framework for the Committee of Sponsoring Organisations (COSO) model was released. It provided companies with a framework for governance, covering a spectrum of internal control environments, including strategic, operating, reporting and compliance.

The Cadbury Report's conclusions are now recognised as the starting point from which all other UK and much international corporate governance guidance has been developed. Many of the recommendations within the Cadbury Report were subsequently adopted into the Principles of Corporate Governance issued by the OECD in 1999 (revised in 2003). These Principles have now passed into other national corporate governance codes and guidance.

Throughout the 1990s, a series of reviews was produced to address particular areas. The Rutteman Report in 1994 addressed the subject of internal financial control; the Greenbury Report in 1995 looked at the area of directors' emoluments and, in 1998, the Hampel Report incorporated the principles discussed within the Cadbury Report and explored the effectiveness of internal control. In that same year, the Combined Code on corporate governance was introduced, pulling all these reports into one code of governance which, while not mandatory, was appended to the London Stock Exchange listing rules. In 1999, Nigel Turnbull issued his report entitled 'Internal Controls – Guidance for Directors on the Combined Code'.

Following the introduction in the US of the Sarbanes-Oxley Act 2002 (SOX), the Turnbull guidance was accepted by the SEC as an approved governance framework to help management comply with section 404 of the SOX Act.[3] In the UK, Higgs (2003) and Smith (2003) provided additional guidance on non-executive directors' roles and audit committees respectively. These were then incorporated into the 2003 revised Combined Code (the Code).

Then in 2004, in response to the impact of SOX, the FRC asked Douglas Flint, the Finance Director of HSBC, to revisit the adequacy and relevance of the Turnbull guidance. Over 100 companies responded to his review, including 56 per cent of the total market capitalisation of the LSE.

The Flint review, published in 2005, concluded that:

> the Turnbull guidance continues to provide an appropriate framework for risk management and internal control. Its relative lack of prescription is considered to have been a major factor contributing to the successful way it has been implemented, and we have therefore decided against recommending substantial changes.[4]

[3] www.icaew.co.uk/index.cfm?route=112276.
[4] Quote from Douglas Flint, www.frc.org.uk/press/pub0822.html.

It is notable that the key guidance on corporate governance in the UK has been written by individuals (Cadbury, Greenbury, Hampel, Turnbull, Higgs and Smith) active in the private sector, with experience of finance, banking and directorships. In comparison, US regulations have been created by federal lawmakers.

Other governance principles

Underpinning the effectiveness of the Code has been the principle of comply-or-explain, which, while putting the emphasis on compliance, does acknowledge that there are circumstances where an alternate approach may be more appropriate for a company's position. In such a situation, the alternative to compliance is clear explanation. It is this principle, which is introduced in the preamble to the Code rather than in the body, which has, together with a requirement for clear guidance, enabled companies to develop appropriate corporate governance practices.

In January 2006, the FRC published the report on their review of the implementation of the Code. This review was conducted in response to questions as to whether a SOX-type regulatory environment was needed in the UK. Fundamentally, should the UK move towards a more financially focused, rules-based approach when assessing the effectiveness of internal controls?

The key message from respondents to the consultation was that the Code was having a positive impact on the quality of corporate governance practice among listed companies. There were some concerns over the increased time commitments needed for directors to satisfy aspects of the Code, and some difficulties were noted in relation to recruiting non-executive members of the audit committee with 'recent and relevant financial experience'.

The 2006 Grant Thornton Corporate Governance Review (the fifth detailed study of disclosures produced by 314 of the FTSE 350 and their compliance with the terms of the UK Combined Code) confirmed that inroads are being made in the area of relevant financial expertise, but with 20 per cent (27 per cent in 2005) of FTSE 350 companies still not identifying the relevant individual, finding these persons still represents a challenge. However, the FRC review concluded that major changes to the Code were not required.

There remain conflicting views as to whether the Code has improved dialogue between shareholders and company boards. The Association of Investment Trust Companies (AITC), in their response to the 2005 FRC review, considered that there had not yet been any added value for shareholders from the introduction of the Code. The FRC, in April 2007, announced further consultation and review of the Code, in particular to address the perception of box-ticking and boilerplating and also the impact and application of the Code to the smaller cap companies. In October, the FRC announced that only two changes were proposed to the Code: to remove the limit on more than one FTSE 100 chairmanship, and to allow the Chairman of a small company to be a member of the audit committee provided he was independent when appointed as Chairman.

The current UK principles-based model appears to be having a positive impact on governance practice. However it still has some way to go in meeting the needs of all stakeholders, a primary requirement being the transparency of directors' activities. So what are the alternatives?

Cross-border harmony

There are different approaches to corporate governance throughout the world, often reflecting the local cultural and economic realities. Should the UK be looking to define and pursue what it considers to be the best approach or should it be working to a common global corporate governance model in order to enable increased global comparability?

The European Corporate Governance Institute (ECGI) is seeking to address the issue of cross-border inconsistencies between governance models within Europe by leading a project: Modernising Company Law and Enhancing Corporate Governance in the European Union.

UK versus US governance environments

The US practice in the field of corporate governance and risk management is to implement a highly regulated environment. Since the introduction of SOX, there has been a decrease in new listings in the US, with only 354 companies listing in 2006[5] compared to 856 companies in 1999 (see Figure 11.1).

This is in stark contrast to the UK's practice, now overseen by the Financial Reporting Council (FRC) which, through the Combined Code, promotes the principles-based approach.

It is this lighter touch to regulation which many believe stimulated the significant increase in the total number of flotations (domestic and foreign) on the LSE which increased to 576 companies in 2006 from 187 companies in 1999.[6] This is also mirrored in the number of new foreign listings, where we are once again seeing growing confidence in UK markets – thirty-two new foreign listings in 2006.[7] This no doubt reflects the liquidity of the UK market (there was a notable decrease in total UK listings from 2000 to 2003). However, the revision of the UK's Combined Code in 2003, at the same time as an apparent market reaction against what is seen as the prohibitively expensive cost of complying with SOX, has turned the spotlight on the issue of principles-based regulation versus prescriptive rules. Recent announcements from the SEC and

---

[5] From World Federation of Exchanges, www.world-exchanges.org.

[6] From World Federation of Exchanges, www.world-exchanges.org.

[7] From World Federation of Exchanges, www.world-exchanges.org.

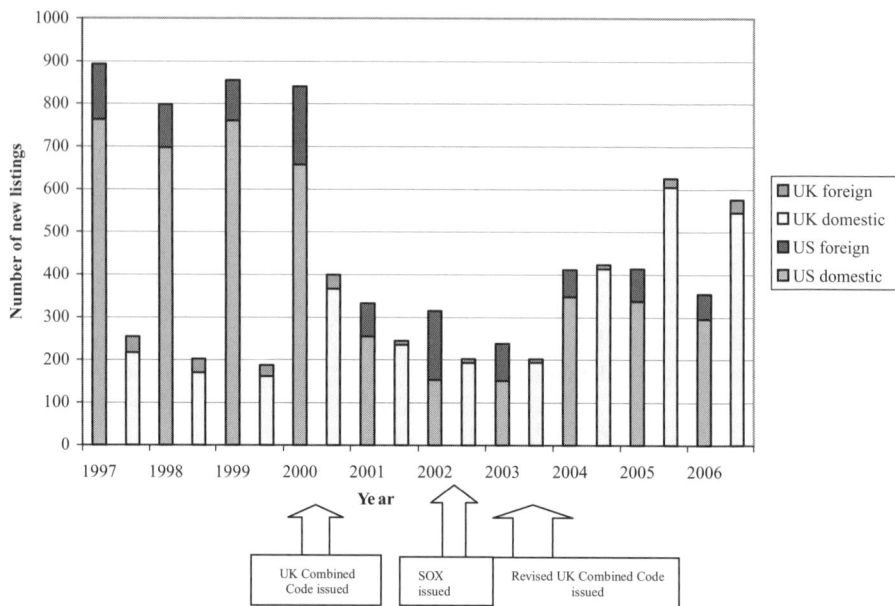

Figure 11.1 Comparison of US and UK listings 1997–2006

PCAOB suggest that the US is seeking to soften its stance, but this may be a case of too little too late.

Figure 11.1 shows the number of Initial Public Offerings (IPO) – both domestic and foreign – in the UK and the US from 1997 to 2006, together with the relevant dates when the UK and US corporate governance guidance was issued.[8]

The decline in US listings is commonly blamed both on the cost and demand SOX places on management resources and also on the reluctance of management, in the heavily litigious environment of the US, to adopt a more risk-based approach to controls assessment. What is reasonable risk to the informed director may not be viewed in the same light by the courts. But other factors are starting to drive a change in governance practice; the competition for new capital is coming from the more loosely regulated emerging markets – China, India, Middle East – not to mention the actual cost of the listing process in the US, where underwriting fees and professional advisory services' costs are considerably more expensive. Economic consultants Oxera found that the same bank would charge higher fees for a listing in the US than in Europe.[9] For

---

[8] From World Federation of Exchanges, www.world-exchanges.org.

[9] *The Cost of Capital: An International Comparison*, Oxera Consulting and London Stock Exchange, June 2006.

example, underwriting fees charged in the US ranged from 6.5 to 7 per cent, compared to 3.25 to 4 per cent in the UK.

Reactions to the US markets' requirements are such that there has been a growing stream of European companies delisting from US exchanges. For example, the Rank Group delisted from NASDAQ, citing that 'complying with the legislation could more than double our annual audit bill'.[10] It appears that companies are no longer willing to pay the premium required, whether as fees or excessive regulatory burdens, to be listed in the US. Indeed Ben Bernanke, the Federal Reserve chairman, went on record in May 2007, urging the US financial watchdog to look at the UK model of principles-based, risk-focused supervision as the basis for future regulation.

The irony is that it is commercial pressure (arguably the driver of many of the US's recent corporate collapses) which could end up driving an easing of the regulatory regime in the US.

Quality of corporate governance disclosures in the UK

One way to judge the extent to which the principles of good corporate governance are considered by company boards is to review the quality of disclosure produced in their annual reports and accounts.

The annual report and accounts is the only regulated medium available to the investor. As such, if a company chooses to disclose only the barest minimum of information, it should be considered to be dissenting from the principles-based approach to UK corporate governance.

A primary objective for guidance in the UK for disclosure is full transparency of governance and risk-management procedures adopted by the company's board. Best practice is when a company chooses to set the standard in governance disclosure by providing clear and transparent information which exceeds the Code's recommendations. Such practice should be considered to be a benchmark for UK governance. However, by 2006, according to Grant Thornton's Review, only a handful of companies in the FTSE had achieved such disclosure.

Have UK companies embraced the principles of the Combined Code?

The Grant Thornton review showed that only thirty-one companies (10 per cent) in the FTSE 350 fully complied with the Code as opposed to choosing the explain rather than the comply option.

The 2005 Ernst & Young Corporate Governance Web Survey[11] found that communicating corporate governance principles within companies could be improved; only a third of management believe the principles are widely disseminated throughout the company. Furthermore 59 per cent of investors indicated

[10] www.financialnews-us.com/?contentid=540316.
[11] Ernst & Young Corporate Governance Web Survey 2005.

227

they did not feel well informed about the principles of corporate governance in the companies in which they invest.

The Flint review reflected strong institutional support (those responsible for £2.4 trillion of funds) in favour of keeping the existing UK approach, but encouraged greater voluntary disclosure by directors, a positive assertion as to the effectiveness of the controls and greater disclosure regarding a company's risks and controls. The conclusions of this review were also supported by the findings of Grant Thornton: that over the past few years UK companies have made great progress in the field of internal control. The 2006 Grant Thornton review found that effectively all boards acknowledged their responsibility for reviewing the effectiveness of the systems of internal control. The review concluded, however, that more could be done to apply the principles of Turnbull through voluntary disclosure of additional information to assist the reader's understanding. It is encouraging therefore to find that 70 per cent of companies in 2006 provided a strong level of additional disclosure in respect of risk and control processes. In addition, it was noted that 40 per cent chose to provide more than the minimum in respect of the roles and responsibilities of committees and how they are appraised. This is a heartening sign that UK companies are starting to adopt the spirit as well as the letter of the Code. However, there is still room for improvement. What the Flint review was looking for in governance disclosures was further detail on how risk management operates and how it is embedded in an organisation. The fact that only 27 per cent of companies gave more than the bare minimum of explanation suggests that the review group's words of encouragement are timely.[12]

There is little doubt that the quality of corporate governance disclosures is improving. However, the Flint review's message was heavily infused with a strong encouragement to forsake boilerplate in favour of giving greater insight into governance practice. The message to the regulators has to be that guidance rather than regulation will be more effective in bringing about lasting change, even though it may take a little longer.

Do they do what they say they do?

There is an ongoing debate as to whether companies and their boards actually practise what they preach in order to comply with the Combined Code. The Code is guidance and not law, so there is an element of trust involved: that what is being disclosed in the compliance statement is a fair reflection of, for example, the risk management and internal control processes in place within the company.

Of course, the report and accounts are a regulated disclosure, and external audit assesses what has been disclosed (directors' report, governance statement,

---

[12] Grant Thornton's Fifth FTSE 350 Corporate Governance Review, 2006.

and so forth) as part of the audit to ensure it does not mislead the reader. However, the extent to which the board implements its governance systems as disclosed may not be entirely clear from the governance statement.

The only way of knowing whether companies actually perform the governance procedures described is to conduct a governance compliance review. Best practice would suggest that this should be conducted by a third party, with the assurance report referenced in the corporate governance disclosure section of the annual report, to substantiate any Code compliance claimed.

As a medium-term goal, a company should set its governance sights on achieving full compliance with the Code and associated guidance, giving clear disclosure and being able to confirm such compliance through external assurance. Such a review could be performed in conjunction with the internal audit effectiveness review which is required every five years, in line with the Institute of Internal Auditors' (IIA) recommendations in the International Standards for the Professional Practice of Internal Auditing.

Resources and investor interest

Market capitalisation may play a significant role in determining how much resource companies will dedicate to complying with the requirements of the Code. There is believed to be a correlation between the level of market capitalisation and the level of compliance, and the FRC in its 2007 review wished to explore this relationship. Grant Thornton's 2006 review considers this by splitting the FTSE 350 into the FTSE 100 and the Mid 250. When looked at over the five years of the review, whether through lack of manpower, funds or commitment from senior management, it is apparent that the Mid 250 have been much slower than the FTSE 100 to react to emerging practice in the field of governance.

There still remains a clear difference between these two groups, with the FTSE 100 displaying greater compliance with the Code and providing a greater level of detail, particularly for softer governance requirements such as Turnbull compliance and corporate responsibility (CR). However, the latest figures show that the gap is now closing. Regardless of the artificial distinction between FTSE 100 and FTSE 250, they all represent significant companies with market capitalisation in excess of £300 million. The greater challenge faces the small cap companies. If it has taken at least five years for the FTSE 250 to catch up to the FTSE 100, it is possible that the small caps may never do so.

Market capitalisation, and by inference their access to resources, may give the advantage to the larger companies as they will have more dedicated resources available to address these compliance areas. For example, a FTSE 100 company will have a more established audit committee, an internal audit function to implement the internal control monitoring required by the Turnbull guidance, and possibly a separate risk and compliance committee, while smaller companies may struggle to justify the costs of such functions.

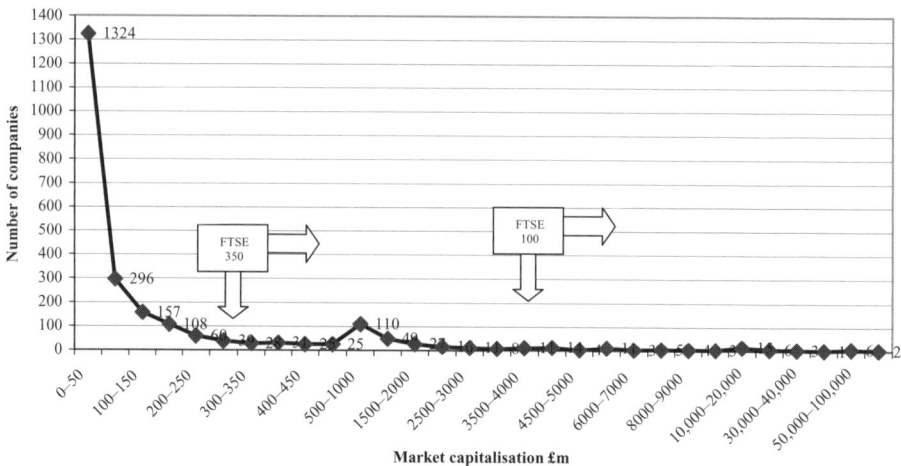

Figure 11.2 Market capitalisation of UK companies

Given that the FTSE 350 are all large companies, perhaps the real driver for compliance is investor interest. The larger the company, the greater the institutional following; the more they are in the public eye, the greater the reputational risk. The result is that typically FTSE 100 companies have more substantial reporting mechanisms in place to implement CR initiatives, and report and monitor these initiatives as directed from the board. They tend to have a dedicated CR website and often provide a separate CR report.

Figure 11.2 gives an indication as to the distribution of companies against market capitalisation. The public companies with less than £300 million market capitalisation probably face the greatest challenge, not to mention those Alternative Investment Market (AIM) companies who aspire to the main market.

The challenge for smaller companies is recognised by the Code which grants certain exemptions to smaller companies, defined as those outside the FTSE 250. Further guidance is provided by the Quoted Companies Alliance (QCA), which makes the following suggestions as 'de minimis compliance':[13]

- Two non-executive directors are recommended.
- Board meetings should be held regularly, at least once in each month, with no fewer than six meetings in each year. The agenda should always include a report on the company's management accounts from the finance director.
- Certain matters should always be put before a board for consideration, for instance appointment of directors, appointment of chairman/managing

---

[13] 'Initial Public Offers on AIM for US Corporations', Taylor Wessing.

director, remuneration, budget, contracts not in the ordinary course of business, significant acquisitions or disposals, and decisions concerning raising capital.

- An audit committee should be established and all non-executive directors should be members of that committee, one of whom must be the chairman. The QCA considers that if a company has only two non-executive directors, it should be sufficient for those directors to constitute the audit committee.
- Companies should seek to define clearly the role which each non-executive director is to fulfil. This may involve discussions with major shareholders to identify areas of perceived board weakness which the appointment of a new non-executive director should address.
- One year is seen as the optimum notice period for executive directors. It is likely that the bonus element of a director's remuneration will form a more significant part of his overall package than in a larger listed company.
- On remuneration committees, the QCA supports the Combined Code principle that remuneration committees should consist wholly of independent non-executive directors, although QCA has stated that remuneration committees should be able to invite individual executive directors to join meetings as appropriate.

So where do the smaller quoted companies need to focus their efforts? Typically, their greatest compliance challenges tend to be in the following areas:

- establishing and maintaining effective internal audit functions
- non-executive directors: quality and quantity on the board
- CR initiatives and disclosure
- Turnbull compliance: risk management and internal control systems.

On a positive note, Grant Thornton's review found that the FTSE 250 companies are taking the spirit of the Code to heart, providing explanations why they may not be compliant with the Code, in line with the comply-or-explain approach. However, for the smaller company, not to mention AIM companies, a significant challenge remains.

Governance versus performance and listings

Alternative Investment Market (AIM) quoted companies

In the UK, AIM is a capital market for smaller companies, outside the FTSE All-Share market, and is not as heavily regulated. AIM provides the opportunity for smaller companies to raise capital in a public market, without committing to the fully listed market and suffering the associated compliance and listing costs. This lighter touch to regulation, coupled with the significant number of small start-up companies, brings with it a greater risk for the investor.

Presently, it is not mandatory for companies quoted on AIM to comply with the principles of the Combined Code. However, the need for additional disclosures and transparency by AIM quoted companies is supported by Sir Derek Higgs, who was quoted in *Internal Auditing and Business Risk Magazine* (August 2006) as requesting 'more disclosures against benchmarks – a light version of the code' for AIM companies.

The Grant Thornton review of corporate governance adoption by thirty-five AIM companies in the south-west of England showed an encouraging result, with 75 per cent of the companies commenting on how they complied with the Combined Code. Few AIM listed companies made statements regarding the relationship between the role of Chairman and Chief Executive, and only one company provided sufficient information regarding performance evaluation of the board, committees and individual directors. Only one company disclosed that it had an internal audit department, with 23 per cent commenting on the required annual assessment for the need for an internal audit department. Disclosures on external audit services, structure of committees and corporate responsibility were largely omitted.

As investors become increasingly sophisticated and the demand for transparency grows, corporate governance in AIM companies will come under greater scrutiny. This will meet fierce resistance, as it is the less regulated environment which is seen as having been one of the main drivers behind AIM's recent rapid growth.

Roles and responsibilities

Shareholders (particularly institutions) look to the disclosure requirements of the Code and related guidance to ensure companies are being governed in line with best practice. Investors may overlook their responsibilities actively to take part by encouraging companies to do more.

Effective shareholder engagement is not a new concept. The Cadbury Report states:

> If long-term relationships are to be developed, it is important that companies communicate their strategies to their major shareholders and that their shareholders understand them. It is equally important that shareholders play their part in the communication process by informing companies if there are aspects of the business which give them cause for concern.

Institutional investors

The UK market is somewhat different from the larger European and US markets in that, in the UK, the majority of shareholders are the financial institutions who control in excess of 60 per cent of total capital.[14]

---

[14] The Europaeum's 'Restructuring Corporate Governance: The New European Agenda' report, 2005. www.europaeum.org

Section D of the Code provides guidance concerning shareholder relations, particularly with institutional investors. The main principle regarding dialogue with institutional shareholders[15] states: 'There should be a dialogue with shareholders based on the mutual understanding of objectives. The board as a whole has responsibility for ensuring that a satisfactory dialogue with shareholders takes place.' The supporting principles take this one stage further, stating: 'The board should keep in touch with shareholder opinion in whatever ways are most practical and efficient.' The main focus of meetings with shareholders continues to be around company strategy and performance updates. So where is corporate governance mentioned? Investors' comments suggest they do not feel well informed about the corporate governance processes in the companies in which they invest. But do they care? And if they do care, what are they doing about it? Ultimately, shareholders can vote with their feet. If they dislike a company's governance principles and systems and feel so strongly about them, they can divest.

One of the key rights of shareholders is to elect, challenge and remove the directors where their actions in managing the company are not satisfactory. This is accepted in law but we rarely see any evidence that this happens in practice. Companies seek to avoid bad publicity at all costs, and institutional investors generally prefer backroom diplomacy and influence.

Shareholder rights in the UK versus the US

Despite many rights of shareholders being accepted internationally, there remain significant differences. For example, Table 11.1 shows the key differences when comparing the UK with the US position.[16]

Shareholder responsibilities

The Institute of Chartered Accountants in England and Wales (ICAEW) has compared the respective responsibilities of directors and shareholders: 'Directors are responsible for acting in the best interests of the company for the benefit of shareholders. Shareholders, in turn, empower directors to lead the company in a fiduciary capacity, whilst maintaining a degree of decision-making control through incorporation rights.'[17]

While directors' responsibilities are defined and supported by numerous principles and laws in the UK, there is more debate around the responsibilities of shareholders since there are no published guidelines. The lack of guidance on shareholder responsibility does not help global investors in today's markets. As a result, conscientious investor bodies such as PIRC and the Association of British Insurers (ABI) are increasingly voicing their views and expectations

---

[15] Section D.1 Combined Code, July 2003.
[16] 'Shareholder Responsibilities and the Investing Public' (ICAEW), June 2006.
[17] 'Shareholder Responsibilities and the Investing Public' (ICAEW), June 2006.

Table 11.1 Shareholder rights: comparison of UK and US positions

Areas of difference	In the UK	In the US
Shareholder pre-emption rights	Rights issue (new shares offered in proportion to existing shareholders first so as not to dilute their ownership). Shareholders can pass a special resolution[a] and vote to disapply this rule if a 75% majority is achieved.	No such law in place – no pre-emption rights.
Director appointment and removal	Right to vote to appoint or remove (and replace) a board director by a simple majority of votes cast on an ordinary resolution.[b] If not re-elected may not be immediately reappointed.	Directors are elected by a plurality[c] of the votes cast by the shares entitled to vote in the election of a meeting at which a quorum is present. Under the plurality voting system an uncontested director is elected on the basis of a single affirmative vote regardless of the number of votes withheld. The US system of plurality voting does not enable shareholders to vote against the election of a director and they must instead rely on the number of votes withheld to express their dissatisfaction. Directors remain on board until a successor is named.
Nomination of directors	Shareholders have a basic right to nominate a director, by a simple majority of votes cast on an ordinary resolution.	Company to exclude shareholder proposals related to the election of new directors from the management proxy statement. The practical effect of this is that shareholders wishing to propose nominees to the board must personally incur the costs for the proposal in soliciting and bringing in other shareholder support. The company can counter-solicit its disagreement with the nomination.

Shareholder communication	The Code provides that the Chairman should ensure that the views of shareholders are communicated to the board as a whole.[d] As principal trading occurs at the same time in London, there are no rules on shareholders acting together.	Shareholders are obliged to follow SEC rules governing communication with each other on voting issues (due to possible numbers and locations of traders) and where shareholders acting together collectively hold more than 5% of the issued share capital they must file Form 13-D with the SEC.
Submit shareholder proposal	Have support of 5% of the votes, or if there are at least 100 shareholders who hold shares in the company on which there has been paid up capital, on average not less than £100 per shareholder.	Must own for at least one year, $2000 in market value of share; or 1% of the company's issued share capital, whichever is less
Votes	Only votes 'for' and 'against' are counted as being cast. Votes 'withheld' are not counted (but this is currently under debate) and proxies are excluded unless a poll is called. 'One share, one vote' is the system by which resolutions are voted upon, but this is restricted to the shareholders in actual attendance at the AGM.	All votes (including proxies) are counted as being cast, including votes 'for', 'against' and 'withheld'. Proxy service providers can influence the outcome of proxy fights and are becoming increasingly prominent.

[a] Passed at a general meeting of which at least 21 days' notice specifying the intention to propose a resolution as a special resolution has been given. A special resolution requires a 75 per cent majority. It is required for important matters such as alterations to the memorandum or articles of association, *a change of name*, or a reduction of capital to be approved by the court.

[b] Used for all matters unless the Companies Act or the company's articles of association require another type of resolution. Passed by a simple majority of members who are entitled to vote at a meeting, notice of which has been properly given. Voting may also be allowed by a member's substitute known as a proxy. The length of notice required for an ordinary resolution depends on the kind of meeting at which the resolution is to be discussed.

[c] Each voter is allowed to vote for only one candidate, and the winner of the election is whichever candidate receives the largest number of votes.

[d] Supporting Principle D1.1 from the Combined Code, July 2003.

for governance practice in the companies in which they invest. By making their views more public and contributing to the various working parties, such as the Flint review, they are having a growing, if not direct, influence on governance practice.

The International Corporate Governance Network[18] (ICGN) has expanded its guidance on the responsibilities of shareholders. Their work aims to:

- provide an investor-led network for the exchange of views and information about corporate governance issues internationally
- examine corporate governance principles and practices
- develop and encourage adherence to corporate governance standards and guidelines
- generally promote good corporate governance.

As the Ernst & Young 2005 survey found, and subsequent reviews have confirmed, shareholders feel strongly that the transparency and adequacy of information they review can be improved.

Board effectiveness

The Code aims to improve the transparency of a company's governance procedures. It is the directors who have legal duties to the shareholders and moral and ethical responsibilities to the wider stakeholder groups. Governance practices are focused on ensuring and enhancing the accountability of those directors. The review of the effectiveness of the board and its individual members is at the heart of that accountability. It is through the process of considering issues such as the existence of a dominant leadership that non-executive directors provide the appropriate challenge. All directors must act in the long-term interests of the company and not their own ego or self-interest. To act otherwise will give early warning to the shareholders of any unhealthy imbalance in authority – a significant contributory factor in some of the major frauds and collapses at the beginning of the decade.

Review of board performance under the Code

The Combined Code includes a further disclosure requirement to confirm that 'a formal and rigorous annual evaluation of [the company's] performance and that of its committees and individual directors' has been undertaken. The board performance review, introduced to the Code by the Higgs review, asks the board to consider not just what its achievements were, but also how they were achieved.

Best practice is to set clear business targets and objectives, and measure activities against these; many companies clearly align the personal objectives

---

[18] www.icgn.org.

of staff with business objectives and then monitor and remunerate according to their achievements. Leading companies include process or behavioural objectives, as well as task-based ones, to ensure that business results are not achieved 'at all costs' and that good results will be sustainable rather than short-lived. In the same way that staff are given personal assessments and business units are reviewed, it follows naturally that the performance of the board itself and its directors should be subjected to the same scrutiny.

It is interesting that only board 'performance' is to be reviewed, while it is the 'effectiveness' of internal control which the Turnbull guidance focuses on, and the effectiveness of internal financial control on which SOX requires opinions. Requiring boards to make greater disclosures and increasing the extent to which they are accountable may be an uncomfortable process.

Boards should have a balance of skills and experience and directors should be committed and contribute effectively, but what does this mean? The expectation is that directors (particularly non-executives) will raise appropriate challenges to ensure that the best courses of action are being followed in the long-term interests of the company.

Guidance is provided on the board performance review, which:

- asks companies to state how their evaluation is carried out
- confirms that it is the responsibility of the Chairman to select an effective process and to act on its outcome
- suggests the use of an external third party to conduct the evaluation will bring objectivity to the process
- includes a list of indicative questions (leading many companies towards a questionnaire-based review).

Soundings taken by Grant Thornton from discussion groups amongst directors suggest that this subject is proving to be a hot topic, with many boards resorting to a mix of outside consultancies and self-assessment techniques such as questionnaires. In practice, many are questioning whether the output really provides sufficient challenge. It is perhaps not surprising that it is the review of the effectiveness of the Chairman which is proving by far the most difficult.

In a survey by RSM Robson Rhodes, *Board Evaluations – Ensuring Your Board Achieves Its Full Potential* released in 2006, the disclosure of 283 of the FTSE 350 companies' annual reports were reviewed and it was found that 264 had undertaken an evaluation.

What gets covered in a board performance review can be broken down into:

- the provision of information to the board
- the composition of the board in terms of background and length of service
- the behaviour in board meetings
- the results of meetings in terms of decisions reached.

The Code's guidance recognises how increased objectivity is likely to result from having external input, so it is surprising that only a third of companies in the FTSE 100 had used external facilitation and as few as 18 per cent in the FTSE 250. Anecdotal feedback suggests the apparent reluctance of boards to expose themselves to independent review, despite the growing number of consultancies now offering the service, is at least partly due to the relative immaturity of the market, and the lack of genuine experience from which to draw and add value. In addition, for the smaller company, the cost of bringing in an external adviser may be difficult to justify.

The form of external review varies considerably. The more enlightened companies may invite behavioural psychologists to observe the dynamics during board meetings. They may even allow proceedings to be interrupted to give timely feedback on ineffective behaviour.

Another level of assessment will be to arrange for interviews of board members to be carried out by independent advisers and the results to be fed back objectively. Among the advantages of this approach are that views are often more freely expressed, and it allows the board to explore the issues giving rise to divergent views. At the very least, an external adviser can be engaged to develop a questionnaire which the Chairman can then use in his interviews with directors.

The Robson Rhodes survey anticipated that more companies would use external facilitation in the future, as boards become more comfortable with the process. The requirement is for a rigorous process to be undertaken. Increasingly, shareholders are more likely to question the rigour of the purely questionnaire-based approach, whether this is facilitated or not.

Results of evaluations

What disclosure is there of the results of the board review process? There is usually acknowledgement that the process has been completed and that this was achieved with or without external help. The Robson Rhodes survey found that less than 43 per cent of both FTSE 100 and FTSE 250 companies discussed the topics covered in the evaluation, while 27 per cent of FTSE 100 companies and 16 per cent of FTSE 250 companies went beyond the basic requirements and disclosed that they believed their boards were effective.

The requirement for boards to take a rigorous look at how well they operate and to challenge themselves to improve, though straightforward to implement, is yet the most personally challenging to the directors. If they are not prepared truly to be judged on their effectiveness, shareholders should consider critically the balance of the long-term rewards they seek against the shorter-term risks being taken by the directors.

Ultimately, it is the shareholders who make the assessment of a board's effectiveness by means of their continuing shareholding. But clearer, more consistent information provided by the company would make their decisions easier.

What makes a company responsible?

Although the institutions play down the importance of corporate responsibility (CR) as a value driver, the wider stakeholder audience increasingly profess themselves to be concerned with CR and the accountability of management. However, caution is required in interpreting such data, as only 8 per cent of all companies submitted their results for external verification. It may be some time before consistency and comparability can be assumed. There has, however, been a year-on-year increase in the quality of CR disclosure, perhaps a reflection of the increased awareness and management of reputation risk. Corporate responsibility reporting in 2006 saw more attention being spent on providing quantified results and obtaining verification of disclosures. Over half of all companies provided quantified data to support their disclosures.

All current governance codes do not touch upon CR, including ethical and environmental issues. Should comprehensive, best-practice international corporate governance guidance include CR disclosure requirements? In the UK, the proposals for the Operating and Financial Review sought to raise the profile of such reporting, but the requirement was suddenly withdrawn by the Government in late 2005. However, this was repackaged into the Companies Act 2006 to incorporate EU directive provisions. The new requirement is in the form of a Business Review, where CR issues are among the list of matters to be addressed. This is covered in more detail in Chapter 7.

There is no single document which is recognised as the standard guidance for CR disclosure. Some available recommendations for CR are general, such as the United Nations Global Compact[19] which suggests best practice in areas of human rights, labour, the environment and anti-corruption. Others are more specific; for example, the 'Equator Principles' are the benchmark for the finance industry to manage social and environmental issues in project finance.[20] Furthermore, there are bodies prescribing best-practice approaches, such as Business Relationships, Accountability, Sustainability and Society (BRASS[21]) and Business for Social Responsibility (BSR[22]), together with Accountability Rating,[23] which analyses and ranks the CR statements of the world's largest companies.[24]

Some industries have informally developed standards for CR disclosures. For example, those companies which have chosen to trade in carbon emissions to meet environmental targets now disclose environmental information, such as carbon units, but this is likely to be as much a response to commercial and financial pressures as for CR purposes alone.

---

[19] www.unglobalcompact.org.   [20] www.equator-principles.com.   [21] www.brass.cf.ac.uk.
[22] www.bsr.org.   [23] Developed by csrnetwork consultants, www.accountabilityrating.com/.
[24] Fortune Global 100.

What is CR and what benefits could reliable disclosures provide for investors?

CR identifies the relationship a company has with its stakeholders and the responsibilities it has towards society. Ignoring these responsibilities could be costly to the company. CR is essentially all about reputational risk management. Risks include public disapproval and suspicion, criticism of the company, damage to customer loyalty, loss of brand equity and a tarnished reputation. Internal risks also include embarrassment, poor morale and reduced commitment from employees. Alternatively, pioneering CR initiatives could provide a company with a strong competitive edge.

Section A.1 of the Combined Code states that the board should set the values and standards of the company, and ensure that the company meets its obligations to shareholders and other stakeholders. The 2006 Companies Act also addresses CR issues by linking them to the duties of directors. Directors should take an enlightened approach to value-creation by taking into account, where relevant, the interests of other stakeholders, the company's social impacts and its reputation for integrity. Another source of information is provided by the FTSE4Good Index Series, which has been designed to measure the performance of companies that meet globally recognised CR standards, and to facilitate investment in those companies.[25] FTSE4Good has issued a report called 'Rewarding Virtue'.[26] The report recommends that 'boards must deal with corporate responsibility in their routine agenda items: approving strategy, reviewing risks, managing executive incentives, overseeing internal control, and setting the tone of the business'. The report also includes recommendations for directors and best-practice guidelines for CR reporting.

Further support for CR disclosures is given by Sir Derek Higgs in his report, describing CR disclosure as 'a useful addition to thinking about corporate governance'.

CR principles or guidance should provide specific comparable metrics for the preparation and comparison of CR disclosures. In the medium term, the most likely development is the emergence of industry-specific metrics. In the longer term, without regulation across industries and countries, there is unlikely to be any directly comparable information, resulting in limited value disclosures.

Is the UK model of corporate governance working?

All stakeholders have a part to play in developing, implementing and monitoring corporate governance practice. Without the buy-in from any one party and continuous pressure from all parties, there is a chance that the principles-based corporate governance framework will not be successful.

The UK approach to corporate governance incurs lower levels of cost compared to those imposed by SOX requirements, in terms both of actual cost as

[25] www.ftse4good.com/Indices/FTSE4Good_Index_Series/index.jsp.
[26] www.ftse4good.com/Indices/FTSE4Good_Index_Series/ Downloads/rewardingvirtue.pdf.

well as of management time and administrative burdens. The UK framework gives the opportunity to provide clear and transparent disclosures, moves away from one single overall claim of compliance and covers a wide proportion of the COSO model, rather than focusing on financial risks only.

The current principles-based, comply-or-explain approach to UK corporate governance is the correct model. It fits well within UK business culture and provides the robust governance framework required by the capital markets to help regulate companies at board level. However, UK companies must beware of complacency, for example in the form of boilerplate disclosures, as it contradicts the spirit of the Code. The recent reviews of the Code have had a positive outcome. As long as the thought leaders and think tanks alike support the Code and the effect it has had on UK companies, the UK corporate governance framework will continue down this same line. Of course, the Code and associated guidance will evolve as governance techniques become more refined and disclosures become ever more sophisticated. This is borne out by the various reviews discussed in this chapter which reflect a year-on-year improvement of governance disclosures among the leading companies. For now the UK model is working, and will continue to do so, as all stakeholders apply governance principles within the spirit of the Code. Is it working? Yes. Is it perfect? No. Can shareholders do more? Yes. Can regulators do much more? No. Can boards do much more? Emphatically, yes.

Index